30

The Good, the Bad and the Fattening

A Dictionary of Food

The Good, the Bad and the Fattening

A Dictionary of Food

Dilys Wells

TIMES BOOKS

Joyce Hughes has given valuable assistance with the research for this book.

Figures given in the analyses of nutrient content of foods are based on those published in *The Composition of Foods*, R. A. McCance and E. M. Widdowson, Medical Research Council Special Report Series No. 297, HMSO.

First published in Great Britain in 1975 by Times Books, the book publishing division of Times Newspapers Limited, New Printing House Square, London WC1X 8EZ

© Times Newspapers Limited 1975

ISBN 0 7230 0117 0

Designed by John Lucioni
Jacket designed by Ken Carroll

Printed and bound in Great Britain by The Anchor Press Ltd and Wm Brendon & Son Ltd, both of Tiptree, Essex

Contents

Introduction

What is a radish? It has a refreshing taste, an attractive colour – but what's in it? An important vitamin? Just water? Could it be fattening? *The Good, the Bad and the Fattening*, a companion to all cookery books, provides the answers to these and other questions.

Nothing is more insidious than the little fictions and pet theories we all develop to justify our eating habits. There's the old 'compensation' trick which prompts us to eat a little of what we don't like, so we can eat more of what we do; there's that wistful conviction that drink can't be fattening because it's *liquid*, after all; and when we are forced to it, there's the lure of the proprietary slimming foods which can lull the unwary into a false sense of security. But what most of us rely on to guide our diets in a general way are dimly-remembered snatches of conventional wisdom: an apple a day . . .; spinach, though nasty, is beneficial; carrots improve the eyesight; bread is simply fattening, and so on.

And in addition to these prejudices, acquired early in life, we are assaulted by conflicting information about food which appears in the press or on radio and which expose us to passing fads and fancies. We become confused as butter is condemned and then reinstated as a *good* food; as health foods gain and lose popularity; as certain familiar foods slide right out of our budgets because of soaring prices. So the first aim of this book is to clear the ground. It is not an ascetic's handbook: its purpose is to present some basic and indisputable facts about food, nutrition and diet. We all accept the view that quality of diet has a direct bearing on looks, health and longevity, but how many people know what properties or constituents of individual foods contribute to these? *The Good, the Bad and the Fattening* provides information about the nutrients in different food; about the nutritional significance of different foods in the average diet; and about how and when to buy and store foods.

One warning: don't take the title of the book too seriously! When it comes to nutrition, the good can be bad if you take too much or too little and, of course, one man's meat . . . . . And every single food mentioned here – whether 'good' or 'bad' – can turn out to be fattening if eaten in excess.

It is estimated that half the people in this country are

overweight and at any time about one quarter of the population is taking steps to slim. Most people want to lose weight because they know they will look better. But a large proportion of the general public is following a variety of special diets for their health's sake. This book is written for those who want to slim, those who follow a special diet because they must, and for those who have the responsibility of producing these kinds of diet.

Choosing a well-balanced diet

Some people automatically associate the word 'diet' with slimming or some other specialised pattern of eating. They think of special diets recommended to speed recovery after illness, or diets such as the vegetarian's chosen for strong moral principles. In fact 'diet' simply describes the sum total of the food eaten daily. Generally speaking, if you eat a wide variety of foods and don't eat too much of any one kind, the chances are you will be having a perfectly adequate diet. You don't *have* to eat certain foods every day. Good nutrition isn't all liver, raw carrots and wholemeal breads – though by all means eat these foods if you enjoy them. Any diet will be a well-balanced one if it supplies the body with all the energy and nutrients it needs, in the right quantitities and in the right proportions.

You can modify your diet to help you lose weight, gain weight, cure constipation, soothe an ulcer or reduce the cholesterol level in your blood. Your chosen diet will still be well balanced if it satisfies the body's needs for essential nutrients. Throughout adult life, your nutritional requirements stay very much the same. The notable exception here is that nutritional requirements increase during pregnancy and lactation, and, to a lesser extent, after severe illness.

We rely on food to provide us with mental and physical energy, and to keep us warm. The body also relies entirely on food for all its own building materials. We are literally made out of the food we eat, so it is obvious that the kind of food we eat has a marked effect on the way we look and the way we feel.

Calories: enough is enough

Carbohydrates,* fats* and **proteins*** are the three major

*For more information, see individual entries in the main section of the book.

8

A WELL-BALANCED DIET

The nutritional requirements of different groups of people listed below will be satisfied if their daily diet includes the given quantities of basic foods.

	MILK pints/litres	CHEESE oz/gram	EGGS number	MEAT OR FISH oz/gram	GREEN VEG. OR CITRUS FRUIT oz/gram	BREAD oz/gram	POTATOES oz/gram	BUTTER OR MARGARINE oz/gram
Children 1–5 years	1/0·57	—	1	1–2/28–56	2/56	1–2/28–56	1–2/28–56	½–1/14–28
Children 5–10 years	1/0·57	1/28	1	2–3/56–84	2–3/56–84	2–6/56–168	2–4/56–112	1/28
Adolescent girls	1/0·57	1/28	1	4/112	4/112	4–6/112–168	4/112	2/56
Adolescent boys	1½/0·85	1½–2/42–56	1	4–6/112–168	4/112	6–10/168–280	6–8/168–224	2–3/56–84
Average women	½/0·28	1/28	1	4/112	4/112	4/112	4/112	2/56
Pregnant women	1/0·57	1½/42	1	4/112	4–6/112–168	4/112	4/112	2/56
Lactating women	1½/0·85	1½/42	1	4–6/112–168	4–6/112–168	4–6/112–168	4/112	2–3/56–84
Average men	½/0·28	1/28	1	4/112	4/112	6/168	6/168	3/84
Very active men	1/0·57	2/56	1	4–6/112–168	4/112	6–10/168–280	6–8/168–224	3–4/84–112
Elderly people	1/0·57	1/28	1	3–4/84–112	4/112	2/56	2–4/56–112	1/28

9

nutrients we get from food, and each of these can be used to give the body energy. In the type of diet most people in the West consume, 50 per cent of our daily energy comes from carbohydrates of different kinds, 35 per cent comes from fats and 15 per cent from proteins.

Energy is often measured in **calories***—the energy-giving value of a food is described as its calorific value. A calorie is such a minute measure, however, that the unit used to measure calorific values of food is always the *kilocalorie* (1000 times larger than a calorie). With the exception of water, synthetic sweeteners and certain seasonings and flavourings like salt, everything you eat or drink provides you with some calories. Some foods or drinks contain more than others and entries for individual foods in this book illustrate this. Compare, for example, bread, butter and honey; or beef, pork and chicken; apples, bananas and dates; milk, beer and whisky.

A common misconception about calories is that they must be avoided when you are trying to reduce weight. But whatever you eat, whether it is lettuce, celery, steak, white fish or caviare, or bread, potatoes and cream cakes, it contains calories. Slimmers need calories like everyone else, but they should have fewer of them.

The actual number of calories any one person needs is almost impossible to determine outside a hospital metabolic unit. Individuals vary in their calorie requirements. What we can say, however, is that daily intake of calories should always match daily expenditure of energy. If you use 2,000 calories a day in energy, you should eat 2,000 calories of food – no more and no less. Unfortunately you don't become more energetic if you eat more than this; the calories left over are usually converted into fat. If you are gradually gaining weight, however slowly the ounces mount up, you have been exceeding your calorie requirement. If your body weight stays perfectly steady for months on end, you can tell that you are eating exactly the right number of calories to suit your own, highly personal, energy needs.

If you are prepared to weigh everything you eat, you can find out how many calories you are eating from the values quoted under individual entries in this book. The same entries will show you where most of your daily calories come from. If we were concerned only with energy, it would not matter whether you were taking your calories mainly as bread and

*For more information, see individual entry in the main section of the book.

Desirable weights for men and women of 25 years and over

MEN

HEIGHT	WEIGHT†		
	small frame	medium frame	large frame
5 ft 1 in/1.55 m	7 st 10 lb/48.9 k	8 st 4 lb/52.5 k	9 st 0 lb/57.1 k
5 ft 2 in/1.57 m	7 st 13 lb/50.3 k	8 st 7 lb/53.9 k	9 st 3 lb/58.4 k
5 ft 3 in/1.60 m	8 st 2 lb/51.6 k	8 st 10 lb/55.3 k	9 st 6 lb/59.8 k
5 ft 4 in/1.63 m	8 st 5 lb/53.0 k	8 st 13 lb/56.6 k	9 st 10 lb/61.6 k
5 ft 5 in/1.65 m	8 st 9 lb/54.8 k	9 st 3 lb/58.4 k	9 st 13 lb/63.0 k
5 ft 6 in/1.68 m	8 st 13 lb/56.6 k	9 st 7 lb/60.2 k	10 st 4 lb/65.2 k
5 ft 7 in/1.70 m	9 st 3 lb/58.4 k	9 st 11 lb/62.1 k	10 st 9 lb/67.5 k
5 ft 8 in/1.73 m	9 st 7 lb/60.2 k	10 st 1 lb/63.9 k	10 st 13 lb/69.3 k
5 ft 9 in/1.75 m	9 st 11 lb/62.1 k	10 st 5 lb/65.7 k	11 st 3 lb/71.1 k
5 ft 10 in/1.78 m	10 st 1 lb/63.9 k	10 st 10 lb/68.0 k	11 st 7 lb/72.9 k
5 ft 11 in/1.80 m	10 st 5 lb/65.7 k	11 st 0 lb/69.8 k	11 st 12 lb/75.2 k
6 ft 0 in/1.83 m	10 st 9 lb/67.5 k	11 st 5 lb/72.0 k	12 st 3 lb/77.5 k
6 ft 1 in/1.85 m	11 st 0 lb/69.8 k	11 st 9 lb/73.8 k	12 st 8 lb/79.7 k
6 ft 2 in/1.88 m	11 st 4 lb/71.6 k	12 st 0 lb/76.1 k	12 st 13 lb/82.0 k
6 ft 3 in/1.91 m	11 st 8 lb/73.4 k	12 st 5 lb/78.4 k	13 st 3 lb/83.8 k

WOMEN

HEIGHT	WEIGHT†		
	small frame	medium frame	large frame
4 ft 8 in/1.42 m	6 st 6 lb/40.8 k	6 st 13 lb/43.9 k	7 st 9 lb/48.5 k
4 ft 9 in/1.45 m	6 st 9 lb/42.1 k	7 st 1 lb/44.8 k	7 st 11 lb/49.4 k
4 ft 10 in/1.47 m	6 st 11 lb/43.0 k	7 st 4 lb/46.2 k	8 st 0 lb/50.7 k
4 ft 11 in/1.50 m	7 st 2 lb/45.3 k	7 st 7 lb/47.6 k	8 st 3 lb/52.1 k
5 ft in/1.53 m	7 st 5 lb/46.7 k	7 st 10 lb/48.9 k	8 st 6 lb/53.5 k
5 ft 1 in/1 55 m	7 st 8 lb/48.0 k	7 st 13 lb/50.3 k	8 st 9 lb/54.8 k
5 ft 2 in/1.57 m	7 st 11 lb/49.4 k	8 st 3 lb/52.1 k	8 st 13 lb/56.6 k
5 ft 3 in/1.60 m	8 st 0 lb/50.7 k	8 st 6 lb/53.5 k	9 st 3 lb/58.4 k
5 ft 4 in/1.63 m	8 st 1 lb/51.2 k	8 st 11 lb/55.7 k	9 st 7 lb/60.2 k
5 ft 5 in/1.65 m	8 st 6 lb/53.5 k	9 st 1 lb/57.5 k	9 st 11 lb/62.1 k
5 ft 6 in/1.68 m	8 st 10 lb/55.3 k	9 st 5 lb/59.3 k	10 st 1 lb/63.9 k
5 ft 7 in/1.70 m	9 st 0 lb/57.1 k	9 st 9 lb/61.2 k	10 st 5 lb/65.7 k
5 ft 8 in/1.73 m	9 st 4 lb/58.9 k	9 st 13 lb/63.0 k	10 st 9 lb/67.5 k
5 ft 9 in/1.75 m	9 st 8 lb/60.7 k	10 st 3 lb/64.8 k	11 st 0 lb/69.8 k
5 ft 10 in/1.78 m	9 st 12 lb/62.5 k	10 st 7 lb/66.6 k	11 st 5 lb/72.0 k

† Weights indicated in this table are average weights. Individual weights may vary by 2–3 lb either side of the average.

potatoes, or as vegetables, fruit and meat. But the body needs foods for building and repair as well as for energy.

Building and repair – protein, minerals, vitamins

There is a constant turnover of cells within all body tissues. Worn-out cells are broken down and new cells, made primarily from the dietary **protein***, take their place. We have a complete turnover of body tissues every seven years. (So if you are 35 years old, now, you have had five new bodies in your lifetime

* For more information, see individual entry in the main section of the book.

already!) The proteins you originally ate as beef, chicken, milk, fish, bread, nuts and green peas are now part of your own body. Children need proportionally more proteins than adults because they are growing, a process which involves building entirely new tissues as well as repairing existing ones. A woman's protein requirements are correspondingly high during pregnancy and lactation, as she has to cover the baby's protein needs for growth as well as the repair of her own body tissues.

Apart from proteins, other nutrients are needed for the building and repair of body tissues. **Calcium*** is an essential constituent of bone; **iron*** is needed to build the oxygen-carrying pigment of the blood, haemoglobin; **vitamins*** are also part of the body construction business. **Vitamin A** (also known as **retinol**) and **vitamin C** (often referred to as **ascorbic acid**) are particularly important for building a healthy skin – both the outer covering of the body and the delicate lining of all internal body tracts. Vitamin C is also required to make connective tissue which binds all body cells together, and it is needed for the absorption and utilisation of iron. **Vitamin D** (also known as **cholecalciferol**) is intimately linked with calcium metabolism in a similar way.

There are thirteen or so members of the **B group** of vitamins. **Thiamin** is the familiar vitamin B_1; **riboflavin** is vitamin B_2. They remain traditionally grouped, as many of them are found together in the same foods, and many have similar roles in the body. As well as being needed for healthy building and repair, B vitamins are vital for releasing energy from food. Vitamin B_1, or thiamin, has been compared with the spark that lights a gas ring, or the sparking plug that ignites petrol in an engine.

Nutritional requirements

What do you need to eat every day in order to stay healthy? As it is almost impossible to determine precise nutritional requirements for any one person, nutritionists are able to estimate only average needs. Their calculations are based on the average amount of food eaten by a large number of healthy people, and allow a certain latitude for most individual variations.

The following table, published by the Department of Health and Social Security, gives average requirements for nutrients and energy (calories) for people in the UK.

*For more information, see individual entries in the main section of the book.

Recommended daily intakes of energy and nutrients

	Age range	Occupational category	Energy in kilocalories	Protein in grams	Thiamin (B1) in milligrams	Vitamin (C) in milligrams	Calcium in milligrams	Iron in milligrams
BOYS & GIRLS	0 to 1 year		800	20	0·3	15	600	6
	1 to 2		1200	30	0·5	20	500	7
	2 to 3		1400	35	0·6	20	500	7
	3 to 5		1600	40	0·6	20	500	8
	5 to 7		1800	45	0·7	20	500	8
	7 to 9		2100	53	0·8	20	500	10
BOYS	9 to 12		2500	63	1·0	25	700	13
	12 to 15		2800	70	1·1	25	700	14
	15 to 18		3000	75	1·2	30	600	15
GIRLS	9 to 12		2300	58	0·9	25	700	13
	12 to 15		2300	58	0·9	25	700	14
	15 to 18		2300	58	0·9	30	600	15
MEN	18 to 35	Sedentary	2700	68	1·1	30	500	10
		Moderately active	3000	75	1·2	30	500	10
		Very active	3600	90	1·4	30	500	10
	35 to 65	Sedentary	2600	65	1·0	30	500	10
		Moderately active	2900	73	1·2	30	500	10
		Very active	3600	90	1·4	30	500	10
	65 to 75	Assuming a sedentary life	2350	59	0·9	30	500	10
	75 and over		2100	53	0·8	30	500	10
WOMEN	18 to 55	Most occupations	2200	55	0·9	30	500	12
		Very active	2500	63	1·0	30	500	12
	55 to 75	Assuming a sedentary life	2050	51	0·8	30	500	10
	75 and over		1900	48	0·7	30	500	10
	Pregnancy, 6–9th mth		2400	60	1·0	60	1200	15
	Lactation		2700	68	1·1	60	1200	15

Food, not nutrients

Because we eat food and not merely nutrients, average daily nutritional needs have been interpreted in terms of basic foods. Eat the quantities of foods listed for your own special category and you will have covered your requirements for essential nutrients.

In addition to these quantities, most people can eat what other foods they like to satisfy their appetites. But if you are inclined to put on weight easily, then your own appetite is *not* a true guide to the actual amount of food you need. You can usually find out, by trial and error, how much you can eat to keep your weight steady – refer to the lists of average weights on page 11 to check that your weight is approximately that recommended for your own height.

Some medical authorities recommend that men in middle and old age should restrict their egg consumption to three each week. If you have been given such advice on medical grounds, increase your meat or fish consumption to six ounces on the egg-free days.

Most people need more roughage than would be provided by the recommended foods. In addition to those listed, have one extra portion of vegetable, but not potatoes. If you prefer, have a mixed salad instead of a cooked vegetable, and have one additional portion of fruit, preferably raw or lightly stewed.

Analysis of the nutritive content of individual foods can help you do this type of dietetic juggling – substituting one food for another without sacrificing the overall nutritional value of your chosen diet.

If for some reason you can't eat eggs, hate drinking milk, and won't eat meat, then individual entries in this book will help you to choose alternative foods which maintain a good dietary balance. Eggs, for example, are valuable for their iron, protein and B group vitamin content, but you can choose a portion of liver or a chicken curry on one day in the week, increase your daily meat consumption to 6oz and you won't omit any essential nutrient from your diet. If you don't like liquid milk, then you can double your cheese allowance. In a diet without meat, you can increase the amount of cheese, milk and eggs and eat more nuts, lentils, dried beans and peas to make good any requirement normally supplied by meat.

Beverages

Unless you have been advised by your doctor to restrict your fluid intake, you can drink as much as you like. This does not apply to alcoholic drinks, which affect the nervous system and are generally high in calories; to drinks which are sweetened with sugar; or to very strong tea or coffee which can aggravate the stomach lining. Keep your milk consumption to within the recommended intake, unless you are one of the lucky ones who can eat and drink what they like and not put on an ounce of surplus weight.

You can freely drink water, unsweetened fruit drinks, weak or moderately strong tea and coffee (sweetened with saccharin if you must take them sweet) and low-calorie mineral waters and soft drinks. Drink at least two pints (about one litre) daily.

Special Diets

When you're slimming or watching your weight

To reduce weight you have to cut down on the amount you eat. When you do this, your daily food gives you less energy than you need for normal mental and physical activity, and your body mobilises some of its fat stores to meet the demand for energy. The more you cut down on your food, the more fat is used up for energy. Do remember, though, that nutritional requirements for protein, minerals and vitamins don't change while you're slimming. A slimming diet must be low in energy but must still contain adequate quantities of the essential nutrients.

You may be restricted in all foods, following a so-called 'calorie-controlled diet'. In this case, you have to count the calories in everything you eat and drink. Look out for calorific values for individual food items. Values for foods are given in the quantities in which they are normally eaten; for example, half an ounce of butter and four ounces of mashed potatoes. If you eat more or less than the average, make the necessary calculations to find the precise calorific value of what you are eating.

Other slimming diets restrict carbohydrate content only, but in practice they are also calorie-controlled diets. You don't have to count calories; just carbohydrate contents. Look out for the carbohydrate content of individual foods, and also note which foods have the golden words 'no carbohydrate'. These are the foods you can, in theory at least, eat in unlimited quantities.

Entries of special interest to you
appetite
carbohydrates
energy
overweight
sugar
synthetic sweeteners

When you're recovering from a heart attack – or doing your best to avoid one

If you have already suffered from a coronary thrombosis, it is likely that you have been recommended *to reduce weight* (the points made on slimming will also help you); and *to modify your fat intake* – it is best to reduce your overall consumption of fats by cutting out very rich foods such as cream, rich cakes and pastries and all fried foods, and then, whenever practicable, to replace saturated animal fats with unsaturated vegetable oils. You can do this by eating a soft margarine instead of butter, and by using corn or sunflower oil in place of solid animal fats in cooking. Individual entries indicate whether foods are high in saturated fats. You will probably have been advised *to limit your cholesterol intake* from foods such as eggs, offal, shellfish and fish roes, and *to reduce your sugar intake*.

Entries of special interest to you
atherosclerosis
cholesterol
fats
fatty acids
fried foods
margarine
overweight
polyunsaturates
oils
sugar

When you're a diabetic

With a mild form of diabetes a low carbohydrate diet alone may be recommended. More severe cases are controlled with insulin. The insulin dose is based on a certain daily carbohydrate intake. In either case – with or without insulin – it is vital to keep strictly to the carbohydrate intake stipulated by the dietitian or doctor. Calculate the carbohydrate content of individual foods in planning daily meals, and check which quantities of different foods can be used as 'exchanges'.

Some diabetics are also advised to keep to a low fat, high protein diet. Check fat content for individual foods in their nutrient breakdowns. Some foods are surprisingly high.

All diabetics are advised to keep to below average weight. See general points for slimmers.

Entries of special interest to you
carbohydrates
diabetes
glucose
fats
sorbitol
synthetic sweeteners

When you're preparing other special diets

High fibre diet recommended for constipation and diverticulitis.

Entries of special interest Bran, cellulose, wholefoods.

Low fibre diet recommended for diarrhoea caused by food poisoning or inflammation of the lining of the digestive tract.

Entries of special interest Those listed above for high fibre diet and also water.

Bland diet recommended for ulcers and dyspepsia. See ulcer.

Low fat diet for jaundice, gall stones and other infections of liver and gall bladder.

Entries of special interest Fats, fried food, oils. See also fat contents of individual foods listed.

Gluten free diet for coeliac disease.

Entries of special interest Flour, gluten, gluten free diets, oats, rice.

How to use the Dictionary

Each food entry includes an analysis of nutrient content. Some of the components of foods may be unfamiliar, and the functions of others may seem obscure. To help the reader, explanations of all listed components and their functions are given briefly in the Introduction and, more fully, under individual entries for calories, protein, fats, carbohydrate, calcium, iron, minerals and vitamins.

In all entries, where a reference is made to another food, constituent or condition which is particularly relevant, it appears in bold type, and the reader may care to turn to the appropriate entry for further information.

Although metric equivalents have been included in the tables in the Introduction, a decision was taken to retain Imperial measures in the Dictionary entries, as readers may be more familiar with them. A table of metric equivalents is given below.

Equivalents are calculated to the nearest gram †			
ozs	grams	lbs	kilograms
½	14	1	0.454
1	28	2	0.907
2	57	3	1.361
3	85	4	1.814
4	113	5	2.268
5	142	6	2.722
6	170	7	3.175
7	198	8	3.629
8 (½ lb)	227	9	4.082
12 (¾ lb)	340	10	4.536

† 1 gram (g) = 1000 milligrams (mg); 1 milligram = 1000 micrograms (microg)

Equivalents are calculated to the nearest centilitre			
fl. ozs*	cls	pints	litres
1	3	¼ (gill)	0.14
2	6	½	0.28
3	9	1	0.57
4	11	2	1.14
5	14	3	1.70
6	17	4	2.27
7	20	5	2.84
8	23	6	3.41
9	26	7	3.98
10 (½ pint)	28	8	4.54

* Imperial measure

ALCOHOL Occurs in beverages such as wines, beers and spirits which are produced by means of fermentation. Two essential ingredients used in making any alcoholic beverage are yeasts, which may occur naturally or can be added to start the fermentation, and some kind of fermentable carbohydrate. During the fermentation process, the yeasts use the carbohydrate as a source of food, and alcohol is produced as a by-product in this metabolic breakdown.

The average amount of alcohol found in drinks:

Beer—half pint (0.28 litre) of	brown ale	6.4 g
	draught bitter	8.7 g
	draught mild	7.4 g
	pale ale, bottled	9.5 g
	stout, bottled	8.1 g
	extra stout	12.1 g
third pint (0.19 litre) of	strong ale	9.4 g

Cider—half pint (0.28 litre)	dry	10·7 g
	sweet	10.5 g
third pint (0.19 litre)	vintage	14.9 g

Sherry—standard ⅓ gill measure dry or sweet   7.5 g

Port—standard ⅓ gill measure   7.5 g

Spirits—all 70° proof, standard measure of ⅛ gill   7.4 g

Table wines—one sixth of bottle   11.9 g

Alcohol is rapidly absorbed into the blood stream, especially if no food has been taken for some time previously. Once in the blood, the alcohol is swiftly carried round the body. Its physiological effect is to depress the higher nerve centres. Taken in moderation, it reduces worry and tension and gives a pleasant feeling of well being. After one or two drinks, most people become more relaxed, sociable and tolerant. Taken in large quantities, alcohol seriously impairs the judgement and makes delicate physical movement almost impossible. In excess, alcohol causes unconsciousness.

In small amounts, alcohol helps to stimulate the appetite. Some drinks with a bitter taste are especially good as appetisers. In large quantities, alcohol dulls the appetite. Many people who regularly consume large quantities of alcohol suffer from nutritional deficiencies as a result. A shortage of protein is thought to cause the liver damage from which many alcoholics suffer.

The alcohol in beers, wines and spirits is used in the body as a source of energy. One gram of alcohol supplies 7 kilocalories (29 kilojoules) of energy. Alcohol follows a similar metabolic pathway to that of carbohydrate. To convert alcohol content into grams of carbohydrate equivalent, multiply by the factor 1.75. The alcohol content of the drink, multiplied by 1.75, *plus* any carbohydrate normally present in the drink, gives the total carbohydrate value of the drink. This type of calculation is required when, for example, low carbohydrate reducing diets are being planned.

ALMONDS Small, flattened nuts of the almond tree with a slightly bitter, characteristic flavour. Used to make almond essence. Like all other nuts, almonds are a good source of protein, calcium and iron.

1 oz almonds, weighed without shells, contains:

```
  164 kilocalories (688 kilojoules)
  5.8 g protein
 15.2 g fat (7.8 per cent saturated)
  1.2 g carbohydrate
   70 mg calcium
 1.20 mg iron
      no vitamin A
      no vitamin D
 0.09 mg thiamin
 0.07 mg riboflavin
      no vitamin C
```

Available all the year round.

Sold whole in shells or without shells whole, flaked or ground. Because of their high fat content, almonds should be kept in an airtight container in a cool, preferably dark, store cupboard to prevent rancidity. If they are not in frequent use, it is best to buy almonds in small quantities only.

Toasted flaked almonds are often used to garnish fruit flans and other desserts. Whole almonds are usually coated with chocolate or icing sugar, while ground almonds are used to make marzipan and almond icing, and to enrich fruit cakes such as the traditional Dundee cake. Almonds are used in many savoury dishes in vegetarian cookery.

ANAEMIA Iron deficiency anaemia, as the condition is more accurately called, occurs when the red blood cells carry less than their full quota of the oxygen-carrying pigment, haemoglobin. Iron is necessary for the manufacture of haemoglobin. Iron deficiency anaemia may be caused by regular consumption of a diet short in iron, by frequent or heavy blood loss, or by defective absorption of iron from the small intestine. Iron deficiency anaemia is the most common nutritional deficiency encountered in countries with a high economic standard. It is found most commonly among women – the incidence in this country is thought to be 10 per cent among the adult female population – and also among pre-school children.

Common symptoms of anaemia are tiredness, breathlessness, headache and a general lack of vitality. Many women who are found to be anaemic do not feel any of these disabilities at all, but nevertheless they cannot be considered to be in full health. Iron deficiency anaemia can be confirmed only by a blood test in which the actual haemoglobin content of the blood is accurately determined.

In most cases, iron deficiency anaemia can usually be corrected within a few weeks by taking a course of iron tablets. It may usually be prevented – but not cured – by eating plenty of foods rich in iron. Meat, and especially liver, kidney and heart are not only good sources of iron, but the iron appears to be readily absorbed by the human body. The absorption of iron from other foods may be improved by the presence of vitamin C. For example, the nutritional benefit of a breakfast egg is improved when it is preceded by a glass of orange juice.

Most pregnant women are given iron tablets to take. This helps to meet the great demand for iron as the foetus grows, and also ensures that the mother does not become excessively weakened by blood loss during the birth of the baby.

ANCHOVIES Small fish of the herring family which are filleted and cured, and packed in either bottles or cans, in brine or olive oil. Although rich in protein and oil, they are rarely eaten in sufficient quantities to contribute anything significant in nutrients and energy to the Western diet.

1 oz (6 small canned fillets) contains:

40 kilocalories (168 kilojoules)

Anchovies are very high in salt. They should be avoided by anyone following a salt-free or low sodium diet.

Their high salt content is often put to good use by serving anchovies, or cocktail savouries with anchovies, at drinks parties. The saltiness helps to stimulate thirst.

ANOREXIA NERVOSA is a fairly rare but serious psychological disorder which prompts the patient to refuse to eat for long periods of time. These may last for several months, or even for several years with relapses. The illness is usually confined to girls and young women. Although it does occur, anorexia nervosa is rare among young males. The cause of the illness is not known, but it is always associated with serious emotional difficulties, frequently with problems of sexual adjustment.

With anorexia nervosa, the patient usually suffers from complete loss of appetite. A few patients admit to feeling hungry, although they still refuse to eat. Many claim to feel quite well and continue to lead very active lives. All sufferers go to extreme lengths to avoid eating and putting on weight. As a result they lose weight at an alarming rate and become quite emaciated. If they are not given the right psychotherapy, patients suffering from anorexia nervosa may starve themselves to death.

APPETITE is the body's food intake meter – the mechanism which keeps the balance between energy requirements and the quantity of food eaten. It is usually a reliable guide to the amount we need to eat. Many people keep a constant weight for years which shows that their food intake has been precisely matched by the energy requirements of their bodies. During periods of increased physical activity when the body needs more energy, the appetite usually increases proportionally. When an individual is less active than usual, his energy requirements are less and his appetite becomes smaller. When energy requirements fall very low, the appetite becomes less accurate as a food-intake controlling mechanism.

Appetite is strongly influenced by past experience of eating foods of certain taste, texture and appearance. Hunger is the more basic, indiscriminate urge to eat food, whatever its flavour. Even when hunger has been satisfied, appetite for foods which are especially attractive may still remain. Our formal meal pattern of a variety of different courses is based on this surmise. But if the appetite is regularly abused – if an individual frequently eats more than his appetite dictates – the control mechanism gradually breaks down. The appetite is no longer a reliable guide to the amount of food needed for energy. The usual result of this breakdown is a gradual increase in body weight.

APPLES One of the most popular fruits in the UK. They can be divided into cooking and eating varieties.

Cooking apples are usually larger than the eating varieties.

One 6 oz cooking apple contains:

        60 kilocalories (251 kilojoules)
       0.6 g protein
        no fat
      16.2 g carbohydrate
        6 mg calcium
      0.48 mg iron
    8 microg retinol equivalents vitamin A
        no vitamin D
      0.06 mg thiamin
      0.03 mg riboflavin
        8 mg vitamin C

Eating apples vary in size but are most frequently sold four to 1 lb. One 4 oz eating apple contains:

        40 kilocalories (167 kilojoules)
       0.4 g protein
        no fat
      10.4 g carbohydrate
       3.2 mg calcium
      0.28 mg iron
    6 microg retinol equivalents vitamin A
        no vitamin D
      0.05 mg thiamin
      0.02 mg riboflavin
        6 mg vitamin C

In the UK the average person eats about 7 oz apples per week. Although the nutrient content of apples is not very high, these popular fruits are valuable for their help in cleaning the teeth and also in preventing gum disorders (see **dental health**). Apples also supply a little roughage to the diet.

Apples are grown in most temperate regions, including the UK. Home-grown apples are available from July to February, and these are supplemented by a large number of imported apples throughout the year.

Cooking apples have a firm, acid-tasting flesh that pulps easily on cooking. Some of the varieties of cooking apples now available are:

Bramley's Seedling
Grenadier
Lord Derby
Newton Wonder
Lord Grosvenor

Eating apples vary from firm to soft according to the variety, but all have a sweeter taste than cooking apples. Some of the varieties of eating apples now widely available are:

Cox's Orange Pippin
Laxton Superb
Granny Smith
Worcester Pearmain
Golden Delicious

They are usually sold graded by size.

Apples keep best in a cool, dark but airy place. If large quantities are produced at home, the apples should be individually wrapped and placed on trays. They may be stored in an outhouse provided this is frost-free. Small quantities can be taken from the store for immediate use.

Cooking apples also freeze very well. The apples may be peeled and sliced, the slices dipped into lemon juice or ascorbic acid solution, and then frozen in dry sugar. Alternatively, the apple may be puréed or poached and then frozen.

APRICOTS Small, soft, stoned fruits. May be purchased fresh, dried or canned. They are a useful source of vitamin A, and contain more than any other fruit.

One 2 oz fresh apricot contains:

    14 kilocalories (59 kilojoules)
   0.4 g protein
    no fat
   3.4 g carbohydrate
    9 mg calcium
   0.2 mg iron
132 microg retinol equivalents vitamin A
    no vitamin D
 0.02 mg thiamin
 0.03 mg riboflavin
    4 mg vitamin C

1 oz dried apricots contains:

   52 kilocalories (217 kilojoules)
   1.4 g protein
    no fat
 12.3 g carbohydrate
 26.3 mg calcium
 1.16 mg iron
170 microg retinol equivalents vitamin A
    no vitamin D
    no thiamin
 0.05 mg riboflavin
    no vitamin C

2 oz canned apricots in syrup contain:

   34 kilocalories (142 kilojoules)
   0.2 g protein
    no fat
    9 g carbohydrate
 6.8 mg calcium
 0.40 mg iron
88 microg retinol equivalents vitamin A
    no vitamin D
 0.01 mg thiamin
  trace of riboflavin
   3 mg vitamin C

Fresh apricots are in season from December to February and June to August.

ARTICHOKES There are two distinct types: globe artichokes and Jerusalem artichokes.

Globe artichokes are buds of a plant and are eaten as a vegetable. They have green, overlapping, fleshy leaves covering a tough hairy part, which is the 'choke' and below this is the 'fond' or 'tender heart'.

One 4 oz globe artichoke, boiled, contains:

 16 kilocalories (67 kilojoules)
 1.2 g protein
 no fat
 3.2 g carbohydrate
 49.6 mg calcium
 0.56 mg iron
 no vitamin A
 no vitamin D
 0.20 mg thiamin
 0.01 mg riboflavin
 4 mg vitamin C

Globe artichokes are imported from France, Italy and Spain and there are a few home-grown varieties.

Available from July to October, globe artichokes should be eaten as soon after purchase as possible; after 2 or 3 days' storage they begin to wilt and lose flavour. They may be cooked whole and served with a simple butter sauce, or with a more elaborate sauce such as hollandaise or vinaigrette. The artichoke hearts may also be served cold with a French dressing as a first course dish, or as part of a mixed salad.

Jerusalem artichokes are small, unshapely, buff-coloured tubers similar to potatoes.

One 4 oz Jerusalem artichoke, boiled, contains:

 20 kilocalories (84 kilojoules)
 2 g protein
 no fat
 3.6 g carbohydrate
 34.4 mg calcium
 0.48 mg iron
 no vitamin A
 no vitamin D
 0.20 mg thiamin
 no riboflavin
 3 mg vitamin C

Jerusalem artichokes are available from October to June. They keep well in a cool, dark place. They are usually peeled before boiling, but are very good simply scrubbed and baked in their skins.

ASPARAGUS The tender shoot of a perennial plant, first cultivated on commercial scale in UK in the seventeenth century. In the nineteenth century they were sold by street traders who cried: 'Sparrow-grass. Buy your sparrow-grass.' Still known today in London's Covent Garden market as 'grass'.

Asparagus contains useful amounts of vitamin C and vitamin A.

4 oz of asparagus, boiled, contain:

20	kilocalories (84 kilojoules)
4 g	protein
no	fat
1.2 g	carbohydrate
29.2 mg	calcium
1 mg	iron
95 microg	retinol equivalents vitamin A
no	vitamin D
0.10 mg	thiamin
0.09 mg	riboflavin
23 mg	vitamin C

Available usually in May and June, asparagus has only a short season of approximately six to eight weeks' duration. Sold bunched and graded, with white base and green tip. Grades: Giant; Extra Selected; Selected; Special; Long Green; Sprue. Bunches vary in size according to the thickness of the stems. The thicker-stemmed ones are the most expensive.

To enjoy asparagus at its best, it should be eaten as soon as possible after gathering. For short-term shortage it should be placed in the salad drawer of the fridge or in a plastic bag on the bottom shelf of the fridge. Asparagus also freezes very well. It can be prepared for the home freezer, or commercially frozen asparagus may be bought. Canned asparagus is also available.

Asparagus is usually served poached as a first course with melted butter, or a richer sauce if preferred. It is an excellent vegetable for soup, or as an ingredient in savoury flans, omelettes and sandwiches.

29

ATHEROSCLEROSIS is the build-up of fatty deposits, known as atheroma, inside the arteries. Atherosclerosis is commonly known as 'hardening of the arteries'. The deposits tend to narrow the arteries and impede the flow of blood. When the arteries are severely congested by atheroma, a blood clot may easily form. If this blocks the narrow blood vessels which bring blood to such vital organs as the brain or heart, severe damage to those tissues, or even death, may occur.

The precise cause of atherosclerosis has not yet been established. A high blood lipid (fat) level, a high blood cholesterol level, high blood pressure and a family tendency to atherosclerosis appear to be strongly implicated. (See also **coronary thrombosis, cholesterol.**)

AUBERGINES Also known as egg plant. A long, oval-shaped vegetable with a smooth, shiny, purple skin.

One 6 oz aubergine, raw, contains:

      24 kilocalories (100 kilojoules)
     1.2 g protein
      no fat
     5.4 g carbohydrate
      18 mg calcium
    0.66 mg iron

The most useful size is 6 to 8 inches long, although they can grow much larger.

The aubergine is an old English vegetable which deserves to be more popular than it is in this country. They are also imported from France, Italy and Israel.

Available all the year round, though more plentiful – and therefore cheaper – around September and October. They keep for 7 to 10 days in the salad drawer in the fridge, or in any cool place. Aubergines may also be quick frozen for the home freezer, lightly cooked in butter or used as an ingredient in dishes such as ratatouille and moussaka. They are also popular vegetables to serve stuffed. Aubergines add their characteristic flavour to other casseroled meat and vegetable dishes, and to cold dishes to serve with dressing as salads or hors d'œuvre.

AVOCADO PEAR A fruit which has a tough, shiny skin varying in colour from bright green to purple. The flesh is pale green, soft and oily. Avocados have a high vegetable oil content of up to 25 per cent.

Available nearly all year round, avocados are usually cheapest from June to September.

One half avocado pear, weighing 3 oz without its stone, contains:*

        132 kilocalories (552 kilojoules)
        1.8 g protein
       10.5 g fat
        3.6 g carbohydrate
          9 mg calcium
        1.4 mg iron
        140 microg retinol equivalents vitamin A
         no vitamin D
       0.09 mg thiamin
       0.09 mg riboflavin
          6 mg vitamin C

*Analyses of Shankman Laboratories, Los Angeles, April 1968–February 1969.

The most popular way of serving avocado pear is simply to fill it with French dressing. It is also very good as a salad ingredient, or puréed to make a delicious chilled soup.

BABY FOODS Foods specially prepared for young babies changing from an all-milk to a mixed diet. The very early introduction of mixed feeding is not recommended. Until a baby is 3 or 4 months old, no food is better than mother's milk. (Modified cow's and powdered milks are the next best for the first few months.) After 4–6 months milk no longer satisfies all the baby's nutritional requirements and other foods should be introduced.

A variety of cereal products prepared from rice, oats, barley, corn and wheat are available. These products are often the first ones offered to the baby. He will usually readily accept the sweetened cereal, reconstituted with hot milk. But cereals should be given in small amounts only. Too much cereal is thought to be responsible for many cases of obesity among children.

Savoury foods, such as meat and vegetable broths, puréed vegetables, purées of creamed chicken or white fish and mild cheese savouries, make good alternatives to the more usual cereal for the first 'solid' food offered. All foods for young babies should be smooth in texture; many automatically reject food with lumps. The food should also be free of fibrous tissue, which may irritate the delicate lining of the baby's gastro-intestinal tract; it should not be too highly flavoured, nor contain too much salt. Flavouring ingredients can also be irritating and the infant's kidneys cannot excrete large quantities of salt.

Obviously, great care must be taken, and scrupulous attention paid to hygiene when preparing foods for babies. Although it is rather time-consuming, there is no reason why all the foods should not be made at home. Many foods prepared for other members of the family may be liquidised in a blender with a little stock, sauce or gravy.

A great variety of canned, bottled and packet baby foods are also offered for sale. As they are specially prepared to appeal to the baby's taste, they are usually very popular. Initially, many home-made baby foods may not be so readily accepted. With regard to nutritive value, many convenience baby foods compare favourably with home-made ones. The vitamin content of some baby foods in cans and jars may be even higher than that of comparable foods prepared at home. Because cans and jars are sterilised during manufacture, baby foods can be stored for *limited periods* in the fridge if all is not eaten at one meal. The can or jar needs to be covered to prevent entry of bacteria or contamination from other foods in the fridge.

Because they are so very convenient, many mothers feed convenience foods exclusively to their babies. The disadvantage of this is that the baby becomes accustomed to a limited range of tastes and textures. He may need to be 'weaned' away from the cans and jars very gradually before he will accept the food the rest of the family eats.

BACON A good source of protein and the B vitamins, available throughout the year. The main bacon cuts used for rashers are back, streaky, collar and gammon. Back resembles chops, with the main meat showing as an 'eye'; streaky has roughly alternate layers of fat and lean, and may be sold joined to the back cut, when it is known under various names, including cut-through and long back. Collar comes from the neck end of the side adjoining the foreleg, and gammon from the thick end of the back leg.

COMPARISON OF NUTRITIVE VALUES OF BACK BACON, COLLAR BACON, GAMMON BACON AND STREAKY BACON 2 oz, FRIED				
	Back	Collar	Gammon	Streaky
Kilocalories (Kilojoules)	338 (1,413)	248 (1,037)	252 (1,053)	298 (1,256)
Protein g	14	15.6	17.8	13.6
Fat g (37.5% saturated)	30.4	19.8	19.2	26.2
Carbohydrate g	0	0	0	0
Calcium mg	6.6	13.2	14.2	29.8
Iron mg	1.6	2.22	1.6	1.82
Vitamin A	0	0	0	0
Vitamin D	0	0	0	0
Thiamin mg	0.23	0.23	0.23	0.23
Riboflavin mg	0.08	0.08	0.08	0.08
Vitamin C	0	0	0	0

Today factory-cured bacon is almost entirely brine-cured, and only hams are dry-salted. After curing, the bacon is dried and either sold 'green' or smoked.

To satisfy modern tastes, bacon is only slightly salted and smoked. This gives the bacon an attractive taste, but does not improve its keeping qualities. In earlier days, bacon was heavily salted and smoked to preserve the meat and keep it fresh for long periods after processing.

Present-day demand is also for lean bacon. Only young pigs which have been carefully bred, and fed on a well-balanced diet, are accepted at the bacon factory. The old-fashioned pig was deliberately fattened up, but the fatty bacon it yielded would certainly not appeal now.

Like other perishable commodities, bacon should be kept in low temperature storage. In a plastic, non-airtight container bacon will stay fresh for 7 to 10 days. If left uncovered, the bacon dries out and becomes stale. Its characteristic flavour may also be absorbed by other foods in the fridge.

For periods up to three months, bacon may be kept in the freezer. If stored for longer, it does not become bad, but its flavour deteriorates.

Traditionally a breakfast food, bacon is also excellent for quick luncheon or supper dishes, and as an ingredient in flans, omelettes and so on.

BANANA The fruit of a tropical tree.

One 6 oz banana (weighed with peel) contains:

78	kilocalories (326 kilojoules)
1.2 g	protein
no	fat
19.2 g	carbohydrate
6.6 mg	calcium
0.42 mg	iron
56 microg	retinol equivalents vitamin A
no	vitamin D
0.05 mg	thiamin
0.12 mg	riboflavin
17 mg	vitamin C

Available all the year round. Bananas are imported while still green and are ripened in this country in special large warehouses before being distributed to the shops.

Bananas should always be kept at room temperature. If kept in the cold, bananas become black and soft; they also discolour when exposed to air. They will keep their own cream colour in fruit salads and so on, if the sliced banana is liberally sprinkled with or lightly tossed in lemon juice.

Because of their soft texture, bananas are very suitable for babies, old people and others who may have difficulty in chewing crisp fruits.

BARLEY A cereal which contains more fat than wheat, but is comparatively poor in protein. The amount of starch in it varies in different samples from 39 per cent to 57 per cent. As a human food it is usually in the form of either 'pearl' or 'patent' barley. The former consists of the whole grain polished after removal of the husk; the latter is simply pearl barley ground into flour, and is most frequently seen as baby food. It contains a little **gluten** and must therefore be eliminated from a gluten-free diet.

1 oz raw pearl barley contains:

    102 kilocalories (426 kilojoules)
    2.2 g protein
    0.5 g fat
   23.7 g carbohydrate
    2.8 mg calcium
    0.19 mg iron
        no vitamin A
        no vitamin D
    0.03 mg thiamin
        no riboflavin
        no vitamin C

The leading barley producing countries are the USSR, France, USA, UK, Canada, and Denmark.

Pearl barley is an important ingredient in traditional dishes such as Scotch broth and Irish stew. But most of the barley grown in the UK is used either for animal feed or for brewing. Barley produces the best malt from which beer and whisky are made.

BEANS There are several varieties, the most popular in the UK being broad beans, runner beans, haricot beans and canned baked beans.

Broad beans are one of the oldest vegetables in cultivation. Along with green peas they contain more energy, protein and thiamin than other fresh vegetables.

4 oz broad beans, boiled, contain:

    48 kilocalories (201 kilojoules)
    4.8 g protein
      no fat
       8 g carbohydrate
      24 mg calcium
    1.12 mg iron
      22 microg retinol equivalents vitamin A
      no vitamin D
    0.20 mg thiamin
    0.04 mg riboflavin
      17 mg vitamin C

In season from the end of May to September, broad beans are at their peak from mid-June to the end of July.

Runner beans have a low energy value compared with the other beans mentioned.

4 oz runner beans, boiled, contain:

>   8 kilocalories (33 kilojoules)
>   0.8 g protein
>   no fat
>   1.2 g carbohydrate
>   29.2 mg calcium
>   0.68 mg iron
>   50 microg retinol equivalents vitamin A
>   no vitamin D
>   0.03 mg thiamin
>   0.07 mg riboflavin
>   5 mg vitamin C

Runner beans are home grown. In season from June to September; at their peak from July to August.

Haricot beans are dried, and are referred to as pulses, as are dried and split peas and butter beans. The dried forms are rich in energy, protein and other nutrients. However, before they can be used, they must be soaked. When this is done the moisture content rises from 12 per cent to 70 per cent and the energy, protein and other nutrient value falls.

2 oz haricot beans, boiled, contain:

>   50 kilocalories (209 kilojoules)
>   3.8 g protein
>   no fat
>   9.4 g carbohydrate
>   36.6 mg calcium
>   1.42 mg iron
>   no vitamin A
>   no vitamin D
>   0.08 mg thiamin
>   0.01 mg riboflavin
>   no vitamin C

In dry storage conditions, haricot beans keep almost indefinitely.

Baked beans are the all-time favourite among canned vegetables in the UK. A useful source of protein, calcium and iron.

4 oz baked beans contain:

    104 kilocalories (435 kilojoules)
    6.8 g protein
    0.4 g fat
    19.6 g carbohydrate
    69.6 mg calcium
    2.32 mg iron
    57 microg retinol equivalents vitamin A
    no vitamin D
    0.07 mg thiamin
    0.04 mg riboflavin
    3 mg vitamin C

The average weekly consumption of baked beans in the UK is just under 4 oz per caput.

Fresh beans, including broad, French and runner beans, should be eaten as soon after gathering as possible. The fresher they are, the better their flavour and the higher their nutritive value. If they have to be stored, fresh beans should be kept in the salad drawer of the fridge, or in a plastic bag at the bottom of the fridge.

All fresh beans quick freeze well, and are excellent for home freezing.

In the United Kingdom, beans are usually served as a hot vegetable. They are also very good to cook and serve cold in a mixed salad.

BEEF Meat from cattle, usually young, castrated male animals. Herefords, Aberdeen Angus, Shorthorns and Charolais are especially good beef cattle.

4 oz of grilled beef steak contain:*

    344 kilocalories (1,445 kilojoules)
    28.8 g protein
    24.4 g fat (50 per cent saturated)
    no carbohydrate
    10.4 mg calcium
    5.9 mg iron

```
      trace  vitamin A
      trace  vitamin D
 0.35 mg   thiamin
  1.2 mg   riboflavin
        no  vitamin C
```

4 oz of stewed beef contain:*

```
      232  kilocalories (974 kilojoules)
     34.8 g  protein
      9.6 g  fat (50 per cent saturated)
        no  carbohydrate
      3.6 mg  calcium
      5.8 mg  iron
      trace  vitamin A
      trace  vitamin D
 0.24 mg   thiamin
  1.2 mg   riboflavin
        no  vitamin C
```

*These are average values and vary slightly with different cuts of beef.

Although the consumption of beef has decreased in recent years, we still eat more beef than any other meat. The national average weekly consumption in the UK is 7 oz per person, which provides 6 per cent of protein and 8.2 per cent of iron in the average diet, as well as important quantities of several different B group vitamins.

Cuts suitable for roasting or grilling should be fine-textured. Coarser meat is suitable for braising or stewing. Flecks of marbling fat within the lean meat ensure tenderness. Other fat should be firm, dry and creamy-coloured.

Beef, like all other meats, should be removed from the butcher's wrappings and kept, loosely covered, in the coolest part of the fridge. If left uncovered, it will dry out. Beef will keep for up to 5 days in the fridge and for up to 12 months in the freezer.

BEER An alcoholic beverage, extremely popular – particularly among the male population – in the UK.

Apart from its energy value, beer contributes little to the diet in the way of nutrients.

COMPARATIVE ENERGY VALUE OF SOME BEERS			
Beer	Measure	Kilocalories	Kilojoules
Brown ale, bottled		159	665
Draught bitter		177	740
Draught mild	1 pint in each case	144	602
Pale ale, bottled		184	770
Stout, bottled		212	886
Stout, extra		223	932
Strong ale		414	1,730

1 pint draught bitter contains:

```
   177 kilocalories (740 kilojoules)
   1.4 g protein
    no fat
  12.8 g carbohydrate
  17.4 g alcohol
    62 mg calcium
    no iron
    no vitamin A
    no vitamin D
  0.08 mg thiamin
     1 mg riboflavin
    no vitamin C
```

1 pint draught mild contains:

```
   144 kilocalories (602 kilojoules)
     1 g protein
    no fat
   9.2 g carbohydrate
  14.8 g alcohol
    60 mg calcium
    no iron
    no vitamin A
    no vitamin D
  0.08 mg thiamin
     1 mg riboflavin
    no vitamin C
```

Sold either as draught beer in public houses, or in bottles and cans in public houses or off-licences.

The bitterness of beer helps to stimulate the appetite, and a glass of beer before, or with, a meal is helpful in stimulating an unduly small appetite. In moderation, beer is also recommended for convalescents.

BEETROOT Round or oval-shaped root vegetable, deep purple in colour.

1 oz boiled beetroot contains:

        13 kilocalories (54 kilojoules)
       0.5 g protein
        no fat
       2.8 g carbohydrate
       8.5 mg calcium
      0.20 mg iron
        no vitamin A
        no vitamin D
 negligible thiamin
      0.01 mg riboflavin
       1.5 mg vitamin C

Beetroot are sold either raw or ready cooked. They are available all the year, but in peak condition in September and October and therefore usually cheapest then.

Beetroot, like other root vegetables, should be stored in a cool, dark place. To avoid excessive 'bleeding', beetroot is scrubbed and cooked in its skin. If not required for immediate use, the boiled beetroot keeps best in its skin, on a covered dish in the fridge.

Beetroot is usually served cold, with or without vinegar or other dressing, as a salad vegetable. It is also delicious served as a hot vegetable with a white sauce, or a sauce of sour cream.

BLACKBERRIES A small soft fruit, dark red to black in colour.

4 oz blackberries, stewed without sugar, contain:

       24 kilocalories (100 kilojoules)
      1.2 g protein
       no fat
      5.6 g carbohydrate

```
   55.2 mg  calcium
   0.72 mg  iron
 13 microg  retinol equivalents vitamin A
        no  vitamin D
   0.02 mg  thiamin
   0.03 mg  riboflavin
      18 mg  vitamin C
```

Blackberries are available both wild and cultivated; the cultivated ones are larger and more juicy than the wild ones and
have a slightly different flavour. In season July to October.

Like other soft fruit, blackberries do not keep well, as they are
inclined to go mouldy in warm conditions. They should be kept
in the salad drawer of the fridge and eaten as soon as possible
after gathering.

Blackberries team very well with apples. Together they make
popular fillings for pies, flans, puddings and other desserts.

BLACKCURRANTS A soft summer fruit with a very strong,
acid flavour. For this reason, blackcurrants are rarely eaten
raw. They are the richest source of vitamin C in the UK diet.

2 oz blackcurrants, stewed without sugar, contain:

```
      12   kilocalories (50 kilojoules)
    0.4 g  protein
       no  fat
    2.8 g  carbohydrate
   26.4 mg calcium
   0.56 mg iron
 14 microg retinol equivalents vitamin A
        no vitamin D
   0.01 mg thiamin
   0.02 mg riboflavin
      80 mg vitamin C
```

In season from June to August and at their peak in July. A very
popular fruit for pies and puddings.

Because they are exceptionally rich in vitamin C, many blackcurrants grown in this country are made into proprietary
vitamin C drinks. So many are used for this purpose that fresh
blackcurrants are rarely offered for sale in parts of the country.
The vitamin C blackcurrant drink itself has a variety of uses.

It makes an excellent sauce for ice cream, pancakes, and steamed puddings, for example.

BRAN The outer husk of the wheat grain, composed of a number of different layers all with a high fibre content. Bran also contains small quantities of protein and certain B group vitamins.

Bran is removed completely when white flour is made. All the bran is retained and finely ground to make wholemeal or wholewheat flour. To make wheatmeal, wheaten or unspecified 'brown' flours, a proportion of the coarser bran particles are removed.

Any bran not included in flour is used to make proprietary bran products, including breakfast cereals, or used for animal food.

Discomfort experienced by those suffering from diverticulitis can often be eased by taking a few tablespoons of bran every day. The bran may be sprinkled on to cereals such as porridge, or mixed into milky dishes like yoghurt. Bran in any form adds roughage to the diet.

BRAZIL NUTS These contribute little to the diet since they are eaten in very small quantities. They are however, a good source of protein.

1 oz brazil nuts without shells contains:

    183 kilocalories (765 kilojoules)
    3.9 g protein
    17.3 g fat
    1.2 g carbohydrate
    50 mg calcium
    0.80 mg iron
      no vitamin A
      no vitamin D
    0.30 mg thiamin
      no vitamin C

Available all the year round, although most popular around Christmas. They may be bought whole in shells or without shells. Brazils are frequently used in confectionery such as brazil nut chocolate and buttered brazils. The nuts themselves make an excellent dessert with fresh fruit, or they may be served with cheese and port wine.

BREAD One of the important staple foods in the typical Western diet, bread provides valuable amounts of protein, carbohydrate, calcium, iron and thiamin. The national average consumption of bread in the UK is about 35 oz per person each week. Of this, 29 oz is white bread, 3 oz brown bread and the remaining 3 oz 'other' breads. This consumption supplies the following proportion of the daily recommended intake of nutrients: protein 17 per cent; energy (calories) 14 per cent; calcium 14 per cent; iron 18 per cent; thiamin 23 per cent.

2 oz white bread (2 thin slices from a large loaf) contain:

    138 kilocalories (577 kilojoules)
    4.4 g protein
    0.8 g fat
    29.8 g carbohydrate
    52 mg calcium
    1.02 mg iron
       no vitamin A
       no vitamin D
    0.10 mg thiamin
    0.01 mg riboflavin
       no vitamin C

2 oz brown bread (2 thin slices from a large loaf) contain:

    136 kilocalories (569 kilojoules)
    5 g protein
    1.2 g fat
    28.4 g carbohydrate
    54 mg calcium
    1.38 mg iron
       no vitamin A
       no vitamin D
    0.16 mg thiamin
    0.04 mg riboflavin
       no vitamin C

2 oz wheatgerm bread (2 slices) contain:

    134 kilocalories (560 kilojoules)
    5.2 g protein

43

                1.4 g fat
                 27 g carbohydrate
                60 mg calcium
              1.52 mg iron
                   no vitamin A
                   no vitamin D
              0.16 mg thiamin
              0.04 mg riboflavin
                   no vitamin C

2 oz starch reduced bread (3 thin slices) contain:

                  133 kilocalories (556 kilojoules)
                  6 g protein
                0.9 g fat
               27.1 g carbohydrate
                57 mg calcium
               0.7 mg iron
                   no vitamin A
                   no vitamin D
              0.10 mg thiamin
              0.02 mg riboflavin
                   no vitamin C

White breads are basically made from pure white flour, water, salt, sugar and yeast. They may be enriched with fats, oils, milk, milk products, malt extract, malt flour. Small specified quantities of rice flour, oatmeal or soya bean flour are also allowed by law to be added to white bread. Other ingredients, such as caraway seeds, poppy seeds, wheat gluten and wheatgerm may also be added. The composition of bread is closely guarded by law, which allows the addition of certain chemical substances which improve the texture, appearance and keeping qualities of bread. Only a certain number of additives may be added, and only in certain small quantities as described in the Government's Bread and Flour Regulations, S.I. 1435, 1963. Some of the permitted additives are yeast-stimulating preparations, anti-mould agents, bleaching and improving agents and preservatives.

A number of proprietary protein and gluten breads are sold as slimming aids, when the bread makes up part of a calorie-controlled diet. These breads contain added wheat protein. Protein bread has a final protein content of 22 per cent; gluten bread a protein content of 16 per cent.

Breads and rolls may only be described as 'starch reduced' ii they contain less than 50 per cent carbohydrate based on dry weight. (Normal bread contains 83 per cent carbohydrate on the same basis.)

Milk bread must contain not less than 6 per cent milk solids from either fresh or skimmed milk added to the dough. Soda bread does not contain yeast and is raised with baking soda. It may contain the same additives as those allowed for normal white bread.

Brown breads include wholemeal bread, which is made from wholemeal flour of 100 per cent extraction; wheatmeal, which must by law contain at least 0.6 per cent fibre and may also contain up to 5 per cent rice or soya bean flour and caramel for colouring; wheatgerm bread with not less than 10 per cent added wheatgerm. Like white breads, additional ingredients may be added to brown breads for extra flavour and enrichment and also to improve texture, keeping qualities, etc.

In the United Kingdom, more than 11 million loaves are baked every day. Over 100 different varieties are made, but by far the most popular, accounting for almost three-quarters of all bread sales, is the sliced and wrapped white loaf.

The so-called 'one pound' or 'two pound' loaves in fact must weigh a minimum of 14 and 28 oz by law. If a loaf weighs more than 10 oz it must be sold as a multiple of 14 oz. Breads that weigh less than 10 oz are usually the fancy loaves like baps, twists and plaits, which do not have to comply with this standard.

BREAKFAST CEREALS The original breakfast cereal food in the UK used to be oatmeal porridge; this has largely been replaced by other cereal products prepared from wheat, maize or rice grains which have been subjected to steam and then toasted, puffed, flaked or shredded. The protein content of the cereals varies: that of puffed wheat is higher than shredded wheat because it is made from a stronger type of wheat. The energy value of breakfast cereals is high because of the low moisture content; the sugar-coated varieties are even higher. Many breakfast cereals are now enriched with the B vitamins, thiamin, riboflavin and nicotinic acid.

2 Weetabix (approximately 1¼ oz), 5 fl. oz milk and ½ oz sugar, an average helping, provide:

   276 kilocalories (1,154 kilojoules)
   8.4 g protein

```
        6.1 g  fat
         49 g  carbohydrate
    182.6 mg  calcium
      2.09 mg  iron
  50 microg  retinol equivalents vitamin A
         no  vitamin D
      0.30 mg  thiamin
      0.57 mg  riboflavin
         no  vitamin C
```

Breakfast cereals of these types are popular in the UK but rarely eaten in the other European countries. Consumption is also high in the USA. Many families eat only a bowlful of cereal with milk and sugar, with perhaps a cup of tea or coffee, for breakfast. Although the milk boosts the overall protein content of this breakfast to some extent, most of the energy value of the meal is derived from carbohydrate. It may be satisfying at the time the meal is eaten, but is not as sustaining as a breakfast with more protein and fat such as the traditional breakfast of bacon and eggs which the cereal-based meal has replaced.

NUTRIENT CONTENT OF 1 oz OF VARIOUS BREAKFAST CEREALS					
Nutrient	Cornflakes	Rice Krispies	Puffed Wheat	Shredded Wheat	Weetabix
Kilocalories	104	100	102	103	100
(Kilojoules)	(435)	(418)	(426)	(430)	(418)
Protein g	2.1	1.6	4.0	2.8	3.1
Fat g	0.2	0.3	0.6	0.8	0.5
Carbohydrate g	25.2	24.2	21.4	22.4	21.9
Calcium mg	1.5	1.7	10.0	9.9	10.1
Iron mg	0.3	0.20	0.93	1.27	1.67
Vitamin A microg retinol equivalents	0	0	0	0	0
Vitamin D microg	0	0	0	0	0
Thiamin mg	0.17	0.30	*	*	0.20
Riboflavin mg	0.30	0.40	*	*	0.30
Vitamin C mg	0	0	0	0	0

* Figures not available

BROCCOLI A green vegetable rich in calcium and vitamin C. 4 oz broccoli, boiled, contain:

          16 kilocalories (67 kilojoules)
        3.6 g protein
          no fat
        0.4 g carbohydrate
      181.6 mg calcium
        1.72 mg iron
      1,668 microg retinol equivalents vitamin A
          no vitamin D
        0.07 mg thiamin
        0.23 mg riboflavin
          45 mg vitamin C

Available throughout the year. Imported from January to March and November to December.

There are several varieties of this vegetable, the main ones being: white broccoli (winter cauliflower), with a fairly large flower head; sprouting broccoli, which have a number of small flower heads. There are three types of sprouting broccoli – white, purple and calabrese (green).

Green vegetables should be eaten as fresh as possible for maximum food value. For short-time storage, keep in the salad drawer of the fridge.

___

BRUSSELS SPROUTS A member of the cabbage family which, like the other members, is a good source of vitamin C.

4 oz brussels sprouts, boiled, contain:

        20 kilocalories (84 kilojoules)
       2.8 g protein
         no fat
         2 g carbohydrate
        32 mg calcium
       0.8 mg iron
       76 microg retinol equivalents vitamin A
         no vitamin D
       0.08 mg thiamin
       0.12 mg riboflavin
        40 mg vitamin C

In season from September to March.

Brussels sprouts originated from the wild cabbage, and although

47

they were known in Belgium for many years it was not until the last century that sprouts were introduced to the UK.

Around the Brussels area any sprouts larger than the size of a small plum were unpopular. These small samples are still highly esteemed for their delicate flavour, but British housewives prefer, on average, sprouts that are about one and a half inches in diameter.

Storage – as for **broccoli.**

BUTTER Contains rather more than 80 per cent butter fat. It has a high energy value and is a good source of vitamins A and D (the amount varying with the season).

½ oz butter contains:

106	kilocalories (442 kilojoules)
0.05 g	protein
11.7 g	fat (55 per cent saturated)
no	carbohydrate
4 mg	calcium
no	iron
141* microg	retinol equivalents vitamin A
0.18 microg	vitamin D
no	thiamin
no	riboflavin
no	vitamin C

*This is an average figure. European winter butter may contain about half this amount, but European and New Zealand summer butter may contain as much as 192 microg per ½ oz.

In the UK the average person eats about 5 oz of butter per week, compared with an average of 3.5 oz of margarine. This average intake supplies about 15 per cent of the total dietary intake of fats, 25 per cent of the total vitamin A and 40 per cent of the total vitamin D in the average national diet.

The flavour of different kinds of butter depends partly on the amount of salt added during manufacture. Some butters are only slightly salted, or may have no added salt at all. Flavour is also determined by whether the butter is made by the lactic method, in which the cream used to make the butter is allowed to 'ripen' before being churned, or by the sweet cream method in which fresh cream is churned straight away. Butters imported

48

from Denmark, Holland and France are lactic butters, while butters made in the UK, Australia and New Zealand are sweet cream butters.

After production, butter should be kept at low temperatures. At home, the fridge is the best place. Butter will keep fresh for up to six weeks in the fridge. For longer periods, it can be stored in the freezer. Care must be taken to keep butter away from highly flavoured foods, as it will absorb their flavour. If it is kept in a warm place, and especially if it is exposed to sunshine, butter develops a very strong flavour – in other words, it goes rancid.

In Europe, butter is more widely used for cooking than it is in the United Kingdom. Most cookery experts claim that the rich flavour butter imparts to the dish cannot be matched by margarine, and certainly not by other cooking fats, such as lard and dripping, which are commonly used by many British housewives in preference to butter.

Even so, many people are limiting their butter consumption as butter contains a high proportion of **saturated fatty acids**. A high consumption of saturated fats appears to raise the blood **cholesterol** level.

In medieval times, butter was regarded as a medicine as well as a food. It was recommended for pains in the joints among children. If, as is likely, these pains were due to rickets (caused by a deficiency of vitamin D), then butter, being a fairly good source of vitamin D, would certainly have helped to cure the condition. Highly rancid butter was also given as a laxative.

CABBAGE A green, leafy vegetable from the plant family *brassica*. Several varieties are available: green cabbage, such as winter, spring or Savoy cabbage; white and red cabbages, mainly imported from Holland. All varieties are good sources of vitamins A and C, and iron.

1 oz raw cabbage contains:

        8 kilocalories (33 kilojoules)
    0.4 g protein
        no fat
    1.6 g carbohydrate

         18 mg calcium
        0.3 mg iron
    14 microg retinol equivalents vitamin A
          no vitamin D
       0.02 mg thiamin
       0.01 mg riboflavin
        17 mg vitamin C

4 oz cabbage, boiled, contain:

           8 kilocalories (33 kilojoules)
        0.8 g protein
          no fat
         1.6 g carbohydrate
        64 mg calcium
        0.4 mg iron
    56 microg retinol equivalents vitamin A
          no vitamin D
       0.04 mg thiamin
       0.04 mg riboflavin
        24 mg vitamin C

Cabbage in one form or another is available all year round. It
has been a popular vegetable in England since medieval times,
when it was served as a side dish with meat. It was cooked in a
little milk or butter, or used as a flavouring in soups and stews.
It is now more popular, perhaps, during winter, when fewer
fresh vegetables are available, though it is an excellent salad
ingredient as well, with more flavour and food value than most
salad vegetables.

Buy only crisp, moist, fresh-looking cabbage. Wilted cabbage
has much less flavour and food value. Eat as soon as possible
after purchase. For short-term storage, wrap in a plastic bag
and place at the bottom of the fridge, or keep in the salad
drawer. If a fridge is not available, keep cabbage in a cool,
dark place.

As vitamin C is so readily destroyed, cabbage should be quickly
washed, shredded with a sharp knife and rapidly cooked in
boiling water. Cook until almost tender, about 7 minutes. Drain
and serve immediately with a knob of butter. Do not keep hot
for any length of time, and do not reheat. The flavour of boiled
cabbage may be enhanced by adding a pinch of grated nutmeg
or a few caraway or celery seeds. It may also be served as
sauerkraut, cooked in vinegar.

CAFFEINE A mildly stimulating drug found in tea, coffee and cocoa. Caffeine works on the central nervous system and prevents fatigue. It is often taken in large quantities by those who drink continual cups of tea or coffee, but there appears to be no addictive effect. It can cause sleeplessness, specially to those who find caffeine produces a marked stimulatory effect. Strong tea or coffee should be avoided by anyone suffering from ulcers or dyspepsia. The caffeine irritates the stomach lining and can cause discomfort.

CALORIE A minute measure of energy. Nutritionists prefer to measure food energy in *kilocalories* (units 1000 times larger than the calorie), although these larger units are often also referred to as 'calories'. Calorific value of foods is always measured in kilocalories. The kilocalorie used to be abbreviated to Calorie, to distinguish it from the smaller unit, the calorie. Now it is more correct to refer to kilocalories, often abbreviated to kcal. In the UK, the conversion to the particular form of metric system known as the SI system (Système International d'Unités) involves the replacement of the familiar calorie by a smaller unit, the *joule*: one calorie is equal to 4.184 joules. To simplify matters, kilojoules and megajoules are gradually being adopted. The daily energy requirement of an active man is expressed as 3,000 kilocalories a day or 12.6 MJ (megajoules).

CANNING A method of food preservation originally devised by a Frenchman, Nicholas Appert, at the end of the eighteenth century. In the very early days, jars were used in place of cans, but in 1812 the first factory for preserving food in tinned iron containers was opened in Bermondsey. The food produced then was quite safe to eat, but it would hardly compare with the quality we take for granted in our canned foods today. In terms of quantity of food preserved and the great variety of food products which are canned, canning remains our most important methed of food preservation.

In the UK, the average man, woman and child each eats over 100 cans of food every year. Even the average baby consumes seven cans of prepared baby foods every week. (Household pets consume even larger quantities of canned foods!) Canned fruit and vegetables, especially baked beans, canned soups and meat meals with either pastry or vegetables, are the most popular of all canned foods. Canned fish and milk puddings are also favourites.

Canned foods continue to be popular because they are so very convenient. Since the food is cooked during processing, it is ready to serve, or at the most may need just to be reheated. Canned foods do not need any special storage facilities, and most of them compare favourably with their fresh counterparts. Canning overcomes the seasonality of foods.

The canning process is basically a very simple one. The food is packed into cans with or without the addition of liquid – brine for vegetables, sugar syrup for fruit, and so on. The can is sealed; the container and its contents are then sterilised by heating in large-scale pressure cookers. Some foods – the alkaline ones like canned vegetables and meat products – require longer heating to ensure complete sterility than do acid foods such as fruit. The actual heating time is determined by the temperature required to kill all harmful bacteria, bacterial spores and toxins which could possibly be present in the food. When the contents of the can reach the required temperature, the can is rapidly cooled by immersion in cold water.

Because of the modern tendency to buy more and more convenience foods, a much wider and more appealing range of canned foods is being produced each year. New canning techniques are being adopted to produce food with a flavour and appearance more similar to good home-cooked food. One of the latest methods is called aseptic canning. In traditional methods of canning, to ensure sterility the food is frequently heated for far longer than is needed to cook the food. Because it is overcooked, the food develops the 'canny' flavour, and loses its good texture and appearance. With aseptic canning, the food is sterilised before it goes into the can. Much higher temperatures are used in order to reduce the overall cooking period. The food is packed into sterile cans, so no further heating is needed. Food produced in this way has a better flavour and appearance, and its nutritive value is likely to be higher than food canned by traditional methods.

Research into the can itself has recently given us the easy-open or ring-pull can. Alternative materials are also being used. In the us aluminium cans are very popular. There, too, cans are often coated inside with lacquer. In Japan, tin-free steel is being used. The cans have a thin inside plating of chromium.

Storage of canned foods

Provided they are kept cool and dry, canned foods will keep well for long periods. Cans of food taken on Antarctic expeditions in the early 1900s, opened some fifty years later, were found to be in first-class condition. If they are allowed to go rusty, or are stored at high temperatures, their contents will deteriorate. Spoilage of canned foods is usually caused by a defect in the can, or incomplete sterilisation. Bacteria which have not been killed can turn the food quite bad. It may become very acid or sulphurous. Some bacteria produce hydrogen gas as they grow. This causes the ends of the can to bulge, making a 'blown' can. The smell of any canned foods spoiled in these ways is usually so offensive there is little chance of its being eaten; it should on no account be consumed.

The Canned and Packaged Foods Advisory Bureau recommends that under good storage conditions canned foods will keep in perfect conditions for these times:

canned fruit, milk, fish in tomato sauce	1 year
canned vegetables	2 years
canned meats, fish in oil	5 years

These are, however, conservative estimates, and foods should keep well for rather longer periods.

Food value

The main nutritive losses during canning are of those nutrients which are destroyed by heat. These are mainly vitamin B1 and vitamin C. Losses may continue during storage at high temperatures.

CARBOHYDRATE This is the chemical name given to a very large group of substances. Nutritionally, the most important are the starches, sugars and celluloses. **Cellulose** cannot be digested by the human digestive system, but has a nutritive value nevertheless. One gram of pure carbohydrate, either starch or sugar, supplies 4 kilocalories of energy (equivalent to about 16 kilojoules).

Starches and sugars are the main sources of energy in the diet. They supply roughly half of the total energy requirement of people in affluent Western societies. In developing countries, the proportion of total energy requirements derived from carbohydrates is an index of both their affluence and the general standard of nutrition.

Carbohydrates are supplied mainly by foods of plant origin. Starches come from cereal foods including flour, bread, cakes, biscuits and other products made with flour; oatmeal and other breakfast cereals made from corn (maize), wheat and rice; other forms of rice, barley and rye. Starch is also supplied by some vegetables. The most important of these is the potato. The most common sugar in the diet is cane or beet sugar, known also as *sucrose*. This is used as a sweetener at the table and in cooking. *Lactose*, or milk sugar, is the chief carbohydrate derived from animal foods. *Fructose* is the sugar which sweetens fruit; *glucose* is yet another type of sugar. Unlike the others, glucose is found in very few natural foods.

In the national average diet in the United Kingdom, cereal foods provide about half our total daily intake of carbohydrate; these foods may contain starch alone, like bread or, like cakes and biscuits, both starch and sugar. Sugar and preserves alone supply about one quarter of our carbohydrates. Potatoes, which are normally regarded as a very starchy food, supply less than 5 per cent of our total energy intake, and less than 10 per cent of our total carbohydrate intake.

CARROTS A popular root vegetable containing a large amount of the deep yellow pigment, carotene. In the body, carotene is converted into vitamin A. In the national average diet in the UK, about 3 oz of carrots are eaten every week and provide about 15 per cent of the daily recommended intake of vitamin A.

1 oz raw carrot contains:

```
       6 kilocalories (25 kilojoules)
     0.2 g protein
      no fat
     1.5 g carbohydrate
    27.2 mg calcium
    0.32 mg iron
567 microg retinol equivalents vitamin A
      no vitamin D
    0.07 mg thiamin
    0.06 mg riboflavin
       7 mg vitamin C
```

4 oz boiled carrots contain:

```
      20 kilocalories (84 kilojoules)
     0.8 g protein
      no fat
     4.8 g carbohydrate
```

         40.8 mg calcium
         0.44 mg iron
2,268 microg equivalents vitamin A
          no vitamin D
         0.08 mg thiamin
         0.04 mg riboflavin
          8 mg vitamin C

New carrots, bought in bunches complete with their feathery foliage, are especially sweet and usually small. There should be no green on the root itself. They are available from late spring. At their best, they should be eaten as soon after purchase or gathering as possible. If not required for immediate use, keep new carrots in the salad drawer of the fridge.

Main crop carrots are allowed to grow to maturity. They are sold without foliage, and are often washed before being sold. If 'old' carrots are to be bought in large quantities for home use, unwashed carrots should be bought as these keep much better than the washed ones. Carrots should be stored in a cool, dark place. Commercially, they are often stored in the fields where they were grown, inside vegetable clamps. If properly kept, the main season's crop of carrots maintains the supply until the next season's 'new' carrots are ready.

Carrots are valued for their colour as well as their flavour. As well as being a very popular vegetable to serve hot, carrots are excellent salad vegetables, especially good in winter salads, coleslaws and so on.

CAULIFLOWER One of the popular green vegetables, although the part of the plant usually eaten is the white flowering head. Like other green vegetables, cauliflower is an excellent source of vitamin C in the diet.

4 oz cauliflower, boiled, contain:

        12 kilocalories (50 kilojoules)
       1.6 g protein
        no fat
       1.2 g carbohydrate
        26 mg calcium
       0.56 mg iron
     6 microg retinol equivalents vitamin A
        no vitamin D
       0.07 mg thiamin
       0.07 mg riboflavin
        23 mg vitamin C

Cauliflowers are available all the year round, although they are more plentiful and often cheaper in autumn and winter.

Choose a cauliflower with a tightly packed head. White heads are usually considered the best; yellow cauliflowers are often thought to be stale. Yellowing is caused by too much sunshine, rain or frost, but it does not affect either flavour or food value. As they are often cheaper than the white ones, yellow cauliflowers may be the better buy. Do not buy cauliflowers which look damaged, or those with a loosely packed head. These may be over-ripe and inclined to be woody.

Eat cauliflowers as soon after purchase as possible for the best flavour and food value. For short-term storage, keep the vegetable in a cool dark place, ideally in the salad drawer of the fridge. Sprigs of cauliflower also quick freeze quite well.

CELERY A popular vegetable or salad vegetable of which only the stem is eaten. Although it has an attractive flavour and crisp texture, celery provides very little in the way of nutrients. Being almost all water and cellulose, it is a useful food for the low calorie diet. Eaten raw, celery adds roughage, and is valued for maintaining dental health.

2 oz raw celery contain:

        4 kilocalories (18 kilojoules)
     0.6 g protein
      no fat
     0.8 g carbohydrate
      30 mg calcium
     0.4 mg iron
      no vitamin A
      no vitamin D
    0.02 mg thiamin
    0.02 mg riboflavin
       4 mg vitamin C

Celery is usually available all the year round, though most plentiful from August to February.

It is best eaten as fresh as possible, although it will stay quite crisp in the salad drawer of the fridge. Alternatively, celery may be prepared and scrubbed to remove any soil and the individual sticks stood in a jug of cold water.

Celery may be boiled and braised as well as served raw. Its attractive flavour may be used to enhance stews and casseroled dishes. Finely chopped, it may be added to stuffings for meat, fish or other vegetables. Celery soup is also very popular.

CELERY SALT A flavouring prepared from dried, powdered celery and table salt. Its flavour is very strong and it should be used sparingly. It is often added to give extra flavour to soups, sauces and casseroled dishes.

CELLULOSE is a carbohydrate made of several thousand units of glucose. It is synthesised by plants for supporting the tissues of stems and leaves. Unlike starch, cellulose cannot be digested in the human digestive system. Although it cannot supply the body with energy, cellulose has the negative food value of providing roughage, or bulk to the food undergoing digestion. The bulk is important for stimulating movement of the intestinal muscles; the rhythmic movements of the large intestine responsible for evacuation of the faeces are especially important.

Cellulose may prevent the absorption of certain mineral substances from food. Calcium and iron are the most important minerals to be affected. The body can make more efficient use of these minerals from food in the intestine if there is little cellulose present at the same time. For this reason, calcium is more readily absorbed from milk than from green vegetables.

CHEESE is probably one of the earliest processed foods devised by man, originating as a means of preserving fresh milk. Different types of cheeses have been produced, quite independently, in many different parts of the world. Today, over 400 different ways of making them are still observed in order to keep the individual characteristics of each cheese. Large-scale production methods have also been introduced to make the most popular types of cheeses.

Most British cheeses are the hard pressed variety. These are produced from pasteurised milk which is turned sour by the addition of specially selected bacteria. Later, the soured milk is separated into curds and whey by the enzyme rennet. The curd is packed into large units of between 60 lb and 80 lb, and is pressed under a great weight. The unripe cheese is then allowed to mature. This takes several months, or even years, depending on whether a mild or mature flavoured cheese is required. British cheeses produced in this way are Caerphilly, Cheddar, Cheshire, Derby, Double Gloucester, Lancashire, Leicester, Stilton and Wensleydale.

Blue veined cheeses like Blue Stilton, Cheshire and Wensleydale are inoculated with special moulds which grow inside the cheese as it ripens.

Small, soft cheeses, such as Camembert and Brie, are not made in the UK. These cheeses are ripened by the action of moulds which grow on the outside of the cheese. This mould growth limits the size of the cheese which can be made.

Unripened cheeses, which include cream and cottage cheese, are becoming increasingly popular. In recent years, a wide variety of unripened cheeses have been produced in Scotland. Some of these are produced according to very old traditional recipes.

In the UK the average person eats about 3½ oz of cheese each week. (Less cheese is eaten in the north of England than in other regions of the UK.) The national average cheese consumption provides the following proportions of the daily recommended intakes of nutrients: 5 per cent of the protein, 10 per cent of the calcium, 4.5 per cent of the vitamin A.

The most popular hard cheese in the UK is Cheddar cheese.

1 oz Cheddar cheese contains:

>117 kilocalories (490 kilojoules)
>7.2 g protein
>9.8 g fat*
>no carbohydrate
>230 mg calcium
>0.2 mg iron
>119 microg retinol equivalents vitamin A
>0.10 microg vitamin D
>0.01 mg thiamin
>0.14 mg riboflavin
>no vitamin C

*The proportion of saturated fat in cheese varies between 50 and 60 per cent.

As it is made from skimmed milk, *cottage cheese* contains very much less fat than ordinary cheeses. This explains why its energy value is so much lower, and explains, too, the popularity of cottage cheese among slimmers. Its calcium content is also lower than that of the hard pressed cheeses.

One 4 oz carton of cottage cheese contains:

        123 kilocalories (514 kilojoules)
      17.92 g protein
       4.52 g fat*
       2.60 g carbohydrate
         56 mg calcium
        0.4 mg iron
    32 microg retinol equivalents vitamin A
  0.04 microg vitamin D
       0.04 mg thiamin
       0.32 mg riboflavin
         no vitamin C

Cream cheese has a very high fat content. The actual amount depends upon whether the cheese was made from full cream or single cream. The protein content of either type of cream cheese is much lower than the protein content of cottage cheese or the ripened cheeses.

1 oz full cream cheese contains:

        232 kilocalories (970 kilojoules)
        0.9 g protein
       24.5 g fat*
         no carbohydrate
          8 mg calcium
       0.04 mg iron
   300 microg retinol equivalents vitamin A
       trace vitamin D
          no thiamin
       0.06 mg riboflavin
          no vitamin C

Most hard cheeses can be stored in the fridge and keep well for a week or more, provided they are well wrapped in plastic or aluminium foil, or kept in a special airtight container. The wrapping is needed to prevent the cheese from drying out. The cheese should be taken from the fridge an hour before it is eaten for its full flavour to be enjoyed. Soft cheeses should be bought when they are just ripe and eaten straight away. Unlike the hard cheeses, soft cheeses stay at their peak of perfection for

*The proportion of saturated fat in cheese varies between 50 and 60 per cent.

a very short time, sometimes a matter of hours only. If bought in advance, the cheese should be slightly under-ripe and allowed to stay in a cool larder until needed. Cheese stales more quickly at a higher temperature. Often it is better to buy a little cheese at a time rather than buying a large piece and risk its going stale if no suitable low-temperature storage is available.

Cheeses most suitable for cooking are Lancashire and Cheddar, especially the much cheaper, imported Cheddar-type cheeses. In cooking, care must be taken not to overheat the cheese. The effect of over-cooking is to make the cheese hard and stringy. Many people find over-cooked cheese very indigestible, hence 'cheese dreams' or the old wives' tale that a cheese dish late at night prevents a good night's rest.

Processed cheese, produced by mixing ripe and unripe Cheddar type cheeses with emulsifiers, is especially good for cooking. It is processed so that the fat does not readily melt away, delaying the stringy stage of over-cooking. Unfortunately, the flavour of processed cheese is not universally popular.

CHERRIES Small, stoned fruit low in vitamin C and most other nutrients.

2 oz raw eating cherries weighed with stones contain:

    22 kilocalories (92 kilojoules)
    0.2 g protein
    no fat
    6 g carbohydrate
    7.8 mg calcium
    0.18 mg iron
    11 microg retinol equivalents vitamin A
    no vitamin D
    0.03 mg thiamin
    3 mg vitamin C

In the UK the best-known eating varieties are the white and black heart cherries, which are juicy and sweet. These are in season from June to July. Cooking cherries, which have a nutrient content similar to eating cherries, are the May Dukes and the morello. They have a much sharper taste than the eating cherries and are in season in August. Processed cherries are also available in cans and jars.

Cherry pie, cherry gâteau and black cherry jam are some of the most popular ways of cooking cherries. The traditional English cherry cake is made with glacé cherries. These are cherries which have been preserved in sugar. Maraschino cherries are cherries which have been cooked in syrup flavoured with maraschino liqueur.

CHESTNUTS The fruit of the sweet horsechestnut tree. This is a native to Spain, but it flourishes in the UK and other European countries. Chestnuts are collected from the tree in autumn and are usually available during the autumn and winter months. Chestnuts are consumed only in very small quantities in the UK. Unlike most other nuts, chestnuts are not a good source of protein and contain little fat.

1 oz of chestnuts, weighed without their shells, contain:

49	kilocalories (204 kilojoules)
0.7 g	protein
0.8 g	fat
10.4 g	carbohydrate
13.1 mg	calcium
0.25 mg	iron
no	vitamin A
no	vitamin D
0.20 mg	thiamin
no	vitamin C

Traditionally, roast turkey is stuffed with a chestnut stuffing made with a purée of chestnuts. This is available in cans and is sold most commonly around Christmas time. Chestnuts are also made into a French speciality, marrons glacés, and other rich desserts. Chestnuts also make an excellent and rather unusual soup. Years ago, roast chestnuts were sold in the streets, but the hot chestnut stalls have largely disappeared now.

CHICKEN Strictly speaking, this term applies to young domestic fowls, either cocks or hens. Nowadays, 'chicken' is used to describe any type of bird of this species. All chicken meat, whatever the age of the bird and however it was reared, is high in protein content and contains useful amounts of several members of the B group of vitamins. The flesh is low in fat, which means that the energy value of chicken is considerably lower than that of other popular meats.

4 oz roast chicken, without bone, contain:

    208 kilocalories (876 kilojoules)
  33.6 g protein
   8.4 g fat (33.5 per cent saturated)
     no carbohydrate
  16 mg calcium
 2.8 mg iron
     no vitamin A
     no vitamin D
0.06 mg thiamin
0.07 mg riboflavin in chicken breast
0.23 mg riboflavin in chicken leg
     no vitamin C

In the UK, the average person eats about 5½ oz of poultry every week. Although there has been some increase in the amount of turkey eaten, chicken is still by far the most popular type of poultry. It is palatable, tender, available all year round and comparatively cheap. Its low cost is the result of streamlined, large-scale production of the birds, and the rapid development of the self-service store and supermarket. Most chickens today are bought quick-frozen from the supermarket. The availability of portions of chicken has also helped its popularity among those who cook for 1 or 2 people.

As a single item of diet, chicken contributes about 4 per cent of the total amount of protein consumed, and 5 per cent of the nicotinic acid, one of the important B group vitamins.

PROTEIN AND ENERGY CONTENT OF CHICKEN COMPARED WITH OTHER MEATS

Meat	g protein/oz	kilocalories/oz
Chicken, roast (weighed without bone)	8.4	54
Beef, roast sirloin (some fat with lean)	6.0	109
Beef, grilled steak	7.2	86
Lamb, roast leg	7.1	83
Lamb, grilled chop ⎫ (weighed without	5.7	142
Pork, roast leg ⎬ bone, lean *and*	7.0	90
Pork, grilled chop ⎭ fat)	5.3	155

Broiler This term is derived from the word 'broil' which Americans use in place of our word 'grill'. A small, tender chicken, such as those produced as battery-reared, quick-frozen birds, suitable for grilling, became known as a broiler. Now the word has come into general use to describe small, quick-frozen birds, reared in batteries as opposed to being 'free range'.

Free range Chickens reared in the old-fashioned way, with freedom of movement in the farmyard or chicken coop, are described as free range. When their muscles are exercised, they develop better flavoured meat, though it can be tougher.

Deep litter chickens are kept in a large shed. They are allowed a certain freedom of movement, but are not allowed to roam outside the building.

Battery chickens are confined to small, usually individual cages. As they are not allowed to move very much, the flesh of battery birds is very tender, but has much less flavour than that of the free range or deep litter bird.

Although flavour may vary, there is no evidence to show that the food value of chickens produced by the various methods differs in nutritional value.

Poussins are very small, young birds, just big enough to serve one or two people.

Spring chickens were, at one time, small, tender young birds. But as chicken production is no longer seasonal, the term has lost it significance.

Roasters are birds which are tender enough to be cooked by roasting. Roasters are young birds weighing between 3 and 4 lb.

Boiling fowl are much older birds. Their flesh is too tough for roasting and must be cooked very slowly in liquid. Often chickens previously kept for egg production are sold off cheaply as boiling fowl. As they are much cheaper than roasters, boiling fowl are a good buy for casseroled dishes.

CHICORY Plants grown in the dark to preserve their delicate flavour; hence the leaves are practically white. Generally eaten raw as a salad vegetable in the UK, but they may also be cooked. They are available throughout the winter and spring.

1 oz raw chicory contains:

            3 kilocalories (13 kilojoules)
        0.2 g protein
          no fat
        0.4 g carbohydrate
       5.2 mg calcium
      0.20 mg iron
            vitamin content unknown at present

Chicory should be stored, like other salad vegetables, in the salad drawer in the fridge.

Since it is extremely low in energy value, chicory is a useful addition in slimming meals, to which its bitterness adds extra flavour.

CHIPS Fried potatoes which enjoy a tremendous popularity in the UK. Also called French fried potatoes in some restaurants.

Chips have a high energy value (see **fried foods**). Like all other methods of cooking, frying destroys some of the vitamin C. There is an average loss of 25 per cent to 35 per cent in the vitamin C content of potatoes when fried.

A 6 oz portion of chips contains:

          402 kilocalories (1,686 kilojoules)
        6.6 g protein
       15.6 g fat
       63.6 g carbohydrate
         24 mg calcium
        2.4 mg iron
          no vitamin A
          no vitamin D
       0.18 mg thiamin
       0.06 mg riboflavin
      12–36 mg vitamin C (according to the age of potatoes – see
              potatoes)

CHOCOLATE A popular confectionery of two main kinds, milk and plain. Both types have a very high energy value derived from their high fat and carbohydrate contents. In addition, plain chocolate contains a little iron.

COMPARISON OF NUTRIENT CONTENT OF 1 oz EACH OF MILK AND PLAIN CHOCOLATE		
Nutrient	milk chocolate	plain chocolate
Kilocalories (Kilojoules)	167 (698)	155 (648)
Protein g	2.5	1.6
Fat g (50% saturated)	10.7	10.0
Carbohydrate g	15.5	13.9
Calcium mg	69.9	17.9
Iron mg	0.49	0.82
Vitamin A microg retinol equivalents	0	0
Vitamin D microg	—	—
Thiamin mg	0.01	0.01
Riboflavin mg	0.10	0.10
Vitamin C	0	0

The essential ingredient in making chocolate is the cocoa bean, which grows in the pods of a tropical palm. When newly harvested, cocoa beans are light violet in colour, but they gradually darken to their characteristic dark brown. To make chocolate, the cocoa beans are roasted and finely ground. These processes convert the beans into a product known as cocoa-mass. This is mixed with a high proportion – about 50 per cent or more – of finely powdered sugar and additional cocoa butter. This last substance is a by-product of **cocoa** manufacture. To make milk chocolate, powdered or condensed milk is added. All the ingredients are very thoroughly mixed together – the mixing may take up to 24 hours to give chocolate its desired velvety texture.

Chocolate for coating biscuits or cakes, or for the centres of individual chocolates, is made with a higher proportion of cocoa butter. This makes a softer product which spreads more easily.

Care must be taken not to use too high a temperature when melting chocolate for use in cookery. Excessive heat causes the individual constituents to separate out. This process cannot be reversed. It is best to melt chocolate over a saucepan of hot water or in a double saucepan.

Chocolate must always be kept in a cool, dry place, well away from bright light, especially sunlight. Heat causes chocolate to melt; heat and light together cause a white 'bloom' to develop, and the chocolate turns rancid.

CHOLESTEROL One of the normal constitutents of the blood. It is associated with the transport of fats around the body. Many important metabolites, including steroid hormones, some vitamin D and the bile salts, are manufactured in the body from cholesterol.

Cholesterol is present in all animal tissues, and consequently in all foods derived from animals. Eggs, offal (including liver, kidney, brains and sweetbreads), fish roes and shellfish are the richest dietary sources of cholesterol. Cholesterol is absent from foods of plant origin.

In addition to being derived from food, cholesterol is made in our own body tissues, especially in the liver and the intestines. The body's own production of cholesterol is not modified in any way by the dietary intake.

The amount of cholesterol carried in the blood – the blood cholesterol level – may vary from 150 mg to 250 mg in 100 ml of blood in seemingly normal adults. A blood cholesterol level of over 220 mg is usually considered undesirable, as coronary heart disease is more common among those with high blood cholesterol levels. The day-to-day level may fluctuate, as it depends not only on the diet, but may also be increased by emotional stress and physical inactivity. Several determinations of the actual average levels are usually required before action is taken to lower the level. This can usually be done by modifying the diet. Blood cholesterol levels are reduced when animal fats are replaced by vegetable oils, when consumption of sugar and sweet foods is reduced and when the consumption of foods which themselves contain cholesterol is also reduced. Exercise also helps to lower blood cholesterol levels, while cigarette smoking tends to raise it. Blood cholesterol also tends to rise with age.

CIDER An alcoholic beverage made by fermenting apple juice. Cider has been described as the *vin ordinaire* of the British, as the apple was the only fruit which could be relied upon to produce the necessary sugar substrate for fermentation. The original cider, nick-named 'scrumpy', was more bitter and less carbonated than the cider which is mass-produced today.

Half a pint of dry cider contains 100 kilocalories (420 kilojoules); half a pint of sweet cider 120 kilocalories (504 kilojoules). A quarter pint of vintage cider contains 140 kilocalories (588 kilojoules).

In addition to being served as a drink, cider is also an ingredient in many traditional recipes, including cider cake, cider sauce for roast pork and cider-baked herrings.

COCKLES See **Shellfish**.

COCOA A beverage as popular today as when it was first introduced into England from the West Indies in the middle of the seventeenth century. Notably rich in iron, cocoa made with milk is a nourishing and refreshing drink.

1 level teaspoon of cocoa contains:

```
      32 kilocalories (134 kilojoules)
    1.45 g  protein
    1.65 g  fat
    2.50 g  carbohydrate
    3.65 mg calcium
    1.02 mg iron
0.5 microg  retinol equivalents vitamin A
      no  vitamin D
    0.01 mg thiamin
      no  riboflavin
      no  vitamin C
```

Cocoa is made from roasting, milling and pressing the cocoa beans. Powerful hydraulic presses remove a proportion of the cocoa butter. Cocoa contains between 20 per cent and 30 per cent of the cocoa butter originally contained in the cocoa beans. Cocoa also contains two substances known as alkaloids – caffeine and theobromine. These alkaloids give cocoa its bitter flavour, and also its refreshing and stimulating properties.

In recent years, the price of cocoa beans has risen enormously. These price rises will undoubtedly be reflected in the rising price of cocoa as well as of chocolate and chocolate confectionery.

Drinking chocolate is made from cocoa which is sweetened and has dried milk added. The powder is treated to make it combine more readily with hot liquids than does cocoa.

COCONUT Much larger than all other nuts, it contains 'milk' as well as kernel. Desiccated coconut, a shredded form with some of the moisture removed, is fairly popular in cake-making in the UK.

1 oz fresh coconut contains:

104	kilocalories (435 kilojoules)
1.1 g	protein
10.2 g	fat (87.5 per cent saturated)
1.1 g	carbohydrate
3.7 mg	calcium
0.59 mg	iron
no	vitamin A
no	vitamin D
0.01 mg	thiamin
negligible	riboflavin
no	vitamin C

1 oz desiccated coconut contains:

172	kilocalories (722 kilojoules)
1.9 g	protein
17.6 g	fat
1.8 g	carbohydrate
6 mg	calcium
1 mg	iron
no	vitamin A
no	vitamin D
0.02 mg	thiamin
0.01 mg	riboflavin
no	vitamin C

The protein content of coconut is lower than that of most other nuts. The most notable difference between coconut and other nuts is that its oil is made predominantly of **saturated fatty acids.** It contains a high proportion of lauric acid, which is unique among saturated fatty acids in being liquid at room temperature.

Commercially, coconut oil is used to make artificial milks and modified cow's milk products. Coconut milk, a slightly sweet liquid with a low mineral content, has no special food value.

COD The most widespread and popular fish eaten in the UK and other countries of the world. It closely resembles the **haddock**, but is generally considered to be inferior in flavour and texture to the haddock. Cod is correspondingly cheaper but still has excellent food value. (For nutrient analysis of cod, see **fish**.)

Most cod landed in this country weigh between six and fourteen pounds. The fish is sold as fillets or steaks and smaller fish may be bought and cooked whole. A great deal of cod is also quick-frozen as fillets or as the universally popular fish fingers.

Cod is available all year round.

COFFEE The dried fruit or bean of the coffee plant which is roasted and ground and then infused with boiling water to make a fragrant and refreshing drink. Coffee became a popular drink in the seventeenth century. Initially, only the upper classes could afford to drink it. Then coffee became cheaper and consequently more popular when it was served in the famous London coffee houses. The first of these was opened in 1652, and soon coffee houses became a feature of London life of that time. Those with literary, artistic and commercial interests often met there to discuss the pressing matters of the day.

When tea became a comparatively cheap commodity, it was drunk in favour of the still relatively expensive coffee. Like tea, coffee also contains caffeine, but it has twice the amount found in tea.

Sometimes the ground and dried root of chicory is added to ground coffee. This is a bitter ingredient added to 'stretch' the expensive coffee grounds to make a cheaper commodity.

Instant coffee is made by extracting the water soluble components from a ground coffee infusion. The resulting liquid may be spray- or roller-dried to a powder or granule. Freeze drying and similar advances in dehydration have given a fresher tasting instant coffee in recent years. Coffee essence is still marketed. This is the thick liquid produced after removing water from the coffee infusion.

Apart from the stimulation provided by the caffeine, coffee has no special nutritive value. It is virtually calorie free, although not when milk and sugar are added to it.

CORN One of the world's important staple cereal foods, known also as **maize.** Corn on the cob is harvested from this cereal crop. Although it is a cereal, it is frequently considered as a vegetable in the UK. Each cob corresponds to the ear of the grain. The kernels are borne on a large, hard core which is the cob. The kernels are often removed to make sweet corn 'off' the cob. In this form, corn is often canned and frozen.

2 oz corn, canned, contain:

54	kilocalories (226 kilojoules)
1.4 g	protein
0.4 g	fat
11.6 g	carbohydrate
2 mg	calcium
0.2 mg	iron
20 microg	retinol equivalents vitamin A
no	vitamin D
0.02 mg	thiamin
0.02 mg	riboflavin
2 mg	vitamin C

In some parts of the world, notably Central and South America, corn is the staple cereal, although it is partly being replaced by wheat. The corn is ground to make gruel, *tortilla* or similar bread-like foods.

In the UK we use ground corn to make cornflour, used in custard and blancmange powders, and also to thicken sauces. It is useful for thickening as it contains more starch and less protein than wheat flour.

During manufacture, the protein in corn is separated from the starch; 0.1 per cent to 0.4 per cent remains.

1 oz cornflour contains:

100	kilocalories (420 kilojoules)
0.1 g	protein
0.2 g	fat
26.1 g	carbohydrate
4 mg	calcium
0.4 mg	iron
no	vitamins

Cornflour is also the basis for many 'instant' quick whip desserts. The cornflour is treated to make it thicken the mixture without heating. Some products may also be beaten to a froth as a result of further treatment of the cornflour.

CORN OIL is an oil extracted from corn (maize) and refined to make it suitable for culinary purposes. It has a bland flavour which does not mask the flavour of the other ingredients with which it is used.

It is high in **polyunsaturated fatty acids**.

$\frac{1}{2}$ fluid oz corn oil contains:

177 kilocalories (535 kilojoules)
no protein
14.2 g fat (10 per cent saturated)
no carbohydrate
no calcium
no iron
no vitamins

Corn oil can be used for all frying, roasting and grilling, for making cakes and pastries, and for salad dressings. It can be heated to high temperatures before the smoke-point (decomposition point) is reached and is, therefore, more suitable for deep frying than lard, dripping or butter.

CORONARY THROMBOSIS is the clotting of blood within the coronary arteries, important blood vessels which carry blood to the heart muscle itself. Like all other body tissues, the heart muscle needs a constant supply of oxygen. If it is deprived of oxygen for any length of time, some of the tissue will be permanently damaged. The severity of a heart attack depends upon the amount of damage caused by blood restriction. If the supply is cut off completely, the patient will die. If the blood clot occurs on one of the smaller blood vessels, or if the clot is quickly dispersed, only part of the heart may be damaged. Although the patient may recover, he will never be as fit as he was before. Anyone who has suffered from a heart attack is always left with a reduced capacity for physical activity.

In America and Britain, coronary thrombosis causes one quarter of all deaths. Every year in the UK 35,000 men die of coronary heart disease before they have reached retiring age.

The basic cause of coronary thrombosis is **atherosclerosis,** i.e. the deposition of fatty materials within the arteries. Coronary thrombosis is more common among men than women, and is also likely to threaten those suffering from either high blood pressure or diabetes, the obese and those who take little exercise. Mental stress is another factor which is associated with the incidence of coronary thrombosis. There are also close statistical relationships between blood cholesterol levels, dietary consumption of animal fats, sugar and the hardness of drinking water and coronary heart disease.

COTTAGE CHEESE See **Cheese.**

COURGETTES See **Marrow.**

CRAB A shellfish. The edible portion of the crab consists of two parts – the white flesh of the claws and the 'brown' meat, a soft, rich, yellow substance which nearly fills the interior of the shell.

2 oz crab, boiled, contain:

72	kilocalories (301 kilojoules)
10.8 g	protein
3 g	fat
no	carbohydrate
16.6 mg	calcium
0.74 mg	iron
no	vitamin A
no	vitamin D
0.06 mg	thiamin
0.08 mg	riboflavin
no	vitamin C

Fresh crabs are at their best from May to August. They can also be bought frozen or canned.

Like other shellfish, crab contains a modest amount of choles. terol. Although it is not especially high, crab would normally be omitted from a low cholesterol diet.

For flavour, and as a health precaution, fresh crab must be very fresh indeed. It should be bought only from a reliable fish-monger. To ensure freshness crabs for eating were once, like lobsters, frequently sold still alive. Now they are usually boiled and dressed for the table by the fishmonger. Crab should be eaten on the day it is bought. For freezing, too, only very fresh crab meat is suitable. Never attempt to freeze crab in its shell.

CREAM That part of the milk with the highest fat content. Being high in fat, cream floats to the top of fresh, unhomogenised milk which is allowed to stand for some time. Butter is made from cream. Cream is also highly valued for serving on desserts and to add richness to cooked dishes.

A number of different creams are offered for sale. The main difference between them is the proportion of fat* they contain. Some creams are also heat-treated to extend their 'shelf life', i.e. their keeping qualities.

Clotted cream is richest of all, with an average fat content of 55 per cent. Double cream must by law contain not less than 48 per cent fat; single cream not less than 18 per cent; half cream not less than 12 per cent.

The actual amounts of fat in each variety may be higher than these figures, which give the minimum required by law.

COMPARISON OF NUTRITIVE CONTENT OF DOUBLE AND SINGLE CREAMS		
	1 oz double cream	1 oz single cream
Kilocalories (Kilojoules)	128 (534)	54 (225)
Protein g	0.5	0.8
Fat g*	13.6	5.1
Carbohydrate g	0.7	1.2
Calcium mg	18	28
Iron mg	0	0
Vitamin A microg retinol equivalents	119	44
Vitamin D microg	0.08	0.03
Thiamin	0.01	0.01
Riboflavin	0.02	0.04
Vitamin C	0	0

*Whatever the proportion of fat in the various types of cream, 55 per cent of the fat is in the form of saturated fatty acids.

Whipped cream Cream will whip, or thicken, provided it has at least 30 per cent fat. Cream is often sold as 'whipping cream' or 'whipped cream' with this amount of fat in it. Double cream whips easily as it has more than this required amount of fat, but it is soon over-whipped and can turn to butter with over-beating. For this reason, it is better, and more economical, to blend double and single cream for whipping, or to add a little milk to double cream. This not only extends the expensive double cream, but gives a lighter whipped cream.

Single cream alone will not whip, but some heat-treated creams will do so even though they have less than 30 per cent fat.

Heat-treated creams Cream sold in small jars or in cans displayed on the grocery shelves and not in a refrigerated display unit is usually found to be *sterilised cream*. This, by law, must have a fat content of 23 per cent. It keeps almost indefinitely, having been sterilised inside its container. The heat treatment gives the cream a slightly cooked flavour and usually a darker colour.

UHT cream – ultra heat-treated cream – is another type of sterilised cream. It will keep for up to 5 months in a cool place. It is retailed in 'tetrapaks', often small ones to give just enough cream for one serving.

Sour cream has been specially soured under controlled conditions by adding cultures of bacteria. This is very similar to the way yoghurt is produced. Sour cream is becoming popular in cooking and for salad dressings.

Fresh pasteurised cream will keep three to four days in summer and up to one week in winter if refrigerated. Sterilised and UHT cream will keep for long periods without refrigeration, provided the containers remain unopened. All types of cream must be treated as fresh once the container is opened.

The use of certain additives – these include sugar, stabilisers and emulsifiers – is now permitted in controlled amounts in specified types of cream. For example, whipped cream may contain sugar and certain stabilisers; ultra heat-treated cream and sterilised cream may contain certain emulsifiers. The inclusion of additives must be declared on the label of any pre-packed cream.

CUCUMBER Usually eaten as a salad vegetable. Next to marrow, it has the highest water content of all the vegetables: 96.4 per cent.

1 oz raw cucumber contains:

        3 kilocalories (12 kilojoules)
    0.2 g protein
       no fat
    0.5 g carbohydrate
    6.5 mg calcium
   0.09 mg iron
       no vitamin A
       no vitamin D
   0.01 mg thiamin
   0.01 mg riboflavin
        2 mg vitamin C

Cucumber is sold graded into various sizes and shapes; all are guaranteed free of blemish and disease. The misshapen samples, which taste just as good as the long, straight cucumbers, are the cheapest.

As they are grown commercially in enormous heated greenhouses under controlled conditions, cucumbers are available at all times of the year. Cucumbers are also grown in summer in unheated greenhouses and cold frames. Although these may not have the ideal long, slim straightness of commercially grown cucumbers, they often have a stronger flavour.

Cucumbers keep well, although to keep them at their best they should be stored in the salad drawer of the fridge.

Traditionally, cucumber dice are used as a garnish for poached salmon. Slices of cucumber also team well with other cold fish dishes.

Cucumbers have also been used from time to time as an aid to beauty, and a means of cooling tired eyes.

CURRANTS One of the popular varieties of dried fruits, currants are prepared from black seedless grapes. Like all other dried fruits, currants have a high energy value and are a good source of iron and calcium. Most of the currants sold in the UK come from Greece and Australia.

1 oz currants contains:

       69 kilocalories (288 kilojoules)
    0.5 g protein
       no fat

        18 g carbohydrate
  27.1 mg calcium
  0.52 mg iron
            no figure available for vitamin A
        no vitamin D
  0.01 mg thiamin
        no vitamin C

The size of the currant has little to do with its quality. Small-
ness can be an advantage, as larger varieties are more likely to
contain seeds.

Currants, and all other dried fruits, should be kept in airtight
containers. Their original carton may be adequate for short
periods, but a storage jar is better. If allowed to dry, the fruits
lose their moist plumpness, and the sugar they contain may
crystallise out.

CURRY POWDER A blend of spices, often very hot ones, used
in the preparation of highly flavoured meat, poultry, fish and
vegetable dishes. Curry contains a large number of minerals but
makes only a small contribution to the Western diet as it is
consumed in very small quantities.

1 rounded teaspoon curry powder contains:

        18 kilocalories (75 kilojoules)
    0.7 g   protein
    0.8 g   fat
    1.8 g   carbohydrate
      45 mg calcium
  5.32 mg   iron
        no vitamins

A variety of formulae are used for curry powders. Spices often
used are: cardamom seeds, chillies, coriander, cumin, fenugreek,
ginger, mustard seed, pepper, turmeric. Salt is also added. As
many as 16 different spices may be included in curry powder.
Originally, these would be pounded together by the cook for
domestic use, but more recently ready-prepared curry powder
has been accepted.

As well as being used to make the usual curries, curry powder
is useful to add extra flavour to other dishes, such as casseroles,
meat loaves and soups. A pinch of curry powder also enhances
the flavour of salad dressings.

Like other spices, the flavour of curry powder deteriorates with age. It is best bought in small quantities and kept in a small airtight tin or jar.

CUSTARD A popular sauce for serving with desserts. There are two main types, the original egg custard and the convenient custard prepared from custard powder. Egg custard is a good source of protein, calcium, iron and vitamins A and D. Custard from custard powder has the same composition as cornflour. It contains approximately the same energy value as egg custard but contains less protein, fat and iron, and more carbohydrate.

COMPARISON OF THE NUTRITIVE VALUES OF EGG CUSTARD SAUCE AND CUSTARD POWDER BOILED WITH MILK		
	2 oz egg custard sauce*	2 oz custard powder boiled with milk†
Kilocalories (Kilojoules)	68 (284)	66 (276)
Protein g	2.6	1.8
Fat g	3.0	2.2
Carbohydrate g	7.6	10.0
Calcium mg	64.2	69.4
Iron mg	0.26	0.08

The figures for the vitamin contents are unavailable.
* Egg custard sauce is prepared from 1 pint milk, 2 eggs, 2 oz sugar and vanilla essence.
† Custard from powder is prepared from 1 pint milk, 1 oz custard powder and 1½ oz sugar.

Apart from custard sauce, there are several other types of custards and desserts which are based on the egg custard recipe. Baked egg custard may be served by itself or with fruit. Baked on top of a caramelised sugar solution, the baked custard becomes caramel custard, or crème caramel. Confectioners' custard is a sweetened version which also contains cornflour. This is used more as a filling for flans, cream slices, etc., or to top the traditional sherry trifle. Custards may also be steamed. These are usually made in individual moulds and are turned out for serving. The homely bread and butter pudding is also based on an egg custard mixture. Unsweetened egg and milk custard can be flavoured with savoury ingredients for flans similar to the French quiche.

CYCLAMATES See **Synthetic sweeteners.**

DAMSONS Small roundish plums, purple to dark blue in colour, with yellow flesh. Damsons are sour, unless really ripe, and are usually cooked in pies or puddings or just stewed.

4 oz damsons, stewed without sugar, contain:

      32 kilocalories (128 kilojoules)
    0.4 g protein
       no fat
    8.4 g carbohydrate
  20.4 mg calcium
  0.36 mg iron
          no figure available for vitamin A
       no vitamin D
  0.08 mg thiamin
  0.02 mg riboflavin
          no figure available for vitamin C. (Plums, however, contain very small quantities of vitamin C.)

Kent and Worcestershire are the two main damson-growing areas, although they are grown in many parts of the country, and even in hedgerows in some districts. Damsons are in season from August to October.

DATES The fruit of the date palm grown in tropical countries. The most popular type of date in the UK is the semi-dried variety, although fresh dates are also available in specialist shops.

THE COMPOSITION OF FRESH AND SEMI-DRIED DATES		
	2 oz fresh dates* (weighed without stones)	1 oz dried dates* (weighed without stones)
Kilocalories (Kilojoules)	80 (374)	70 (295)
Protein g	0.6	0.6
Fat g	0	0
Carbohydrate g	22.8	18.1
Calcium mg	17	19
Iron mg	0.85	1
Vitamin A microg retinol equivalents	8	3
Vitamin D	0	0
Thiamin	negligible	0.02
Riboflavin mg	0.06	0.01
Vitamin C	0	0

* Average quantity for a single portion.

Fresh dates are imported, usually frozen to preserve their freshness. Semi-dried dates, the most popular sweet, sticky kind, are allowed to dry before harvest. They are known as a tree-dried fruit. Dried dates may be sold carefully packed, complete with stones, as dessert dates, or stoned and compressed into blocks as cooking dates.

Like other dried fruits, dried dates keep very well. They should be wrapped in plastic film or similar airtight wrapping to prevent excessive drying, or the absorption of extra moisture from the air.

DENTAL HEALTH The term used to describe the state of the teeth and gums. Strong, healthy teeth are determined largely by heredity, but the food eaten by the mother during pregnancy, and by the young child in the first few years of life, also have an important part to play. If, when the teeth are first forming, there is a shortage of calcium or vitamin D, the teeth cannot be as healthy and strong as they would be if there were no deficiency. After the teeth have erupted, diet still plays a vital role in good dental health. It depends not only on what you eat, but also on when you eat it, whether you eat foods which act as natural teeth cleaners, and whether you use a toothbrush efficiently as well as regularly.

Sugar and especially sweet sticky foods, above all, have a considerable local effect upon the teeth. The high incidence of dental decay among children has been blamed upon our high consumption of sugar and sweet foods. If sweet food particles are left sticking to the teeth, or wedged between them, dental plaques are formed in which bacteria thrive. The bacteria themselves live off the sugary residues, and produce acids as a by-product. The acid then eats away the protective enamel coating on the tooth. With its protection eroded away, the tooth begins to decay. However thick and strong the enamel, it cannot withstand the acid's attack. If the teeth are cleaned thoroughly after eating sweets and sticky sweet foods, the dental plaques cannot be formed. Sweets eaten at the end of a meal are not so dangerous as sweets eaten between meals. After a meal, the flow of saliva induced by the meal continues to clean the teeth, but does not act as efficiently between meals.

Crisp, hard foods like apples, pears, celery or raw carrots work as excellent tooth cleaners. They gently scour the teeth, removing all traces of sticky particles. The same crisp foods, and other hard ones like crusty bread, crispbreads, nuts and crisps are also helpful in keeping the gums healthy. If these hard foods are avoided – as may be the case if the teeth are bad – soft foods become impacted between the teeth. The hard foods would normally remove them. The impacted articles are attacked by bacteria which can later infect the gum tissues. Very severe gum disorders can result if minor infections are neglected. Gingivitis is the name given to the minor gum infection, but it can lead to periodontal disease, in which not only the gums but also the bones and other supporting tissues of the teeth are badly infected.

Gum disorders are more common among adults than among children. But dental decay, or dental caries, is chiefly found in children. (See also **fluorine**.)

DIABETES A disease in which there is total or partial breakdown in the body's production of the hormone insulin, which enables cells to remove glucose from the blood and utilise the glucose for energy. Although carbohydrates may be digested in a perfectly normal way, the blood glucose cannot be utilised. It accumulates in the blood and is finally excreted by the kidneys in the urine. Sugar in the urine is one of the first tests for diabetes.

Diabetes often runs in families. Those who inherit the genetic factor for diabetes tend to develop the disease at an early age. Such patients usually need to take insulin in some form. Some women develop diabetes during pregnancy, especially after several previous pregnancies. The disease can occur at any age, but the majority (80 per cent) of all cases begin after the age of 50. Many cases occur even later in life. Those who become diabetic in middle and later life are often severely overweight. It is thought that the insulin-producing cells simply become worn out with constantly being required to produce large amounts of insulin to deal with excessively large carbohydrate intakes. Such patients can often be kept quite healthy by dietary control of the diabetes without the additional need for insulin.

Provided diabetics follow their doctor's advice very closely, there is no reason why they should not lead perfectly healthy lives. It is important, of course, to keep to the prescribed diet, especially when insulin is taken. Too much carbohydrate will cause excretion of glucose in the urine; too little carbohydrate could cause faintness and even coma.

Special care must be taken to note the carbohydrate content of all foods. Carbohydrates, usually starch, are used in a great many manufactured or prepared foods such as soups, gravy powders, mousses and similar desserts, while bread or breadcrumbs are freely used in hamburgers, sausages, meat loaves and so on.

When cooking for a diabetic, it is easy to replace sugar with saccharin, though it is better to encourage the diabetic to change his taste for sweet foods. Care must also be taken to serve meals regularly. On excursions or journeys, some emergency food supply should always be taken. Diabetics simply cannot go for long periods without food, and even the best-laid plans for meals to be taken away from home can go wrong.

DOUGHNUTS Deep fried, yeasted bun with a high energy value. The composition of the doughnut will depend on the recipe used in production, since small variations are found in different bakeries.

An average composition for one 2 oz doughnut is:

202 kilocalories (844 kilojoules)
3.4 g protein
9 g fat
27.6 g carbohydrate
38 mg calcium
1.10 mg iron
no figures available for vitamin content

DRIED FOODS Historically one of the oldest kinds of preserved foods. Originally, meat and fish, fruit and vegetables were allowed to dry in the sun or by a fire. Reduction in moisture content inhibits the growth of food spoilage organisms, which extends the keeping qualities of the food.

With old methods of drying, both flavour and food value deteriorated. Recently, improved methods of drying, such as rapid air- and freeze-drying, give a product with a very fresh flavour which has lost little in food value.

Liquids such as milk, fruit juices and coffee, may be roller-dried as the liquid is trickled over heated rollers; spray-dried, when a fine jet of liquid, introduced at the top of a warm chamber, dries as it falls; or freeze-dried by freezing the liquid and then evaporating its moisture content by heating under reduced pressure.

Solid foods such as fruit, vegetables, meat and fish are dried by passing currents of air through perforated trays carrying a thin layer of the diced, minced or chopped food. The trays may be agitated to hasten the drying process. Drying may also be speeded up by heating in a vacuum. This latter method is described as 'puff' drying, as reduced pressure causes the drying food to expand. (Puffed wheat is produced in this way.) Freeze-drying is also used for some solid foods, usually the more expensive foods such as prawns and ready-prepared, complete main meals.

Traditional methods of drying fruit and vegetables are still used. Raisins, currants and sultanas are all allowed to dry in the sun, while still on the vine. They are described as vine-dried fruits. Prunes, figs and dates are tree-dried. Legumes, including the popular peas and beans, are allowed to dry in the summer sun as the annual parent plant withers and dies.

In drying, nutritive losses are confined mainly to those nutrients which are unstable to heat. The chief losses are of B group vitamins and vitamin C. The longer the drying process and the higher the temperatures used, the greater the nutritional losses. For example, traditionally dried peas contain negligible amounts of vitamins B and C, whereas freeze-dried peas have a vitamin content very near to that of the newly-harvested vegetable.

DUCK A richly-flavoured poultry. Because it is less suitable for large-scale production, duck remains more expensive and therefore more of a luxury than either chicken or turkey. Like goose, the flesh of duck has a higher fat content than other poultry, and therefore a higher energy value.

8 oz duck, weighed with bone, contain:

    384 kilocalories (1,605 kilojoules)
     28 g protein
   28.8 g fat
     no carbohydrate
   23.2 g calcium
   7.04 g iron
     no vitamins A, D and C and small quantities of thiamin
         and riboflavin

Because of the high fat content, duck is not as digestible as chicken. Fattiness may be offset by serving a light, piquant sauce – orange sauce with duck is very popular. Duckling is usually a small bird weighing between 1 lb and 2 lb. Ducks are usually 2 lb to 5 lb in weight. Because duck has a larger proportion of bone than chicken, the portion size, weighed with bone, needs to be bigger. A 2 lb bird will be sufficient for only 2 people.

Choose a young bird for tenderness. This will have a white skin, and soft, pliable feet. The feet and bill should be yellow. Fresh duck is not as freely available as fresh chicken, but frozen ducks are always on sale. Wild duck has an especially rich flavour but, like other game, tends to be tougher than the domestically reared bird.

DYSPEPSIA Discomfort in the stomach region after taking food or drink. Dyspepsia is also known by other names such as indigestion or heartburn. Although it may be the result of some disorder of the digestive system, dyspepsia is most commonly caused by anxiety or over-work; eating meals too quickly or when extremely tired; by heavy smoking or drinking alcohol. Dyspepsia may also be caused by eating foods which are very highly flavoured, seasoned or spiced. For immediate relief of discomfort, antacid preparations may be helpful. If the symptoms persist, a doctor should certainly be consulted.

EGGS Among the most nourishing foods in the typical Western diet. Eggs are also a rich source of **cholesterol** (see **yolk**).

One 2 oz egg contains:

90	kilocalories (376 kilojoules)
6.8 g	protein
7 g	fat (33.5 per cent saturated)
no	carbohydrate
32 mg	calcium
1.4 mg	iron
170 microg	retinol equivalents of vitamin A
0.86 microg	vitamin D
0.06 mg	thiamin
0.20 mg	riboflavin
no	vitamin C

In the UK, the average person eats between four and five eggs a week. This consumption provides the following proportion of essential nutrients in the national average diet: protein 5 per cent; iron 7 per cent; vitamin A 8 per cent; vitamin D 17 per cent.

Eggs are available all year round, though more plentiful, and therefore cheaper, in the summer months. They are sold graded by size in the UK, mainly as large, standard, medium and small. Very few extra small eggs are also available. In the rest of the EEC there are seven weight grades (see table) and three grades of egg quality: grade A, for fresh eggs; grade B for second quality or preserved eggs; grade C, eggs for manufactured foods only.

EEC GRADES	UK GRADES	
1 over 70 g	large	$2\frac{3}{16}$ oz (62 g) or more
2 65 g to 70 g	standard	$1\frac{7}{8}$ oz to $2\frac{3}{16}$ oz
3 60 g to 65 g		(53.2 g to 62 g)
4 55 g to 60 g	medium	$1\frac{5}{8}$ oz to $1\frac{7}{8}$ oz
5 50 g to 55 g		(46.1 g to 53.2 g)
6 45 g to 50 g	small	$1\frac{1}{2}$ oz to $1\frac{5}{8}$ oz
7 under 45 g		(42.5 g to 46.1 g)
	extra small	less than 1 oz (42.5 g)

Whatever the size of the egg, roughly 10 per cent is shell, 60 per cent white and 30 per cent yolk. Of these, egg white is roughly 90 per cent water, 10 per cent protein, with traces of fat and carbohydrate; egg yolk roughly 50 per cent water, 17 per cent protein, and 33 per cent fat.

Eggs should be stored pointed end downwards in the fridge, away from the freezing unit. Keep away from strongly-flavoured foods which may taint the eggs. If a fridge is not available, keep them in the coolest place possible. In the fridge, eggs stay fresh for three weeks after laying; they stale more quickly at room temperature. Remove eggs from fridge an hour or more before using, as cold shells crack if eggs are boiled, and eggs whisk more easily at room temperature.

Eggs may be kept in a domestic freezer for long-term storage, provided they are shelled. It is best to beat egg lightly with a pinch of either salt or sugar. They keep for up to 6 months; remember to label them.

The colour of the shell depends only on the breed of hen; the yolk colour is determined by the hen's diet. Neither shell nor yolk colour affects flavour or nutritive value. There is very little difference in flavour, and no difference in food value, between free range and battery eggs.

Most egg dishes are easily digested. They are especially suitable for elderly people, young children and for anyone needing a light diet. Because of the high fat content of the yolk, eggs should be omitted in a fat-free diet. Eggs contain more cholesterol than most foods, and must be restricted in a low cholesterol diet. Overcooking eggs makes them tough and indigestible. Egg-thickened sauces may curdle if overcooked. To avoid a blackened yolk, hard-boil eggs for no more than 12 minutes, and then plunge them into plenty of cold water.

Unlike hens' eggs, ducks' eggs may be contaminated with salmonella bacteria. Duck eggs must always be hard-boiled, and used only in dishes which are thoroughly cooked.

ENDIVE Looks a little like a peculiarly shaped, curly-leaved lettuce. A salad vegetable which has never been a bestseller in this country. Its characteristic bitter flavour may be responsible. Like lettuce, it has a high water content, 93.7 per cent, and consequently contributes few nutrients to the diet.

1 oz raw endive contains:

3	kilocalories (13 kilojoules)
0.5 g	protein
no	fat
0.3 g	carbohydrate
12.4 mg	calcium
0.79 mg	iron
95 microg	retinol equivalents vitamin A
no	vitamin D
0.02 mg	thiamin
0.03 mg	riboflavin
3 mg	vitamin C

Although still not grown in large quantities in Great Britain home-grown endive is now available from May to October.

Like other salad vegetables, it should be kept cool, ideally in the salad drawer of the fridge. Endive keeps better than most other green salad vegetables. Because it is not so inclined to wilt and become limp, and also because of its attractive curled leaves, endive is very good for garnishing and for serving as a side salad at meals prepared in advance.

ENERGY The basic nutritional requirement of any living organism. Energy is needed for **metabolism,** growth, activity and warmth. Animals rely almost exclusively on food for energy. Each of the three major nutrients – **carbohydrates, fats** and **proteins** – may be broken down in the body for this purpose. If food intake is severely restricted, the building and repair function of protein is bypassed in order to satisfy the body's need for energy.

The energy requirement of any one individual is the amount of food which keeps him healthy and feeling well, and at a constant body weight. Most people vary in their energy requirements from day to day. Over a period of seven days or so, food intake is usually adjusted to match energy requirement in most people whose weight stays at a constant level (see **appetite**).

Energy requirements vary a lot from person to person. Requirements are increased through activity, increase in body size, during growth and pregnancy, and also, to a small extent, by living in a colder climate. Energy requirements usually decrease with age: it is often said that they begin to decline from the age of 25. Men usually need more energy than women because of their greater body weight.

These general factors apart, two individuals of the same age, sex, weight and degree of activity can still vary in their energy requirements. Some may need two or three times as much as others. For information about average requirements, see table on page 13.

ENZYMES Organic substances controlling all the chemical reactions which take place in living tissues. Although enzymes are made by living cells, they are not themselves alive. All are complex molecules of protein. Several thousand different enzymes exist in the human body. Only certain enzymes will be found in any specialised tissue. Each enzyme is highly selective; it is specific to one reaction only.

Some enzymes regulate the building up of the organic molecules which are the component of living cells. Other enzymes bring about the breakdown of food materials to release energy. Perhaps the best known enzymes are those of the digestive system, which break down complex food materials into their simple components.

Enzymes have been described as organic catalysts. Although they speed up chemical reactions, they remain unchanged themselves. Animal enzymes work best at the temperature of the animal's body. All enzymes are inactivated by both excessive heat and cold, and each has its own optimum degree of acidity or alkalinity in which to work. Some enzymes require activation by substances called co-enzymes. Several members of the B group of vitamins function as co-enzymes in the complex chain of chemical reactions by which energy is released from food.

FATS Rich energy-giving foods derived from both plants and animals. Animal fats, like lard, suet, and butter made from the fat of milk, tend to be solid at room temperature. Fish fats are the exception. Fats from plants, such as olive oil, corn oil, sunflower and peanut oils, are liquid at room temperature. Liquid fats are usually called oils. Whether liquid or solid, one gram of pure fat supplies 9 kilocalories (37 kilojoules) of energy.

Being a very concentrated source of energy, fats are helpful in increasing the energy value of the diet without greatly increasing its bulk. This is important in providing high energy value diets required by those doing extremely hard manual work or for athletes.

Fats are digested very much more slowly than either proteins or carbohydrates, and thus stay in the stomach longer. While they are there, they reduce the stomach's mobility. In other words, fats are very sustaining, as they have a good satiety value and help to delay hunger pangs. This is why, in spite of the high energy value, some fat is desirable in meals for slimmers.

Most popular foods have a high fat content. An average cut of meat may contain 20 per cent to 30 per cent by weight of pure fat. Cheese is also 30 per cent fat, and even eggs contain 12 per cent fat. Pork has more fat than other meats, and duck and goose have the highest fat content among poultry. Herrings and other fat fish store oils within their muscle fibres. During summer, when food is plentiful, the herring has far more fat than during winter months, or immediately after spawning. Fat which is not evident in foods like lean meat, cheese, milk and eggs, is called invisible fat.

In the average British diet, individual foods supply the following percentages of the total fat intake:

butter, margarine and other fats	35.0 per cent
all meats	30.0
milk, cream and cheese	18.2
bread, cakes, biscuits, pastries	9.0
eggs	3.4
vegetables	1.2
fish	1.1
fruit	0.5

A *low fat diet* may be prescribed for patients suffering from obstructive jaundice; from diseases of the pancreas or liver; for patients recovering from a coronary thrombosis and some patients wishing to reduce weight.

The *high fat foods* to be avoided are butter, margarine, cooking fat, lard, dripping, vegetable oils, fried foods, mayonnaise, pastry, suet puddings, cream cheese, any rich cakes or desserts, cream in any form (including buttercream or mock cream), chocolates, toffees, nuts, potato crisps, any fat meat or fat fish, duck, goose.

The *low fat foods* which will be allowed are very lean meat, with all visible fat trimmed off, chicken or turkey, cottage cheese, yoghurt – especially the low fat variety, skimmed milk, white fish, all fruit and vegetables (except chips and other fried vegetables, avocado pear and olives).

See also **fatty acids** and **polyunsaturates**.

FATTY ACIDS (saturated and unsaturated) Organic acids which combine with glycerol to make fats and oils. A number of different fatty acids exist in the variety of fats eaten in a normal mixed diet. Each fatty acid is made of a chain or ring of carbon atoms, to which atoms of oxygen and hydrogen are linked. *Saturated fatty acids* carry as many hydrogen atoms as their molecular formulae will allow. In general, fatty acids from the fats in meat, butter, cream, cheese, milk, lard and other foods made with a high proportion of these ingredients are the main sources of saturated fatty acids in the average British diet. Some fatty acids, called *unsaturated fatty acids*, do not have their full quota of hydrogen. A molecule of a *mono-unsaturated fatty acid* is short of two hydrogen atoms. The most widely distributed fatty acid of all, oleic acid, is a mono-unsaturated fatty acid. It is found in both animal fats and vegetable oils. In *polyunsaturated fatty acids* – conveniently abbreviated to PUFA – four or more hydrogen atoms are missing. Two PUFA, known as linoleic and linolenic, are essential for good health, yet they cannot be made within the body. Because they are dietary essentials, linoleic and linolenic acids are called *essential fatty acids*. (A third fatty acid, arachidonic acid, is sometimes considered as an essential fatty acid but it can be made in the body provided there is an adequate supply of linoleic acid.) Essential fatty acids, EFA, are found mainly in vegetable oils. Cottonseed, soya bean, corn and peanut oils are some of the richest sources. Linoleic acid is also found, though in smaller quantities, in some animal fats.

Generally speaking, the higher the proportion of unsaturated fatty acids, the lower the melting point of the fat or oil. Hence liquid vegetable oils and solid animal fats. Olive oil contains predominantly the mono-unsaturated fatty acid oleic acid, and becomes solid in the fridge. Corn oil or sunflower oil, which mainly consist of polyunsaturated fatty acids, do not solidify in even the coldest part of the fridge.

Dietary fats and their component fatty acids are known to have an effect on the cholesterol level of the blood. They are also thought to be implicated in some way, as yet unknown, with the development of atherosclerosis and coronary thrombosis (see **atherosclerosis**, **cholesterol**, **coronary thrombosis** and **polyunsaturates**).

FISH A great many varieties of fish are caught for food in seas, rivers and lakes. Over one hundred kinds are offered for sale in the UK. The type of fresh fish available at any one time depends upon the season – some fish are more plentiful and in better condition at certain times of the year than at others – and also upon the weather. In very bad weather, fresh fish cannot be landed, but quick freezing has overcome many potential supply problems.

In addition to fresh fish – the white fish, fat or oily fish and shellfish – we have canned, bottled, smoked and marinated fish as well as fish products such as fish cakes and fish fingers.

Many types of fish and fish products may be bought quick frozen.

Most fish contains roughly the same amount of protein as meat, but smaller quantities of B vitamins and some minerals. **Shellfish** are a rich source of iron. The amount of fat in fish varies widely, from 2 per cent in white fish like cod, haddock, plaice, halibut and sole, to 10 per cent or even 20 per cent in the fat fish like herrings, salmon, sardines and tuna. The higher the fat content, the greater the energy value of the fish. White fish is especially useful for low energy value slimming diets.

Unlike the fat of meat, the oils from fish contain vitamins A and D. Fish oils are also highly unsaturated, unlike meat fat.

COMPARISON OF NUTRITIVE VALUES OF WHITE AND FATTY FISHES (4 oz PORTIONS, WEIGHED WITH SKIN AND BONES)

	Cod steamed	Haddock steamed	Herring fried in oatmeal	Kipper baked	Salmon canned
Kilocalories	76	84	236	124	152
(Kilojoules)	328	352	988	520	632
Protein g	16.4	18.8	21.6	14.4	22.4
Fat g (highly unsaturated)	0.8	0.8	15.2	6.8	6.8
Carbohydrate g	0	0	1.6	0	0
Calcium mg	13.2	47.2	38.8	39.6	76
Iron mg	0.44	0.6	1.92	0.88	1.6
Vitamin A microg retinol equivalents	0	0	52	52	104
Vitamin D microg	0	0	25.5	25.5	14.2
Thiamin mg	0.08	0.08	0.04	0	0.04
Riboflavin mg	0.12	0.12	0.32	0.32	0.12
Vitamin C mg	0	0	0	0	0

In the UK, the average person eats about 5 oz of fish each week. About half of the fish eaten is sold in fried fish shops and is eaten with chips. In the national average diet, fish provides about 5 per cent of the total protein intake, and small amounts of various members of the B group of vitamins. Fat fish supply 20 per cent of the total dietary intake of vitamin D.

Popular varieties of white fish like bream, brill, cod, haddock, halibut, plaice and sole are available all year round. They are usually at their best during the autumn and winter months. Herrings are landed at some English and Scottish ports almost all year round. Most shellfish are also available throughout the year, though crabs, lobster, prawns and shrimps are usually at their best during the summer. Salmon and trout are also at their best in summer although imported fresh or frozen salmon and trout are available all year round.

Choose fresh fish by its firm white flesh and fresh smell. If the head is still on, the eyes should look bright and the gills still red. Stale fish has an unpleasant 'fishy' smell and pinkish, slimy flesh.

When judging the comparative value of whole fish, cutlets and filleted fish, bear in mind that 70 per cent of whole fish may be waste, and even cutlets may have 20 per cent inedible bone and skin. Fillets have very little waste, and none at all if skinned fillets are bought.

Fresh fish must be eaten as soon as possible after purchase. It will keep only 1 or 2 days in the fridge, where it should be well wrapped to avoid the contamination of the flavour of other foods.

Treat smoked fish as fresh fish. To suit modern tastes, smoking is done for flavour only. It does not extend keeping qualities.

If fish needs to be purchased well in advance, it is better to choose frozen fish, which keeps well. The storage period depends on the star marking of the freezer cabinet. For domestic freezing, fish must be processed within a few hours of the fish being caught. Fish from even the most reputable fishmonger is not really fresh enough for freezing.

FLOUR The product of milling wheat grains. Predominantly starch with varying amounts of protein (7 per cent to 14 per cent). The protein content depends on the variety of wheat and on the climate in which it is grown. Flour also contains valuable amounts of calcium, iron and B vitamins.

In flour milling the term 'extraction rate' means the percentage of flour which is separated from a given weight of wheat. Wholemeal flour – 100 per cent extraction – contains the whole of the cleaned wheat grain. Wheatmeal or brown flours usually contain 80 per cent to 90 per cent of the grain. White flours usually contain 70 per cent to 72 per cent of the grain, although lower extraction flour can be produced.

The distribution of nutrients within the wheat grain is not uniform: the concentration of protein and vitamins is higher in the germ and outer layers of the grain than in the inner part of the grain, the starchy endosperm.

There is and always has been a greater demand for white flour than for brown. To safeguard the nutritional value of flour (and bread), the government instituted certain Orders and Regulations. The latest, the Bread and Flour Regulations of 1963 (amended in 1972), states that all flours must contain the following minimum quantities of nutrients:

	per 100 g
iron	1.65 mg
thiamin	0.24 mg
nicotinic acid*	1.60 mg

*The Food Standards Committee has recommended that nicotinic acid should no longer be added to flour and their recommendation is being considered.

These are the approximate levels occurring naturally in 80 per cent extraction flour; flours below this level are enriched with these nutrients. The Regulations also require that all flour, other than self-raising flours, which already have a calcium content of not less than 0.2 per cent (by the addition of a raising agent), and wholemeal flours, must contain not less than 235 mg and not more than 390 mg calcium carbonate (*creta praeparata*) per 100 g flour. No additions are made to wholemeal flour.

Today, when we eat such a wide variety of food, there is little significant difference in the nutritional values of flours, apart from the higher fibre content of brown flours.

In the UK the average person obtains the following proportion of essential nutrients from the bread and flour in his diet:

protein	20 per cent
kilocalories (energy)	18 per cent
calcium	18 per cent
iron	22 per cent
thiamin	28 per cent
nicotinic acid	13 per cent

Flour is sold in 1 lb and 3 lb packs for the domestic market. It should be stored in its bag on a cool, dry and airy shelf. If the

COMPOSITION OF VARIOUS FLOURS USED FOR BREAD (15 per cent moisture)

	Wholemeal	Brown flour	80% extraction	White enriched
Extraction rate %	100	90	80	70
Protein %	12	11.80	11.50	11.10
Fat %	2.49	1.90	1.40	1.16
Carbohydrate %	64.30	68.50	70.10	72.30
Kilocalories (approx) per oz	95	99	99	99
Kilojoules (approx) per oz	397	414	414	414
Calcium mg/100 g	30	148	145	142
Iron mg/100 g	3.50	2.70	1.70	1.70
Thiamin mg/100 g	0.40	0.33	0.24	0.24
Nicotinic acid mg/100 g	5.70	3.50	1.60	1.60

kitchen, pantry or storage cupboard is at all damp, transfer the flour to an airtight container. Plain flour will keep for 4 to 6 months; self-raising flour for 2 to 3 months; brown flours for up to 2 months.

The strength of flour is largely determined by its protein content. A strong flour, which makes an elastic dough which rises well, contains 10 per cent to 15 per cent of the wheat protein known as gluten. Strong flours are made from hard wheats grown in extreme climates, and are imported from Canada and central Europe. Strong flour is recommended for bread and all yeast cookery, for puff pastry, steamed puddings and batters.

A soft flour which makes a dough with a light, soft texture contains between 7 per cent and 10 per cent gluten. Soft flours are made from home-grown wheats and others grown in a milder climate, such as French and Australian wheats. Soft flours are recommended for rich cakes and puddings, shortcrust pastry and biscuits (see also **gluten**).

FLUORINE One of the so-called **trace elements** found in minute amounts in nearly every tissue of the body, but particularly in the teeth and bones. Drinking water is the chief source of fluorine, but water supplies vary in the amount of fluorine they contain. Some drinking water contains none at all; other supplies contain more than 10 parts per million (ppm). Many foods contain minute amounts of fluorine, but fish and tea are the only ones which contain significant amounts.

A fluorine level of 1 part per million in the drinking water increases the resistance of children's teeth to decay. There is a marked reduction of dental caries in a 'fluoride area' compared with the incidence of decay in a 'no-fluoride area'.

For years, dental associations have strongly advocated the artificial addition of fluorine to water at source where none exists naturally. In the United States, fluoridation of water has been a common practice since 1966. Reduction in tooth decay has been considerable. So far, proposals to add fluorine to water supplies in the UK have been strongly opposed.

So that children's teeth may benefit from the small level of fluorine required to build more decay-resistant teeth, parents can buy fluorine tablets. Fluoride toothpastes and mouthwashes are also available, but they are not as effective as fluorine in the drinking water. They are also limited in being effective only when the teeth are developing and actually erupting from the gums.

FRIED FOODS Foods cooked in hot fat or oil. In shallow frying, only enough fat to cover the bottom of the pan and to prevent sticking is used. In deep fat frying, the food is completely immersed in the hot fat or oil.

Because of the high cooking temperatures used – these range from 160°C to 200°C (about 325°F to 400°F) – the food is cooked quickly and evenly. Frying is suitable only for small or thin pieces of food, or the outside will be cooked while the inside remains raw. Frying must also be restricted to very tender foods. Unlike long, slow moist methods of cooking, frying does not help to tenderise food.

To help keep its shape, food for deep frying is usually coated before being cooked. Egg and breadcrumbs or batter are often used. The coating cooks quickly, giving a firm outer covering to the food. This helps to stop it breaking up. The coating also stops excessive absorption of fat into the food. To keep its crispness, food should always be well drained on kitchen paper after frying. If fried food is kept hot before serving, it inevitably absorbs some of the fat from the coating. In turn, the coating takes up moisture from the food and becomes soggy. Ideally, fried food should be well drained and served immediately.

The high temperatures of frying cause unavoidable loss of some heat-unstable nutrients. But as it is a quick method of cooking, high temperatures are not maintained for very long, and the short cooking time usually balances the high temperatures in determining nutritional losses during frying. Generally speaking, frying is one of the best ways of conserving food value.

One of the drawbacks of frying is that some fat is always absorbed by the food. This increases the overall energy value of the food. The energy value of a slice of bread when fried is increased from 70 kilocalories an ounce to 160 kilocalories an ounce. A poached egg has only 90 kilocalories compared with the 140 kilocalories of a fried egg of the same size. Potatoes treble their energy value when they are fried as chips – boiled potatoes have 23 kilocalories an ounce, chips 68 kilocalories per ounce.

Like other foods with a high fat content, fried foods can be very indigestible. Many people prefer to grill instead of frying. On the other hand, others find fried foods very palatable, attractive and satisfying, a fact which is illustrated by the enormous popularity of chips, which are eaten in great quantities with almost everything, and on their own.

Fried foods will be forbidden to anyone for whom a low fat diet has been prescribed. They will be severely restricted for many patients who have suffered from a coronary thrombosis, or who appear to be predisposed to a coronary. Foods fried in vegetable oils may be permitted in a less severe diet.

FROZEN FOODS Foods which have been preserved by chilling them to such low temperatures that the activity of food spoilage enzymes and organisms is completely stopped.

Most frozen foods eaten are commercially quick frozen although domestic freezer ownership is increasing quite quickly. After quick freezing, the frozen food needs to be stored at low temperatures. Commercial cabinets or holding rooms are kept at $-18°C$ ($0°F$). At this temperature, frozen foods will keep safe almost indefinitely. Actual storage times are largely determined by any deterioration in flavour and appearance likely to occur during long storage. Although the food stays safe to eat, it very gradually loses its palatability.

The temperature of the domestic fridge, 5°C (40°F) is enough only to slow down the action of food spoilage. The keeping times of perishable foods is extended by just a few days. Frozen foods which are not required for immediate use should be stored in the frozen food compartment. (None exists in some old fridges still in use, though the ice-making compartment may be used for one or two days' storage.) British Standard specifications for refrigerators allow a system of star marking which indicates the length of time for which frozen foods may be safely stored in the frozen food compartment. One star shows safe storage for one week; two stars for a month; three for three months.

Buying quick frozen foods A great variety of frozen foods is produced for sale. All kinds of meat and meat products, fish and fish products, poultry and dairy products are available, as well as quick frozen fruit and vegetables, ice cream, mousses and other frozen desserts, pies, puddings and pastries. A good range of complete meals which only require reheating are also sold. The more unusual meals like meat curries, paella and lasagne seem to be as popular as quick frozen versions of well-known favourites like shepherd's pie and steak and kidney pudding.

As quick frozen foods save a great deal of time – time which would otherwise be spent in shopping and cooking – they are becoming increasingly popular in the UK. Every week, the average person eats in meals produced at home at least 5 oz of commercially quick frozen food. Marketing trends indicate that this figure will soon be doubled. In large-scale catering, caterers have found that it is both cheaper and more convenient to use ready-prepared frozen foods instead of employing staff to prepare and cook fresh foods. Any meal taken away from home, whether it is in a restaurant or café, industrial canteen or staff restaurant, in hospital or at school, is likely to include some item of quick frozen food.

See also **quick freezing**.

FRUCTOSE See **Carbohydrate.**

FRUIT Botanically speaking, the fruit is the seed-bearing organ of the plant. By this definition, ears of wheat are fruit, and so, too, are peas, beans and tomatoes. On the other hand, rhubarb is not.

In more general terms, we regard fruit as those sweet parts of the plant that are harvested when ripe, and served, sometimes with sugar, as dessert. But the same 'fruits' may be served to accompany savoury dishes – apple sauce with pork, pineapple or peaches with grilled gammon, redcurrant jelly with mutton, cranberries with turkey, and so on. There is thus no hard and fast rule for distinguishing fruit and vegetables, or even for defining what we mean by fruit!

There can be no doubt that home-grown produce provides some of our most popular fruits: apples and pears, cherries, currants – black, red and white; damsons, plums and green-gages; gooseberries and grapes; loganberries, raspberries and strawberries; medlars, nectarines and peaches. The same varieties have been grown in Britain since gardening details were first recorded.

Fruit is also imported to the UK from all parts of the world. Imported fruits include citrus fruits – grapefruit, oranges, lemons and limes, bananas, melons, peaches and pineapple, as well as the more unusual fruits like passion fruit, guavas and green figs.

Our own, highly seasonal, summer fruits may be flown from other parts of the world to give a year-round supply. The cost obviously makes these fruits a luxury out of season.

In the UK the average weekly consumption of fresh fruit is about 1 lb per person. An average diet also includes another half pound of fruit which has been canned, bottled, dried or frozen, and canned and frozen **fruit juice**.

Although these are average figures, there is quite a variation in the amount of fresh fruit eaten in different parts of the country. In London, the south-east and the south-west of England people eat about 20 per cent more fruit than the national average amount. People in Scotland and the north of England eat considerably less fruit than the average.

The main contribution of fruit to the diet is vitamin C. Al-most 40 per cent of the total daily intake is derived, on average, from fruit. More than 10 per cent of our total daily intake comes from oranges alone.

Fruits vary in the amount of vitamin C they contain. The quantities of different fruits listed below contain 30 mg of vitamin C, which is the daily recommended amount for most adults and older children. The quantities are based on edible portions of *fresh* fruit unless otherwise stated.

stewed blackcurrants: $\frac{3}{4}$ oz
orange, lemon or strawberries: 2 oz
grapefruit: $2\frac{1}{2}$ oz
raspberries or stewed gooseberries: 4 oz
melon: $4\frac{1}{2}$ oz
bananas: 10 oz
peaches: 13 oz
stewed rhubarb: 15 oz
cherries or eating apples: 21 oz
canned peaches: 27 oz
plums or pears: 35 oz

Some fruits are plentiful and fairly cheap all the year round; they may be home-produced, imported or both. These fruits can be found in the shops throughout the year: grapefruit, lemons, oranges (see Seville oranges and tangerines below), bananas, grapes, pineapple, apples, pears, melons.

Other fruits may always be found in certain very high-class shops, but they are not generallly available in all months of the year. The times of the year when these seasonal fruits are plentiful and fairly cheap are:

apricots   December to February and June to August
cherries   June to August
damsons   August to October
peaches   February and March and June to October
plums   January to April and June to September
blackcurrants   June to August
blackberries   July to October
gooseberries   May to July
raspberries   May to August
strawberries   June to August
rhubarb   April to June
Seville oranges January to March
tangerines   November to January

Buying fruit Care should be taken to buy unblemished, unbruised fruit. Soft fruit such as strawberries and raspberries should be dry with no squashed fruit, which soon turns mouldy. Some fruit is harvested before it is ripe, and may need to be kept for a few days at room temperature after buying to ripen it for eating. Buy only very fresh fruit for immediate consumption.

Storage of fruit Hard fruits like apples will keep from one season to another if stored correctly; see **apples**.

Citrus fruits keep fairly well if kept in the cool. The salad drawer of the fridge is suitable, or a cool outhouse.

Bananas should never be kept in the cold or they will turn soft and brown. Buy in small quantities as they become over-ripe within a few days. Buy greenish bananas if they will need to be kept for any length of time.

Pears are best bought hard and allowed to ripen at room temperature.

Soft summer fruit should be eaten as soon as possible after harvesting. Keep in a dish in the fridge, carefully covered to prevent their flavour from contaminating other foods. Peaches, apricots, dessert plums and grapes are usually sold ripe for eating. Take care not to bruise them, and eat them as soon as possible.

In addition to the vitamin C it contains, fruit is valuable for cleaning the teeth and for keeping the gums healthy. Fresh fruit is best for this purpose, and crisp fruits like apples are better than soft fruits like bananas. Fruit also adds roughage to the diet.

Centuries ago, the laxative properties of a diet high in fruit was confused with diarrhoea resulting from a variety of intestinal infections. Summer diarrhoea was very common among babies and small children, every year causing the death of thousands. This disease was thought to be transmitted through fruit, as were other fevers. The acid of fruit was also thought to corrode the teeth and cause tooth decay. In the middle of the eighteenth century an eminent doctor, William Cadogan, strongly recommended that children should have plenty of fruit, and dismissed any views that fruit was dangerous for them. At roughly the same time, the value of fruit in preventing scurvy was accepted. Gradually, views on fruit were reversed. It was accepted as a nourishing and healthy food; so much so that by the end of the nineteenth century fruit cures became very popular among wealthy people. These were diets based on fruit, which excluded almost all other food. In this way the fruit cures were very similar to the diets followed at many so-called health farms today.

FRUIT JUICES Juices extracted from fruit; usually citrus fruits, pineapples and tomatoes. Fresh citrus fruit juices are a rich source of vitamin C.

COMPARISON OF NUTRITIVE VALUE OF 4 fl. oz OF FRESH ORANGE JUICE AND CANNED, UNCONCENTRATED ORANGE JUICE		
	Fresh orange juice	Canned natural orange juice
Kilocalories (Kilojoules)	44 (184)	52 (216)
Protein g	0.8	0.8
Fat g	0	0
Carbohydrate g	10.8	13.2
Calcium mg	13.2	12
Iron mg	0.36	0.4
Vitamin A microg retinol equivalents	9	8
Vitamin D	0	0
Thiamin	0.10	0.08
Riboflavin	0.03	0.04
Vitamin C	57	44

Canned orange juice may be sold as natural or sweetened. When sugar is added during processing the product label must be marked 'sweetened orange juice'. 4 fluid ounces of 'sweetened' canned orange juice contains between 56 and 64 kilocalories (234–67 kilojoules).

Frozen concentrated orange juice contains when reconstituted 10 mg of vitamin C per fluid ounce.

3 fluid ounces of fresh, canned or frozen orange juice will provide the daily recommended intake of vitamin C for most children and adults.

Vitamin C content of 1 fluid ounce of various other fruit juices:

Fruit juice	*Vitamin C mg*
Fresh lemon juice	14
Fresh grapefruit juice	11
Canned grapefruit juice	10
Canned pineapple juice	2–5
Bottled blackcurrant juice, concentrated	75

Canned fruit juice should be stored in a cool dark cupboard. Warmth, which is absorbed through the can, can lead to destruction of the vitamin C. Canned juices keep well for at least one year. After opening, treat as fresh juice. Transfer the canned juice into a glass or plastic container, cover and keep in the fridge. (Glass-packed juice can of course be stored in its own container.)

FRUIT SQUASHES Soft drinks flavoured with fruit extracts or artificial flavourings. The more expensive products will include juice extracted from fruit. They may contain vitamin C from the juice, or vitamin C may be added to the drink. Other squashes are made with the complete fruit, peel included. The cheapest varieties may rely heavily on synthetic flavourings and have no vitamin C at all.

Squashes are made to be diluted with water. They are often heavily sweetened with sugar, or with saccharin. If saccharin is used, this must be clearly stated on the label. If vitamin C is added, this must also be stated.

In general, fruit squashes have negligible food value, apart from any vitamin C they may contain. Most are equivalent just to flavoured, sweetened water.

GAME Wild birds and animals which are shot, both for sport and also for eating. For the protection of certain rare and threatened species, only some types of bird may be shot as game. The game birds themselves are protected at breeding times and when the young birds are recently fledged. In the UK game animals are restricted to hare and deer, and again there are also close seasons for shooting.

Game	Season
pheasant	1 October to 1 February
partridge	1 September to 1 February
woodcock, plover, snipe, wild duck and geese	November to March
grouse	12 August to 10 December
blackcock	20 August to 10 December
ptarmigan	September to May
quail	all year round
buck venison (deer)	June to September
doe venison	October to December
hares	August to March

The nutritive value of most game is similar to that of chicken and turkey, except that game is richer in iron than the domestic fowl. Hare and venison have a nutritive value very similar to that of beef.

Game can be bought only from a butcher or poulterer with a special game licence. Some game is quick frozen to meet out-of-season demand.

Buying game birds Young female birds are the most tender. Choose a small-boned, plump bird with soft quills and tender pinions. Avoid birds mutilated by shot.

Buying hare Young hares are most tender. They have short necks and long joints, their claws are smooth and sharp and their ears are soft. Young hares also have a narrow cleft in the upper lip.

Buying venison Good quality venison has plenty of creamy-white fat. It should have a pleasant smell. The meat of the doe is more tender than that of the buck.

Hanging After shooting, most game is stored complete with feathers or skin and viscera. It must be stored in a cool, airy place. Hanging allows the flavour to improve and the flesh to tenderise. The length of time for hanging depends on personal taste; it is usually enough to hang birds until the breast feathers can be easily plucked.

After dressing game, it should be eaten within one or two days. Keep it wrapped in the fridge until required for cooking.

To keep the flesh moist, a piece of steak often used to be placed inside the game bird during cooking. Nowadays, it is more practical to place a knob of butter inside the bird and cover it with foil to conserve moisture.

Prime cuts of venison may be roasted, but both venison and hare are more reliably tender when pot roasted or braised. Game soups and game pâtés are delicious ways of using up trimmings and left overs.

GARLIC A plant of the onion family with a nutrient content similar to that of onions. Garlic has been grown in Britain for many centuries, and was used liberally in traditional British cooking, as its strong and distinctive taste was useful as extra flavour for insipid meat, or to mask the flavours of less-than-fresh meats. Today garlic is often regarded as a continental ingredient, but it can still be bought in most parts of the UK.

It is available all the year round, although supplies may wane or may be of inferior quality shortly before the new season's garlic is harvested.

Because it is used sparingly, garlic does not add to the nutritional value of the diet. Although standard textbooks on nutrition make no reference at all to any therapeutic properties of garlic, this vegetable is greatly acclaimed by the health food devotees. They maintain that it helps to cure colds, pulmonary congestion and coughs; and that it may also be used externally to cure abscesses and earache.

GELATINE A protein extracted from the bones and tissues of animals. After prolonged cooking in water or steam, tough gristle is converted into gelatine (hence the tenderising of meat gently stewed, braised or pot roasted). Stock made with bone and trimmings 'sets' because it contains gelatine. Good stock made in this way is considered very nutritious, but although it is derived from animal tissues, the nutritional value of gelatine is not very high. It supplies a number of amino-acids required by the body (see **proteins**), but it is deficient in at least one of the essential amino-acids.

Commercially prepared and crystallised gelatine is used to set a variety of different types of sweet and savoury jellies, moulds, mousses and cold soufflés. It is often sold in pre-measured envelopes containing sufficient gelatine to set one pint of liquid. Gelatine is also the main ingredient in table jellies which are dissolved in hot water and then set in a mould.

Home-made soup can often be improved by the addition of a little gelatine powder.

GHERKINS Small pickled cucumbers. Like cucumber itself, gherkins are practically all water. They have no special nutritive value, but their piquant flavour helps to stimulate the appetite, and they are often served with aperitifs for this reason. Gherkins are also used to accompany curries, when they help to refresh the palate; and as a mouthwatering garnish to a variety of savoury dishes.

GIN A distilled spirit, flavoured principally with juniper berries. Unlike other spirits, it is flavoured by additives rather than by ingredients in its basic recipe. Originally introduced from Holland by William of Orange, cheap and crude gins were widely sold to the poor in many large cities in the eighteenth century. Gin is now a more sophisticated drink and is used as a basis for many cocktails.

A standard measure of gin ($\frac{1}{8}$ of a gill) contains about 50 kilocalories (210 kilojoules).

GLUCOSE A simple sugar of which most **carbohydrates** are made. Starch, for example, is made of chains of glucose units, and sucrose is composed of glucose linked with fructose. During digestion, carbohydrates are once again reduced to their simple constituent molecules. Then, mainly as glucose, they are transported in the blood stream to every cell in the body. Between meals, the glucose supplies become used up. A low glucose level in the blood is thought to be one of the mechanisms which give rise to the feeling of hunger. If the blood glucose level falls too low, it causes a feeling of faintness. If the glucose level is not replenished, the individual may lose consciousness.

Glucose which is manufactured commercially from starch is used to make a variety of proprietary drinks, sweets and powders. These are usually advertised as rapid sources of energy and general pick-me-ups. There is no evidence, however, that glucose has any therapeutic advantage over sucrose.

GLUTEN The name given to the elastic substance formed when the wheat proteins in **flour** combine with water. In consistency, appearance and, to some extent in its behaviour, gluten is like bubble gum. As the dough is kneaded, the gluten becomes tougher. If a raising agent is incorporated in the dough, the gases it produces blow up the gluten to small balloons, or gas pockets. When the dough is baked, the blown-up gluten sets, giving a sponge-like texture to the baked dough. Gluten is really the skeleton of the baked flour product. The way a dough behaves is the way the gluten is behaving inside it.

The stronger the flour, the stronger the gluten, and the greater the amount of it. Doughs made with a strong flour rise well and have an elastic, springy texture. In a soft flour, there is less gluten and it is not nearly so elastic. It cannot be blown up to give a good rise to the dough. Doughs made with soft flour do not rise well, but they have a softer, more tender texture.

Gluten is softened by sugar and fat. A richly fruited loaf, for example, does not rise very well and has a closer texture than a loaf with only a little fruit. Gluten is toughened by kneading, so while bread dough is thoroughly kneaded, a sponge cake is worked as little as possible. Gluten is also toughened by acids. Lemon juice added to a puff pastry mix helps to strengthen the gluten so the layers of dough are strong enough to keep separate the layers of fat and pastry. This layering gives the flakiness to the puff pastry.

Gluten is added to some proprietary breads chosen by slimmers following a low carbohydrate diet. Breads sold as gluten breads have at least 16 per cent protein; protein breads have added gluten, which brings their total protein content to 22 per cent.

These percentages are based on dry weight. Starch-reduced products are also enriched with gluten so that the starch content of rolls, breads, crispbreads and so on is effectively reduced. Starch-reduced products are required by law to contain no more than 50 per cent carbohydrate, again based on dry weight.

Gluten, being a protein, has roughly the same energy value as an equivalent weight of carbohydrate. So these products are not especially helpful to slimmers who are following a calorie-controlled diet. As they contain more gluten than ordinary products, the gluten-enriched foods rise extremely well. Slice for slice, the gluten-enriched breads contain fewer calories because they are so much lighter. Weight for weight, they have an energy value similar to ordinary bread.

A gluten-free diet is prescribed for those suffering from coeliac disease. In this complaint, the gluten causes an acute inflammation of the intestine and an abnormal secretion of mucus which severely interferes with the absorption of most nutrients, and especially fats, in the intestine.

Gluten is widely distributed in foods. Those which are forbidden in a gluten-free diet are all foods made with wheat flour, including bread, biscuits, cakes and puddings; pasta, such as spaghetti and macaroni; products containing breadcrumbs, such as stuffings, meat loaves, rissoles and sausages; all packaged foods, mixes, canned soups, sauces and ready-made desserts. Many breakfast cereals, including all those made with wheat, are also forbidden.

Gluten-free flour is prepared for gluten-free diets, and oatmeal, rye or barley flours may also be used. Cornflour, from which gluten is removed during normal production, may also replace wheat flour to some extent.

When coeliac disease is confirmed, a special diet will be planned for each patient, and a complete diet list supplied of foods which must be omitted or restricted.

GOOSE One of the poultry meats which has a high fat content·

8 oz roast goose, weighed with bone, contain:

    424 kilocalories (1,772 kilojoules)
    36.8 g protein
    14.8 g fat
    no carbohydrate
    6.8 mg calcium
    3.08 mg iron

Geese are available all the year round, but are at their best from December to March. A young bird, which has more tender flesh, is recognised by soft, yellow feet and a yellow bill. The fat should be yellow and the flesh pinkish in colour.

Roast goose was once more popular than roast turkey for a traditional Christmas dinner. The fat collected from the dripping was kept for medicinal purposes. A rubbing with goose grease was thought to be a cure for a bad chest.

GOOSEBERRIES Seeded fruits, normally classed as soft, summer fruit, which are a good source of vitamin C.

4 oz green gooseberries, stewed without sugar, contain:

    16 kilocalories (67 kilojoules)
    1.2 g protein
    no fat
    2.8 g carbohydrate
    24.8 mg calcium
    0.28 mg iron
    26 microg retinol equivalents vitamin A
    no vitamin D
    0.04 mg thiamin
    0.02 mg riboflavin
    32 mg vitamin C

Sold as dessert or cooking varieties. Cooking gooseberries are usually green, very sour, with firm flesh and a fairly large number of seeds. Dessert gooseberries may be green, yellow or a russet colour, often with a hairy skin. They usually have soft, pulpy, sweet flesh and large seeds.

Gooseberries are in season from May to July. They are popular for pies, flans and other desserts. Gooseberry sauce also makes an unusual accompaniment to pork or roast goose.

GRAPEFRUIT A citrus fruit with a somewhat bitter flavour. Like other citrus fruits, grapefruit is a rich source of vitamin C.

One half grapefruit, weighing 4 oz, contains:

24	kilocalories (117 kilojoules)
0.8 g	protein
no	fat
6 g	carbohydrate
30 mg	calcium
0.4 mg	iron
no	vitamin A
no	vitamin D
0.04 mg	thiamin
0.04 mg	riboflavin
44 mg	vitamin C

Grapefruits vary in size from that of a large orange to giant fruits weighing several pounds. Most have a thick yellow skin, though some do have thin skins with a brown mottling; this is not an indication that the fruit is going bad, but is characteristic of West Indian fruit.

Grapefruit are imported from various countries and are available all year, although the price varies.

Large quantities of grapefruit are canned, especially in the United States and the West Indies, both as segments and as grapefruit juice.

Unlike other citrus fruits, grapefruit is rarely used in cooking, though grapefruit marmalade has a pleasant and unusual flavour.

GRAPES Small, sweet, very juicy fruit grown in bunches on vines. Dessert grapes come in two main types – 'white', which are green or yellow, and 'black', which are a dark purple. They contain small quantities of vitamin C. White and black grapes have a similar nutrient composition.

4 oz white grapes contain:

        68 kilocalories (284 kilojoules)
      0.8 g protein
       no fat
     17.6 g carbohydrate
     20.8 mg calcium
     0.36 mg iron
       no vitamin A
       no vitamin D
     0.04 mg thiamin
     0.02 mg riboflavin
        4 mg vitamin C

Grapes are usually imported to this country, though a small quantity is grown in hothouses. They are available all the year round, although the price varies considerably.

In grape-growing countries, smaller grapes are grown especially for wine-making, and are also dried as raisins. Very small grapes can be grown out of doors in this country on sunny, south-facing walls. Although traditionally the fruit given to convalescents, grapes have a lower food value than most fruits.

Peeled green grapes are sometimes used to garnish poultry and fish dishes, the best known being *sole véronique*. Black grapes make a particularly attractive garnish for sweet dishes.

 HADDOCK One of the most popular fish eaten in the UK. Like all white fish, it is an excellent source of protein. It is low in fat, and consequently in the fat-soluble vitamins A and D.

6 oz fresh haddock, steamed, contain:

      126 kilocalories (527 kilojoules)
     28.2 g protein
      1.2 g fat
       no carbohydrate
     70.8 mg calcium

0.90 mg iron
    no vitamin A
    no vitamin D
0.10 mg thiamin
0.17 mg riboflavin
    no vitamin C

Haddock is a round-bodied fish, distinguishable from cod by a black line running along its body. It also bears marks resembling fingerprints on the black line behind the head. Haddock has a firm white flesh with a better flavour than cod. It is sold fresh, fried, frozen and smoked; whole, filleted or as cutlets.

Haddock is available all year round, but is usually best from November to February. Store as described under **fish**.

There are three main varieties of smoked haddock available: golden cutlets, which are fillets from larger haddock; finnan haddock, medium-sized haddock split and smoked, sold on the bone; and Aberdeen smokies, small haddock smoked whole.

HALIBUT The largest of the flat fish caught and landed in the UK, it is more elongated in shape than other flat fish. It is described as a 'prime' white fish. (In the trade, 'prime' is used to describe its slightly oily flesh.) Halibut, like sole, has more fat than other white fish; it is also one of the most expensive fish, with fine, milky flesh of excellent flavour. Smaller halibut, between 2 lb and 3 lb, known as chicken halibut, have a more delicate flavour. Most halibut caught measure between 3 ft and 7 ft in length. 'Jumbo' halibut, as long as 20 ft, are landed from time to time. Smaller fish may be sold as fillets; the larger are usually sold as cutlets.

Halibut is available all the year round, but is usually best from August to April.

6 oz fresh halibut, steamed, contain:

    168 kilocalories (702 kilojoules)
    29.4 g protein
    4.8 g fat
    no carbohydrate
    16.8 mg calcium
    0.78 mg iron
    205 microg retinol equivalents vitamin A
    1.7 microg vitamin D

0.13 mg thiamin
0.17 mg riboflavin
　　no vitamin C

Halibut caught in the Pacific usually contain some vitamins A and D. Atlantic-caught fish contain much less of these vitamins, and sometimes none. Halibut liver oil is rich in both vitamins A and D. The oil is often made into capsules. Halibut liver oil contains 900,000 microg retinol equivalents of vitamin A per 100 g, and 255,000 microg per ounce.

HAM The hind leg of pork which is cut from the carcass and salt-cured. Usually more expensive than bacon, ham is similar in its nutritive value. Like bacon, ham is an excellent source of protein and B vitamins, in particular vitamin B1, thiamin.

One 4 oz portion boiled ham (lean and fat) contains:

　　492 kilocalories (2,056 kilojoules)
　18.4 g protein
　44.8 g fat (37.5 per cent saturated)
　　no carbohydrate
14.4 mg calcium
2.84 mg iron
　　no vitamin A
　　no vitamin D
0.57 mg thiamin
0.23 mg riboflavin
　　no vitamin C

Special curing and finishing methods give us the famous English hams like York and Wiltshire. The less well-known Seager ham is cured with a sweet brine, while the black outside of the Bradenham ham is derived from special applications of spices and molasses. Sweetcure ham is based on an American recipe for a short curing process in a sweetened brine. Sweetcure ham is usually pressed after bone and fat have been removed.

The curing of ham in a common salt solution with added nitrites and nitrates improves its keeping qualities. Uncut and uncooked hams will keep for several months in a cool, airy place. Traditionally, hams were prepared in the autumn, and stored in a cool cellar to provide meat throughout the winter months. Curing also enhances the flavour of the meat and gives its characteristic pink colour. This is derived from the action of the curing salts on the natural pigments of the meat. Curing also tenderises the meat. The curing processes, though most are carried out in modern factories, are based on the traditional farmhouse methods, and it still takes four to six months to cure a York ham.

Hams may be bought whole, in joints or slices, both cooked and uncooked. Canned ham is also very popular. Joints and slices of raw or cooked ham should be kept wrapped in the coolest part of the fridge. In this way, ham stays fresh for one week. In a cool larder, ham can be kept for 4 to 5 days. If no cool storage is available, buy cooked or uncooked ham in small quantities for immediate use.

HEALTH FOODS In the *Health Food Guide* to organisations, shops, restaurants and hotels that specialise in health foods, Michael Balfour and Judy Allen define a health food as one which 'has been produced from or reared on soil that is unpolluted by chemical fertilisers, is free of chemical sprays, artificial stimulants to growth and additives, has not had the goodness refined out of it, and is prepared for the table with the least possible delay and loss of nutrients'. Professor A. E. Bender, a leading nutritionist, defines health foods as 'substances whose consumption is advocated by various health movements. They include foods for vegetarians, wholegrain cereal foods, foods free from chemical additives, and foods grown on organic compost without the additional use of fertilisers and pesticides'. Another eminent scientist argues that all foods are 'health foods' if they provide man with the right quantities of nutrients in the right balance of those entities essential to his well being. Most people accept Arnold Bender's definition of health foods.

It does not follow that to be as healthy as possible, you should eat only health foods – nor that you will be in perfect health through eating normal, non-health foods! Although health-food advocates claim that enormous advantages are gained from following their chosen diet, the nutritional benefits of health foods are still being argued by nutritionists. As yet, there is no conclusive scientific evidence to prove that health foods are more nutritious than comparable foods produced by the usual commercial methods.

Some people claim that health foods have a better flavour. Many wholegrain foods certainly contain more roughage than their refined counterparts.

Health foods are usually more expensive than ordinary food. Most of them cost between 30 per cent and 100 per cent more than similar food bought in a supermarket. Apart from the extra cost, it would be impossible to produce enough food for everyone to eat without the use of chemical fertilisers and preservatives.

In the UK, the annual turnover for health foods was £18 million in 1970. This figure was predicted to rise to £25 million within a few years. In the United States health food stores sold $400 million worth of health foods in 1972. In both the United States and Britain, most health foods are bought by customers under the age of 30.

The first health food to be produced is reputed to be the now-familiar cornflake, first marketed by Dr John Kellogg in 1898. Cornflakes were devised and sold as a purifying food for Seventh-Day Adventists. Peanut butter is another health food originally devised by Dr Kellogg.

HEART A muscular organ derived from animals butchered for meat. Heart is very nutritious, being especially rich in iron and B vitamins. It also contains some cholesterol: 150 mg in 100 g of food. It is, however, one of the least popular offals.

4 oz braised heart contain:

272	kilocalories (1,137 kilojoules)
28.4 g	protein
16.8 g	fat
no	carbohydrate
10.8 mg	calcium
9.20 mg	iron
68 microg	retinol equivalents vitamin A
	no figures available for vitamin D
0.45 mg	thiamin
1.10 mg	riboflavin
no	vitamin C

The older the animal, the tougher and drier its heart will be for eating. Ox hearts weigh between 3 lb and 4 lb. They are usually very tough and need long, slow, moist cooking. Calves' hearts are the most tender of all, and weigh about 8 oz, a generous portion for one person.

Hearts may be bought either fresh or frozen. Fresh hearts should be bright red and have a pleasant, fresh smell. Like all offal, hearts should be bought for immediate consumption and not kept for more than one day in the fridge.

Braising is the best cooking method for heart. Ox heart is sliced and lambs' hearts cooked either whole or in halves. Lambs' hearts may also be stuffed before cooking.

HERBS Plants grown mainly for their aromatic and flavouring properties. In the past, herbs were widely used as medicines. The ancient Egyptians, Greeks and Romans were familiar with both the culinary and medicinal value of herbs. Many herbs grown in Britain today are thought to have been introduced by the Romans; some species survived in the gardens of monasteries and apothecaries. The herbaceous border of the modern garden has descended from the old-fashioned herb garden, and some plants grown today for their flowers or foliage were originally grown for their flavour or medicinal properties.

Until the agricultural revolution in the eighteenth century, few farm animals were kept during the winter. Consequently, from late autumn to late spring little fresh meat was available. Herbs were widely used to improve the flavour of meat that was either insipid or putrid. The medicinal properties of the herbs would have been some safeguard against the hazards of eating meat which was bad.

In England today, herbs are not so widely used. The most popular ones are thyme, sage, mint and parsley. In France, tarragon, chervil and dill are more popular; in Italy, basil, marjoram and oregano are widely used. These herbs will all grow quite happily in most soil and weather conditions found in the UK. A small area of land planted as a herb garden gives the cook great scope for improving the flavour of many dishes. Consult a good cookery book to find which herbs blend especially well with the flavour of individual foods.

Most herbs die back in all except the mildest of winters in Britain. For use during the winter months, herbs can be bought dried, or they can be dried at home. Many fresh herbs can be deep frozen, too. Frozen herbs resemble the fresh herb more than the dried ones. Drying concentrates the flavour and dried herbs should be used with discretion.

Although they are still widely acclaimed by the herbalists, the nutritional value of most herbs is confined to supplying useful quantities of vitamins A and C, provided the herb is eaten in sufficient quantities. A handful of chopped parsley added to a mixed green salad will boost its vitamin content considerably, but a tiny sprig of parsley or just a few snips of chives are useful only as decoration.

HERRING One of the fatty fishes caught in great numbers around the British coast; the total catch of herring is about one eighth by weight of all fish landed in the UK.

Herring have a higher nutritive value than most fish. They are also one of the cheapest fish, but the average consumption in the UK of herring in all its different forms (see below) is less than one fish per person per year.

6 oz HERRING, WEIGHED AFTER HEADING, BONING AND TRIMMING, CONTAIN:		
	herring fried in oatmeal	herring baked in vinegar
Kilocalories (Kilojoules)	402 (1,688)	324 (1,360)
Fat	25.8	25.22
Carbohydrate	2.4	0
Protein	37.2	28.4
Calcium	66	99.6
Iron	3.2	2.7

6 oz raw herring contain these quantities of vitamins:

vitamin A	8.1	microg retinol equivalents
vitamin D	34.2	microg
thiamin	0.06	mg
riboflavin	0.54	mg

Herring are small, round-bodied fish. They can weigh from 4 oz to over 1 lb. Weight depends on the variety of herring, and on the season. Before spawning, the fish are fatter, with a higher proportion of oil. Herring are generally sold whole, or headed and boned; quick frozen herrings are usually boned. They are available all year round, though caught at different fishing grounds around the coast.

Herrings are also prepared in several different ways. Varieties of smoked herring include kippers, bloaters, buckling and red herrings. Herrings may be salted or, like rollmops and Bismarck herrings, marinated in spiced vinegar. Soused herrings are baked in vinegar. Marinated herrings are uncooked.

HONEY A very sweet substance made by bees from the nectar they collect from flowers. Honey is a mixture of natural sugars. Its flavour comes from the presence of small amounts of volatile, aromatic substances derived from the flowers. Roughly 20 per cent by weight of honey is water.

1 oz (2 tablespoons) honey contains:

82	kilocalories (344 kilojoules)
0.1 g	protein
no	fat
21.7 g	carbohydrate
1 mg	calcium
0.1 mg	iron
no	vitamin A
no	vitamin D
no	thiamin
0.01 mg	riboflavin
no	vitamin C

The colour of honey varies from almost white to deep brown and depends upon the species of flower from which the bees collected the nectar. Heather honey, for example, is darker than clover honey. Colour and flavour tend to change a little during storage. On keeping, liquid honey tends to crystallise.

Most brand-name honeys are blended to give a standard colour, flavour and price. Unblended honeys are always more expensive. Honeys produced by bees feeding on rare or unusual plants are the most expensive of all, like that collected from the bees feeding on the wild thyme which grows on Mount Hymettus in Greece.

Honey has been collected for many centuries. There are many references to honey in the Bible, and drawings from Egyptian tombs show the ingenious ways the Egyptians had of collecting honey from 'wild' bees. Until comparatively recent times, honey was the only sweetener man had.

As it has such a long tradition, honey has in the past been claimed as a medicine as well as a food. It was used in Hippocrates' day as a healing agent for burns, ulcers and wounds. Even today, honey is claimed to act as a mild sedative, a cure for constipation, and to bring relief from hangovers and irritating coughs.

Honey is widely recommended by health food advocates. They claim, correctly, that honey contains iron, copper, calcium, manganese, magnesium and several other mineral elements, but the minerals are present in such minute traces that they cannot make any real contribution to dietary requirements. For example, a man would need to eat 100 oz of honey to derive enough iron for one day; he would need 500 oz of honey to give him a day's recommended intake of calcium! (Women would need even larger quantities of honey to meet their higher dietary requirements of these two minerals.)

Although honey has no real advantages over ordinary sugar from the point of nutritional value, it has a more pleasing flavour. When used in cookery, honey improves both flavour and texture. Cakes and puddings made with honey stay moist longer than those made with sugar as the only sweetener. (See also **treacle**.)

ICE CREAM Originally a mixture of eggs and milk with cream, or equal quantities of cream and fruit purée which were churned during freezing. Most commercial ice creams available today are made from milk, cream and milk products, or non-milk fats with sugar, permitted stabilisers, emulsifiers and flavouring ingredients. Dairy ice creams must contain at least 5 per cent milk fat. No fat, apart from milk fat and the fat from a small quantity of egg yolk, is permitted. In non-dairy ice creams, other fats such as vegetable oils may be used.

1 oz brickette of vanilla ice cream contains:

    55 kilocalories (230 kilojoules)
    1.2 g protein
    3.2 g fat
    5.6 g carbohydrate
    39 mg calcium
    0.1 mg iron
       no vitamin A
       no vitamin D
    0.01 mg thiamin
    0.06 mg riboflavin
       no vitamin C

Composition, manufacture and labelling of ice cream are rigorously controlled by government food standards. For example, no artificial sweetener may be used, and minimum standards are stipulated for different kinds of ice creams, such as dairy ice cream, fruit ice cream and so on.

After the ingredients are mixed together, they must be pasteurised before cooling and freezing. During the freezing process, air is beaten into the mixture. There is no legislation about the amount of air that may be incorporated. The actual volume of air beaten into the mixture determines the colour, volume and texture of the final product. The very soft ice creams contain a very large volume of air.

Ice creams may be kept for several months in the freezer.

ILLNESS A modified diet plays an important part in the treatment of certain illnesses. These include jaundice, gall stones, other liver and kidney disorders, gastric and duodenal ulcers, colitis and diverticulitis. Blood cholesterol levels may also be controlled by dietary adjustment. Some illnesses are caused by the breakdown of certain metabolic pathways required for the normal use of food. Examples of these are diabetes and coeliac disease, where a specially modified diet must be followed at all times. Therapeutic diets must be kept under close medical supervision.

During and after most illnesses, slight changes in the daily food are usually needed. After surgical operations, or severe accidents in which body damage has occurred, extra vitamin C is needed to speed the healing of wounds. Extra quantities of body-building nutrients, including proteins and iron to make good any blood loss, are also required. An iron-rich diet is needed after childbirth, too.

Any bout of sickness and diarrhoea increases the patient's need for fluids. Liquids only may be taken for a day or so if he cannot face solid foods. Fruit juices, weak tea and coffee, milk if possible, and hot drinks made with yeast or meat extracts are all suitable. The same beverages need to be served regularly to anyone suffering from a severe cold to replace fluids being lost as a result of the infection. Liquids should also be given at frequent intervals to anyone with an increased body temperature.

Many ill people have a small appetite. They may not be hungry or the very thought of food may nauseate them. Because a good diet will aid their recovery, attempts should be made to encourage them to eat. (On no account *force* anyone, especially children, to eat.) Provided the patient is taking enough fluids, you can be guided by his own fancies. A little of what you fancy goes a long way to help the appetite recover. Don't try to make him eat steamed fish and mashed potatoes if all he fancies is a thin slice of toast with Marmite. Small portions of attractively prepared and served, easily digested food provide the light diet that is needed. Milk in any form, chicken, white fish, cottage cheese and eggs (if they are tolerated) will provide protein in an easily digested form. Fresh fruit, fruit juices, a few teaspoonsful of boiled peas or carrots will satisfy the vitamin requirement. Sponge cakes, bread and butter, jellies, ice creams and mousses are other dishes suitable for a light diet.

IODINE One of the **trace elements** and an essential mineral substance required daily in small quantities for health. It is needed for the manufacture of the hormone thyroxin which is one of the hormones controlling the metabolic rate. Sea fish and shellfish are the best dietary sources of iodine. Vegetables, cereals and other plant crops provide iodine if they are grown on soils containing iodine. Drinking water often contains traces of iodine, and it is frequently added to table salt. In the UK and the USA iodisation of salt is voluntary. The Food and Nutrition Board of the United States has recommended that it should become a legal requirement to add iodine to table salt. Because coastal areas are rarely short of iodine, the UK being a small island, fares well.

A regular and persistent shortage of iodine causes cretinism among babies and young children, and endemic goitre among adults.

IRON One of the minerals essential for growth and health supplied by the diet. In the UK, roughly one-third of our total iron intake comes from cereal foods, some of which are enriched with iron (see **flour**); one-third comes from meat; about one-fifth from vegetables; and the remainder from other foods, including eggs. The richest sources of iron are liver, kidney and heart; egg yolk, wheatgerm and shellfish; canned meats, especially corned beef (some canned foods absorb iron from the can). Curry powder is extremely high in iron, which is derived from the iron vessel in which the spices are blended. Cooking pots and knives can also add iron to food.

The body of a 11 stone (70 kg) man contains between 4 and 5 grams of iron. Most of this is incorporated in haemoglobin, the red, oxygen-carrying pigment of the blood. Some iron is stored as an emergency supply in the liver. A little iron is used to make the muscle pigment myoglobin, and traces of iron are used in enzyme systems. Normally, the body uses the same iron over and over again. When old blood cells are broken down, their iron is used to make the haemoglobin of their replacements. The turnover of iron is quite efficient, but there is an unavoidable loss of about 1 mg each day. This amount needs to be made good by dietary iron.

The amount of iron is normally maintained at a constant level by a special mechanism within the intestinal cells. If the body is short of iron, as a result, perhaps, of bleeding, more iron is absorbed from food. If the body has an adequate supply of iron, the absorption is suppressed even though an especially iron-rich meal is eaten. In very large doses, iron is toxic. The absorption mechanism is overcome if excessive amounts are taken, so iron tablets must be kept well out of reach of small children.

Individuals vary in the efficiency with which they can absorb iron. A shortage of iron causes iron deficiency **anaemia.** Anaemia may be brought about by poor diet, poor absorption, blood loss, or increased iron requirements during rapid growth or pregnancy.

IRRADIATION OF FOOD The exposure of food to measured amounts of irradiation as a method of preservation. Although this method of preservation has been accepted in certain other countries, it is not generally allowed in UK. Irradiation is only permitted here in the preparation of special diets which must be completely sterile. (Sterile diets are needed, for example, for patients suffering from leukaemia.)

The advantages of radiation are that little change is made in the taste, texture, appearance or nutritive value of the food. Irradiation might be used to delay ripening of quality produce such as strawberries, mushrooms and asparagus, to prevent the sprouting of vegetables, to kill insect pests in stored foods such as grain, and to stop food spoilage by yeasts, moulds and bacteria.

JAM A traditional way of preserving fruit in a very high concentration of sugar. As the fruit is boiled for long periods, it loses most of its vitamin C. Jam is mainly a pleasant source of carbohydrate.

1 oz (1 tablespoon) jam contains:

74	kilocalories (310 kilojoules)
0.1 g	protein
no	fat
19.6 g	carbohydrate
5 mg	calcium
0.3 mg	iron
1 microg	retinol equivalents vitamin A
no	vitamin D
no	thiamin
no	riboflavin
3 mg	vitamin C (blackcurrant jam contains up to 12 mg vitamin C)

Jams are prepared by boiling together fruit and sugar, usually in the proportions of ¾ lb fruit to 1 lb sugar. Cooking apples, black and red currants, damsons, gooseberries and plums are easy to make into well-set jams. These fruits have the right amount of pectin (the setting ingredient) and sufficient acidity. Apricots, blackberries, raspberries and loganberries make a medium-setting jam, but cherries, strawberries, pears and ripe blackberries make a poor-setting jam unless extra pectin and acid are added.

Fruit for jamming should be as fresh as possible and dry. Underripe fruit is better than over-ripe, as fruits lose pectin in ripening. Acidity is needed to extract the pectin from fruit. Acid is added as lemon juice, citric or tartaric acid, or as the juice from acid fruits like gooseberries.

Preserving sugar is specially made for jamming. The large sugar crystals dissolve slowly without frothing. This cuts down the need for skimming during the early stages, and the jam is less likely to burn.

A great range of jams is sold ready-made. These vary enormously in quality – the higher the price, the better the quality. Some bought jams are made from preserved fruits to spread the jamming process over the year, instead of confining it to the fresh fruit season.

Jams were first made in the 1880s, when sugar became a very cheap commodity. Originally, jam was a cheap alternative to butter as a spread on the bread of the poor. The jam they ate was made from the cheapest fruits and vegetables available, coloured and flavoured to taste like fruit jams. It is said that bread and jam made up two out of the three meals eaten by the poor children of those times.

JELLY Sweet or savoury liquids set by the addition of gelatine. Savoury, or aspic, jelly is used to set small pieces of solid foods, such as prawns, lobster, veal and ham, chicken or turkey, hard-boiled eggs and salad vegetables, in a mould. Aspic jelly may also be chopped and used to garnish other cold dishes.

Sweet jellies are often set with fresh fruit, or used to glaze the top of fruit flans and similar sweet dishes. Sweet jelly is also used to line a mould to be filled with another sweet mixture.

Because of their convenience, packet table jellies and flavoured jelly crystals are extremely popular. These are made into jelly by the simple addition of water.

One 4 oz serving of a made-up jelly contains:

       73 kilocalories (305 kilojoules)
     1.7 g protein
      no fat
    17.7 g carbohydrate
     8.9 mg calcium
    0.49 mg iron
      no vitamins

Packet jellies may be made with milk, whisked with cream or evaporated milk, or set with fresh fruit to improve the food value of the jelly.

Jellies are popular with young children, and are useful for preparing light diets, or for patients with sore mouths or throats.

To prevent melting, jellies should always be kept in a cool place. When ready-cooked meat or fish is set in aspic, it should be eaten as soon as possible. It should be kept in the coolest part of the fridge for no longer than 2 days.

Sweet jellies can be kept longer. They will lose their fresh flavour after 2 or 3 days, but are safe to eat after one week or more, provided they have not been made with milk, cream, eggs or similar perishable items.

JOULE The unit of energy destined to replace the **calorie** in the conversion to the metric, or S.I. system. To convert calories into joules, multiply calorific value by 4.2.

JUNKET A cold dessert made from flavoured milk set by the addition of the enzyme, rennin. Rennin is bought as 'rennet'. It is the same enzyme as that used in the preliminary stages of cheese making. Rennet is added to lukewarm milk and then left undisturbed for two hours or so in a cool place.

The nutritional value of junket is the same as that of the quantity of milk from which it was made. The cheif dietetic values are that junket is easily eaten and digested, and also nutritious.

Junket should be eaten as soon as it has set sufficiently. If kept too long, it separates into the well-known curds and whey. The watery whey cannot be mixed back into the more solid junket, which becomes rather unpalatable.

KIDNEY An offal meat with a very high nutritional value. Kidney, liver – and, to a lesser extent, heart – are the only meats to contain more than a trace of vitamin A. They may also, unlike other meats, contain a little vitamin C. Kidney and liver are also higher than carcase meat in many of the B group vitamins, and also in iron. A rich dietary source of **cholesterol.**

A 4 oz portion stewed or braised kidneys contains:

> 180 kilocalories (752 kilojoules)
> 29.2 g protein
> 6.4 g fat
> no carbohydrate
> 24.5 mg calcium
> 80.8 mg iron
> 342 microg retinol equivalents vitamin A
> no vitamin D
> 0.25 mg thiamin
> 2 mg riboflavin
> no vitamin C

The flavour and tenderness of the kidney depends upon the animal from which it was taken. Ox kidney has a strong flavour. It is rather tough and needs long, slow cooking. Ox kidney is usually the cheapest and best choice for stewing and braising. Calf's kidney is slightly more tender. Pig's kidney is larger than lamb's, and not quite as tender as lamb's kidney, which is generally considered to be the best. Lamb's kidneys are sufficiently tender to grill or fry.

Fresh kidney should look bright red, be of firm texture and have a pleasant, fresh smell. For storage, see **heart.**

Dietitians recommend the weekly inclusion of kidneys or liver in the menu. Kidneys are especially valuable for anyone suffering from, or prone to, anaemia.

Traditionally, kidneys are stewed with beef to make steak and kidney pies and puddings. Devilled kidneys are another traditional dish, originally served at breakfast. Kidneys team well with mushrooms and are often served in grills, risottos and omelettes, or incorporated into soups.

KWASHIORKOR A disease in children caused by a dietary shortage of protein. The disease is characterised by wastage of the muscles, failure to grow, oedema leading to swelling of the abdomen, irritability and mental apathy. In a mild attack, only growth may be stunted and resistance to infection decreased. In severe cases, the liver and pancreas may be irreparably damaged, and even death may be the final result.

FAO and WHO studies have shown that kwashiorkor is very common in eastern and western Africa, the Near and Far East, the West Indies, and northern provinces of South America. In eastern and western Africa it has been said that most children suffer from some degree of kwashiorkor at some stage of their infancy.

Kwashiorkor was the name given to the disease by the Ga tribe living in and around Accra. Roughly translated, kwashiorkor means 'the disease the older child gets when the next baby is born'. Children are commonly breast fed for two or three years in developing countries, until the next baby is born. Up to this time, the child's protein intake is adequate, but when it is taken from the breast it is weaned on to starchy porridges which have inadequate protein for the child's needs. Kwashiorkor thus develops during the early weaning period.

Dried skim milk has proved to be effective in treating cases of kwashiorkor. UNICEF have done a great deal in distributing this food among races whose children suffer from the disease.

LACTOSE See **Carbohydrate**.

LAMB One of the most popular carcase meats. In the UK the average person eats about 5 oz of lamb and mutton each week. Lamb contains slightly less protein and iron than beef. Because of the difference in individual cuts of lamb, and also in different carcases, it is difficult to give an accurate figure for the total energy value of lamb. The values below are for meat of average fatness:

A 4 oz portion of roast lamb contains:

```
    324 kilocalories (1,352 kilojoules)
 28.4 g protein
 23.2 g fat (54.5 per cent saturated)
     no carbohydrate
   4 mg calcium
 4.8 mg iron
     no vitamin A
     no vitamin D
0.12 mg thiamin
0.28 mg riboflavin
     no vitamin C
```

Fresh English lamb is available mainly in spring and early summer. For the rest of the year, frozen carcases supplement the supply. Imported lamb comes mainly from New Zealand. 60 per cent of our total consumption of lamb and mutton is imported.

The number of different breeds of lamb reared in this country provide carcases of varying sizes. New Zealand lambs are always small. Size is not a reliable indication of the age and tenderness of English lamb. Young animals give smooth, moist, pinky-red meat with a thin, pliable skin covered with a thin layer of creamy fat. Generally speaking, the darker the fat, the older the animal.

There is little difference in the nutritive value of cheap and expensive cuts. Cheap cuts do, however, have more fat and usually more bone. The quantity of wastage must be considered when choosing good value for money.

Roasting cuts of lamb include leg, shoulder and loin. Chops and cutlets are ideal for grilling, and the better cuts are also suitable for kebabs. An excellent flavour is derived by using one of the traditional recipes for Lancashire hot-pot, Irish stew, etc., for cheaper, stewing lamb. Stewing lamb may also be minced for pies, rissoles and meat loaves.

For storage, see **meat**. Lamb keeps for up to 3 days in the fridge and up to 6 months in the freezer.

LARD A pure white, hard animal fat produced by rendering pork fat. Years ago lard was the most popular fat used in cooking. It gives a fine short pastry but cannot be creamed for cake making. Its bland flavour is considered by some to be an advantage for pastry making, but lard does not give the richness of butter. Lard contains very little moisture and supplies no nutrients apart from fat (of which 38 per cent is saturated). Its calorific value is 262 calories per ounce.

LEEKS An onion-flavoured vegetable, which looks rather like a very large spring onion. Leeks contain useful quantities of vitamin C and iron.

4 oz boiled leeks contain:

28	kilocalories (117 kilojoules)
2 g	protein
no	fat
5.2 g	carbohydrate
68.8 mg	calcium
2.28 mg	iron
8 microg	retinol equivalents vitamin A
no	vitamin D
0.08 mg	thiamin
17 mg	vitamin C

Chiefly a winter vegetable, leeks are at their best and cheapest from November to February. They will keep for one week or more in a cool, dark place.

Leeks may be used raw, thinly sliced in winter salads, and are especially good in coleslaws. Leeks have a more subtle flavour than onions, and may be substituted for onions in stews, soups and so on. The well-known chilled soup, crème vichyssoise, features leeks. (This soup is just as good served hot.) As a vegetable, leeks may be boiled, steamed or braised. They are usually served with sauce.

LEMONS One of the citrus fruits. Widely used as a flavouring in both sweet and savoury dishes. Because of their acidity, lemons are not eaten raw as fruit. They are an excellent source of vitamin C.

1 oz lemon juice contains:

2	kilocalories (8.4 kilojoules)
0.1 g	protein
no	fat
0.5 g	carbohydrate
2.4 mg	calcium
0.04 mg	iron
no	vitamin A
no	vitamin D
trace	thiamin
no	riboflavin
14 mg	vitamin C

Lemons are available all the year round but, like oranges, usually best during winter months. The best buy is the thin-skinned variety, which contain the most juice.

Recipes often call for the outer skin, or **zest**, of lemon to be grated. If the skin is to be used, choose blemish-free lemons.

Keep lemons in a cool place. If long storage is required, the salad drawer of the fridge is most suitable. In the warmth, lemons dry out and the skin toughens. Lemon juice should be kept in a closed container in the fridge.

As early as 1600, lemon juice was recognised as a cure for scurvy, the disease which killed so many sailors on long voyages. The curative effect was attributed by some to the acidity of lemons. Vinegar and oil of vitriol (sulphuric acid) were often used as substitutes for lemon juice. But it was not until 1854 that lemon or lime juice became compulsory supplies for any merchant ship at sea for more than 10 days. Enough juice was needed to give each crew member one ounce daily. As a result of this regulation, British seamen became known abroad as 'limers' or 'limeys'.

LENTILS One of the vegetables described as pulses, which are dried seeds of plants. Lentils are rich in carbohydrate and contain more protein than most vegetables. Lentils have been called the poor man's meat, though this may need to be changed because of recent dramatic price increases.

1 oz dry lentils contains:

      84 kilocalories (351 kilojoules)
     6.8 g protein
      no fat
    15.1 g carbohydrate
      11 mg calcium
     2.2 mg iron
    2 microg retinol equivalents vitamin A
      no vitamin D
    0.14 mg thiamin
    0.07 mg riboflavin
      no vitamin C

Lentils can be used to extend a meat dish, without proportionally increasing the cost. They blend very well with the flavour of ham or bacon, and are used to make the *dahl* served as a side dish with curry.

Like other dried foods, lentils should be stored in an airtight container, where they will keep almost indefinitely.

LETTUCE Probably the most popular salad vegetable eaten in the UK. Lettuce is low in food value, containing 95 per cent water and very few minerals and vitamins. It is a fairly good source of roughage.

1 oz lettuce contains:

       3 kilocalories (12.6 kilojoules)
     0.3 g protein
      no fat
     0.5 g carbohydrate
       7 mg calcium
     0.2 mg iron

47 microg retinol equivalents vitamin A
        no vitamin D
    0.02 mg thiamin
    0.02 mg riboflavin
       4 mg vitamin C

Because of its low energy value, lettuce is ideal for adding bulk to a low calorie diet.

Two main varieties are sold commercially – the cabbage lettuce and the cos lettuce. A more interesting selection may be home grown. Seed catalogues feature tender miniature lettuce, lettuce with very curly leaves, extra crisp leaves and even leaves streaked with bronze.

Lettuce wilts rapidly. It should be kept cool and moist in the salad drawer of the fridge. Lettuce should be well dried before placing in the fridge, or it will yellow more rapidly. Slightly wilted lettuce will crisp up in the fridge, and some people advocate soaking the lettuce in cold water to which a small piece of coal is added. Lettuce is best eaten as soon as possible after gathering.

LIMES Citrus fruit, similar to lemons in shape but with a green skin and a sharp flavour. A very good source of vitamin C, but, like lemons, they are not eaten as a fresh fruit. 1 fluid oz lime juice contains approximately 12 mg vitamin C. The juice is used to prepare drinks and in cooking or marmalade making.

Limes, like lemons, have long been known for their medicinal properties. They were eaten as a protection against scurvy (lack of vitamin C).

Limes are in season from February to July.

LIVER The most popular of the offal meats in the UK diet. Liver is one of the most useful sources of iron, vitamin A, riboflavin and other B vitamins. It also contains less fat than most meat.

4 oz calf's liver, fried, contain:

        296 kilocalories (1,237 kilojoules)
        33.2 g protein

       16.4 g fat
        2.8 g carbohydrate
         10 mg calcium
      24.60 mg iron
    6,804 microg retinol equivalents vitamin A
     0.84 microg vitamin D
       0.36 mg thiamin
       3.96 mg riboflavin
         24 mg vitamin C

The price, flavour and tenderness of liver depend on the
animal from which it comes. Liver should look moist, be quite
firm to touch, not at all slimy, and have a fresh smell. It is
usually best freshly cut by the butcher, or bought in a piece for
home slicing. Ox liver is the cheapest, has a strong flavour and
is often rather tough; most suitable for casseroles. Calf's liver
is regarded as the best and is, therefore, the most expensive;
suitable for frying and grilling. Lamb's liver is the nearest to
calf's liver in price and flavour, and is also suitable for frying
and grilling. Pig's liver is cheaper than calf's or lamb's liver. It
has a very pronounced flavour and a soft texture, ideal for pâtés.

Before the active constituent of liver which prevented pernicious
anaemia was isolated, patients were required to eat large
quantities of raw liver. Now, patients suffering from pernicious
anaemia are given injections of the life-giving vitamin B12.

100 g (about 3½ oz) of raw liver contains 300 mg of **cholesterol**.

LOBSTER An expensive shellfish eaten as a great delicacy
in the UK. Although it is costly, lobster does not have any
nutritional advantage over more homely fish like the haddock.

One small whole lobster weighing ½ lb with its shell, boiled,
contains:

       96 kilocalories (401 kilojoules)
     17.6 g protein
      2.4 g fat
         no carbohydrate
     50.4 mg calcium
     0.72 mg iron
         no vitamin A
         no vitamin D
         no figures available for thiamin
     0.40 mg riboflavin
         no vitamin C

Lobsters are usually sold ready-boiled. A female or 'hen' lobster is usually considered the best, but the flesh of the male is firmer after cooking. A 2 lb lobster weighed in the shell will serve two people. Like crab, lobster must be very fresh.

Lobster is in season all year round, but best in summer. Fresh lobster may be difficult to buy during the winter, when quick frozen lobster may be substituted. Several gourmet dishes may be bought ready prepared and quick frozen. Lobster is also canned as lobster meat or as pâté.

Lobsters contain 200 mg of **cholesterol** in 100 g (about 3½ oz).

LOGANBERRIES A soft fruit similar to, but slightly larger than, a raspberry. Like all soft fruits, it is a good source of vitamin C.

4 oz loganberries, stewed without sugar, contain:

    16 kilocalories (91 kilojoules)
    0.8 g protein
    no fat
    2.8 g carbohydrate
    30.8 mg calcium
    1.20 mg iron
    Trace of vitamin A
    no vitamin D
    0.03 mg thiamin
    0.02 mg riboflavin
    28 mg vitamin C

They are in season from June to August, but are also obtainable canned in syrup.

MACARONI See **Pasta**.

MAIZE Also called Indian corn, it is a cereal not widely used as a human food in the UK.

It is richer in fat than any other cereal except oats, containing twice as much as wheat or barley, and three times as much as rye. It contains fewer minerals and protein than wheat.

THE AVERAGE COMPOSITION OF MAIZE PRODUCTS

	Whole Maize meal, bolted	Maize flour	Cornflour (Corn starch)	Flaked Maize
Protein %	8.9	7.1	0.5	0.3
Fat %	4.9	1.3	0.7	3.5
Carbohydrate %	72	77.5	92	72.43
Fibre %	1.2	0.9	—	1.77
Ash %	1	0.6	—	1.18
Water %	12	12.6	—	11.84

Maize is prepared for food in many different ways. The following are all maize products: maize meal; maize flour; cornflour; cornflakes; corn oil; popcorn.

Maize does not contain **gluten** and can, therefore, be used in a gluten-free diet.

The most popular maize products in this country are cornflour, cornflakes and corn oil (see also **corn**).

MALNUTRITION is the result of long-term dietary imbalance. It is most often caused by under-nutrition. It has been estimated that half of the world's population suffers from the effects of under-nutrition. One and a half thousand million people exist on a diet which provides too little of one or more essential nutrients, or a diet that does not satisfy the individual's energy requirement. Long-term malnutrition causes disease. Some of these diseases have signs and symptoms related to the deficiency of one particular nutrient. Often the diet is inadequate in several respects and the symptoms are not so clear-cut.

Children are frequently the victims of under-nutrition. It is estimated that 60 per cent of the world's population under the age of 5 suffers from the effects of a shortage of total food, or from a specific shortage of protein. These children are said to be suffering from either protein-calorie malnutrition or **kwashiorkor.** During growth, their nutritional requirements are relatively high, and the staple foods which support an adult may not provide the right proportion of nutrients to overall energy value. In other words, the child cannot eat enough of them to derive the nutrients he needs.

Children are also more susceptible to disease than adults. Malnutrition reduces the body's resistance to disease and infection; an infection can increase the physiological demand for certain nutrients, which in turn aggravates the malnutrition – and so the vicious circle continues.

The World Health Organisation lists the most important nutritional diseases, on a global basis, as **xerophthalmia** which is widespread in the Near and Far East and some parts of Africa and is caused by a deficiency of vitamin A; nutritional **anaemia** resulting from a shortage of certain B vitamins and/or iron; and endemic goitre caused by a severe shortage of **iodine**.

In the developed affluent countries of the western world, malnutrition is evident in different forms, although the total incidence of malnutrition may be as widespread. **Obesity,** the result of over-nutrition, may be as detrimental to health as a shortage of a specific nutrient. Obesity may prove to be a fatal condition, although its effects are insidious rather than acute. Dental caries is another kind of disease which springs from poor dietary balance, coupled with poor dental hygiene.

Widespread deficiency diseases are not found in the UK. The only likely nutritional deficiency is iron deficiency **anaemia**. From time to time, cases of rickets among children are reported, but these are only isolated cases. Elderly people may also be marginally short of certain vitamins, especially vitamin C and certain of the B group vitamins.

MARGARINE The first-ever manufactured food, margarine was originally devised as a **butter** substitute in 1869. Many modern margines have advantages of their own. Margarine has the same energy value as butter.

½ oz margarine contains:

109	kilocalories (457 kilojoules)
0.05 g	protein
12.1 g	fat (18–19 per cent saturated)
no	carbohydrate
0.5 mg	calcium
0.05 mg	iron
128 microg	retinol equivalents vitamin A
1.13 microg	vitamin D
no	thiamin
no	riboflavin
no	vitamin C

Margarine may be made from vegetable, animal or marine oils. Some margarines are made exclusively from vegetable oils, a fact clearly stated on the wrapping. Margarine may also contain up to 10 per cent butter.

Liquid oils are hardened when hydrogen is added to some of the unsaturated bonds in their constituent **fatty acids**. A nickel catalyst helps to bring about this reaction. The flavour of margarine comes either from specially cultured milk, or from the substances known to flavour butter, which can also be added to margarine.

Vitamins A and D are required, by law, to be added to margarine. The vitamin A addition is equivalent to the average amount found in butter. Vitamin D in butter fluctuates over the year; margarine contains about 5 times more vitamin D than the average sample of butter.

By law, margarine may contain no more than 16 per cent water.

In the UK the average person eats $3\frac{1}{2}$ oz of margarine each week. In the national average diet, margarine provides 10 per cent of the total fat intake, 10 per cent of the vitamin A and almost 40 per cent of the vitamin D intake.

The price difference between butter and margarine has always been crucial to consumption figures. For some, margarine still carries the image of a second-rate butter substitute. However, the consumption of margarine is increasing, mainly because of the introduction of soft, 'luxury' margarines, which have properties butter lacks. They are always soft enough to spread straight from the fridge; they are suitable for one-stage cooking because they aerate easily; and as they are made from a high proportion of, or exclusively from, vegetable oils, they are higher in PUFA (see **fatty acids**) than either butter or the harder margarines.

The softness of margarine depends upon the blend of fats and oils used, i.e. in the proportions of saturated and unsaturated fats; and on the size of the water droplets incorporated in the emulsifying and plasticising process.

Margarines can usually be divided into three main groups: the super-grade, soft, or luxury types, sold in tubs, which are the most expensive of all; medium-grade margarines, wrapped in parchment or foil, which are medium-soft products, cheaper than the soft margarines; and standard-grade margarines, the cheapest and hardest of all, wrapped in parchment and sold for cooking.

Fats synthesised from coal and petroleum were used to make margarines in Germany during the Second World War. Even then, the cost of these 'artificial' margarines was much higher than if traditional ingredients had been used. More recently, scientists have been juggling with the fatty acid constituents of fats to make a low energy value margarine. A more viable product has proved to be a highly whipped, low calorie spread made with the usual fats but a higher water content. This low energy spread cannot be described as a margarine as the permitted water content is exceeded. It has roughly half the energy value of normal margarines or butters. The high water content makes this low energy spread unsuitable for cooking.

MARMALADE A preserve of citrus fruits in a high concentration of sugar. It may be prepared from one or more citrus fruits. For the purpose of preserving, the bitter variety of orange is generally used, but sweet oranges and tangerine oranges are frequently combined with lemons, grapefruit and bitter oranges to make different kinds of marmalades. Lime marmalade is also popular.

The underlying principles of marmalade making are essentially the same as those for making **jam**. A high proportion of sugar is required – hence the high energy value of marmalade. Much of the vitamin C content of the citrus fruits is lost during marmalade making.

1 oz (1 rounded tablespoon) marmalade contains:

74	kilocalories (310 kilojoules)
no	protein
no	fat
19.7 g	carbohydrate
10 mg	calcium
0.2 mg	iron
2 microg	retinol equivalents vitamin A
no	vitamin D
no	thiamin
no	riboflavin
3 mg	vitamin C

Many varieties of marmalade are available in jars and cans. Bitter oranges used to prepare marmalade are imported from late December to the end of February and are usually at their best and cheapest at the end of January.

MARROW Has the highest water content (97.8 per cent) of all vegetables, and as a result has a low nutritive value.

4 oz boiled marrow contain:

       8 kilocalories (33 kilojoules)
    0.4 g protein
        no fat
    1.6 g carbohydrate
  15.6 mg calcium
  0.33 mg iron
        no vitamin D
        no thiamin
     2 mg vitamin C
        no figures available for riboflavin or vitamin A

In season from July until November. The tiny marrows known as courgettes, which are available at the beginning of the season, have the best flavour. Courgettes are easily grown at home.

Large marrows keep quite well in a cool cupboard or outhouse. Courgettes should be kept in the fridge salad drawer, and quick freeze well if fresh. Some commercially frozen courgettes are watery and flavourless.

Courgettes are best cooked in butter, either whole in a covered dish in the oven, or sliced and gently fried in a pan. They are also delicious with tomatoes and onions. Large marrows need a savoury stuffing to give them flavour: bake the stuffed marrow whole or in slices.

In the early days of commercial jam making, marrow was widely used to extend the more expensive fruits. Marrow and ginger jam is still a good combination.

MAYONNAISE A seasoned blend of egg yolks, oil and lemon juice or vinegar. One tablespoon of mayonnaise contains about 100 kilocalories (420 kilojoules) and about 11 g of fat. The fat is largely unsaturated as **olive oil** is commonly used to make mayonnaise.

Because it contains a high proportion of egg yolk, the home-made version is more nutritious (see **eggs**). It is also a fairly rich source of **cholesterol**.

MEAT The flesh and organs of animals, mainly domestic animals such as cattle, pigs and sheep, killed and cooked for food. Carcase meat is the animal's flesh; offal (or 'variety meat', as it is more attractively called in the United States) comes from the animal's internal organs. Carcase meat may be trimmed away from the animal's skeleton, or it may be cut into joints containing bone. Liver, kidney, heart, sweetbreads (thymus glands), tongue, tripe (the white muscle of the cow's ruminant stomach), brains and chitterlings (small pieces of small intestine) are offals considered fit to eat in the UK. Of these, liver, kidney and tongue are the most popular.

Meat is an extremely popular food, and more money is spent on meat than on any other single item of food bought for the average British household. About a third of the total food budget goes on meat alone. This expenditure provides these proportions of the daily intakes of essential nutrients: roughly a third of the total intake of protein, fat and iron; from a fifth to a third of the B group vitamins; and a quarter of the vitamin A intake.

Although meat is very nutritious, it is also comparatively expensive. The price of meat is usually determined by the tenderness of the cut. Price is no indication of nutritional value. Cheap meats are not necessarily less nutritious, but they do need more careful cooking to make them palatable.

Tender cuts, such as steaks, chops, cutlets and top-quality joints may be cooked quickly at high temperatures. Grilling, frying and roasting are all suitable methods. (These are known as dry cooking methods.) Tougher cuts need long, slow, moist cooking methods, such as braising, pot roasting and stewing. Moist cooking changes gristle into gelatine and tenderises and softens tough muscle fibres.

Meat shrinks during cooking because of the contraction of proteins. As they contract, juices are squeezed out of the meat. As vitamins and minerals, as well as flavourings, are contained in these juices, they should be served with the meat. In moist cooking, the juices help to enrich the cooking liquid. Overcooked meat can be dry or stringy. It is always tasteless, and has a lower food value than meat cooked for the right length of time.

For advice on buying meat, see individual meats such as **lamb**, **beef**, etc.

For storing, meat should be taken from the butcher's wrappings and placed in a covered, non-airtight container. A casserole, a covered roasting tin, or a plate covered with foil are all suitable. The container should be placed on the top shelf of the fridge. Use raw carcase meats within 2 or 3 days; mince, offal or bought cooked meats should be eaten on the day of purchase or the following day.

Meat keeps extremely well in the freezer. It should be well wrapped to prevent drying out and freezer burn. Sausages, mince, offal, bacon and any other fatty or highly seasoned meats keep for up to three months; pork for 3 to 6 months; lamb and beef up to 9 months. Allow meat to defrost thoroughly before cooking. Slow defrosting in the fridge reduces dripping and consequent loss of food value and flavour.

MELON A fruit grown in many of the warmer European countries. It contains useful quantities of vitamin C, and as melon is eaten raw, little of this is lost in preparation.

One 6 oz portion of melon, weighed with skin, contains:

         24 kilocalories (100 kilojoules)
        0.6 g protein
         no fat
        4.5 g carbohydrate
       14.4 mg calcium
       0.24 mg iron
  180 microg retinol equivalents vitamin A
         no vitamin D
       0.04 mg thiamin
       0.04 mg riboflavin
         28 mg vitamin C

Water melons have less vitamin C. A 6 oz serving would supply between 6 mg and 8 mg.

Several types of melons are usually available. The *canteloup* is almost round, with dark green skin and pinkish-yellow flesh. *Honeydew* is oval with either a pale, greenish-white skin, or dark green ridged skin. It has greenish-yellow flesh. The *water melon* is the largest of all melons. It is usually round with dark green, smooth skin and pinkish-red, watery flesh and large, flat seeds. Although it looks so attractive, water melon often has little flavour. *Charentais* melon is generally considered to be the best of all, but it is usually the most expensive. The melons are small, with yellowish-green skin and deep yellow flesh; they are very sweet and strongly perfumed. These melons are mainly imported from Israel.

All types of melon are best, and cheapest, during the summer months. Honeydew melons are most generally available during the rest of the year.

Melons are harvested before they are fully ripe to allow ripening to continue during transport. To be ripe enough for eating, the tips of the melon should be fairly soft. Hard melons ripen more quickly in a warm place: an airing cupboard or warm spot in the kitchen are suitable.

Chill melon before serving. If melon is prepared in advance, cover with film or foil to prevent the smell being passed to other foods. Similarly, wrap well any portion of melon stored in the fridge. Keep unripe melons in a warm place to ripen; ripe melons may be kept for 3 or 4 days in the fridge.

METABOLISM A collective term for all the chemical reactions which take place in the body. Some of these reactions are concerned with the breakdown of food materials to supply the body with energy. Other chemical reactions build different tissues of the body from materials derived from food. The breakdown reactions are called 'catabolism'; the building reactions are called 'anabolism'.

Basal metabolism The automatic reactions which are essential for life, and which continue even when we are asleep or unconscious, form our basal metabolism. The reactions include those required for the beating of the heart and circulation of the blood, respiratory movements, digestion, excretion and temperature regulation. The amount of energy required for basal metabolism varies from person to person. For an individual who leads a fairly sedentary life, basal metabolism may account for half of the day's total energy requirement. (The remaining energy will be used by the muscles during physical activity.) Basal metabolism is stimulated by exercise, and the energy requirement for basal metabolism may be increased for several hours following a period of sustained physical activity.

MILK The most nutritionally complete of all foods.

Half a pint (10 fluid ounces) of milk contains:*

    180 kilocalories (770 kilojoules)
      9 g protein
     11 g fat (55.5 per cent saturated)
     14 g carbohydrate
    340 mg calcium
    0.2 mg iron
120 microg retinol equivalents vitamin A
0.1 microg vitamin D
    0.1 mg thiamin
    0.4 mg riboflavin
     10 mg vitamin C

*Although by weight milk is 85 per cent water, it has over 100 different constituents. The major ones are listed here.

In the UK, the average person consumes just over 4½ pints of milk each week, which supplies the following proportions of energy and essential nutrients: energy value 10 per cent; protein 18 per cent; calcium 46 per cent; thiamin 13 per cent; riboflavin 33 per cent; vitamin A 12 per cent; vitamin C 8 per cent.

With the exception of farm-bottled milk, all milk sold in England and Wales must be heat-treated to ensure that it is free from infection. Heat treatment also extends the keeping quality of milk. All heat treatment of milk causes some loss in food value, especially of those vitamins which are unstable to heat. These include thiamin and vitamin C. The more vigorous the heating, the greater the loss. However, milk is not an important source of these vitamins. The advantages gained by pasteurisation, sterilisation and drying of milks far outweigh the disadvantages of these small nutritional losses.

Fresh milks

Pasteurised milk is rapidly heated and kept at 161°F, 72°C, for 15 seconds, then quickly cooled and bottled. (The law also allows milk to be pasteurised by heating to a lower temperature but maintaining this for a longer time.)

Homogenised milk is heat-treated, then processed to break up the fat globules. They stay evenly distributed in the milk, so no cream rises to the surface.

Sterilised milk is homogenised, then heat-treated in bottle to a temperature of 212°F, 100°C. Has a cooked taste but keeps longer – up to one week – than other fresh milks.

Channel Islands and South Devon milks have higher fat contents than other milks; they contain not less than 4 per cent butter fat, and usually cost 1p a pint more than plain pasteurised milks.

Farm bottled milk is 'raw' or unpasteurised milk, and may cost a little more than pasteurised milk.

UHT milk is heat-treated at a much higher temperature – 270°F, 133°C – than other milks. Packed in specially sterilised containers, it will keep for up to five months even without refrigeration. When opened, it keeps as long as ordinary pasteurised milk.

With the exception of unopened UHT milk, all these fresh milks still contain some harmless bacteria. These feed on the milk sugar, lactose, converting it to lactic acid. It is this acid which turns milk sour. Although not very palatable, sour milk is quite harmless and can be used in cooking.

Processed milks

Evaporated and condensed milks are prepared by removing some of the water originally contained in the fresh milk. The milk may be skimmed – i.e. have the cream removed – before evaporation. This must be clearly stated on the can label. Sugar may or may not be added, and this too must be stated on the label.

Dried milks are products from which practically all the moisture is removed. They may have all or a proportion of the butter fat removed before drying. Details must be indicated on the label.

Instant non-fat dried milks are prepared from skimmed milk. The dried powder is given a subsequent treatment to make it readily reconstituted in cold or warm liquids. By removing the fat, the energy value of the reconstituted product is halved compared with fresh milk.

Manufactured milks

Filled milk contains fats or oils (other than milk fat) combined with milk solids derived from liquid, evaporated or powdered skimmed milk.

Imitation milk is a milk-like liquid which is made from ingredients such as coconut oil, soya beans, corn syrup. It has a much lower food value than other true milk products.

Synthetic milks, for feeding infants, invalids, or others who are allergic to any of the constituents of cow's milk, are specially formulated to produce a comparable liquid of high nutritive value.

Human milk

Human milk has 50 per cent more lactose (milk sugar), less protein, and considerably less calcium and phosphorus than cow's milk. Pure cow's milk is unsuitable for feeding very young human babies and must be diluted and sweetened with sugar to make its nutritional content more like that of human milk.

Storage

Canned milks need no special storage conditions. Dried milk should be kept in an airtight container in a cool, dry cupboard (see also **canning**). Fresh milks which are prone to souring must be kept as cool as possible. The acid-producing bacteria are more active in the warmth. Milk should also be stored in the dark. Its riboflavin content is reduced if milk is kept in a bright light, such as on a sunny doorstep.

A rich source of the bone-building nutrient, calcium, milk is an important food for infants, growing children, adolescents and pregnant women. It is very easily digested and is usually the basis of a light convalescent diet. It is excellent food for the elderly, too.

MINCEMEAT A sweet filling for pies, traditionally eaten at Christmas.

Many recipes for mincemeat are available, but all contain the dried fruits – currants, raisins and sultanas – and also apples, suet, sugar, spices and cut mixed (candied) peel. Some contain any of the following; lemon rind and juice, brandy, rum, nuts and glacé cherries. The ingredients are minced or chopped and mixed together and then allowed to mature before using as pie fillings.

1 oz mincemeat contains approximately:

    37 kilocalories (155 kilojoules)
    0.2 g protein
    0.9 g fat
    7.2 g carbohydrate
    14.9 mg calcium
    0.60 mg iron

Actual values for the vitamin content are not available, but mincemeat contains small quantities of thiamin and riboflavin and other B vitamins.

Mincemeat may be prepared at home or bought in jars or cans.

One 2 oz mince pie made from shortcrust pastry and min ce meat contains:

    222 kilocalories (928 kilojoules)
    2.8 g protein
    12.6 g fat
    25 g carbohydrate
    36 mg calcium
    0.84 mg iron

The name 'mincemeat' dates back to the time when meat was included in the mixture. Preserved, pickled and otherwise somewhat tasteless meats were often sweetened in medieval and Tudor times by cooking them with fruit and spices.

MINERALS A well-balanced diet must provide small quantities of inorganic substances, commonly known as minerals or mineral elements. About twenty different minerals are needed for health. These include calcium and phosphorus, which make bone tissue; iron and copper for making the blood's haemoglobin; magnesium, manganese and zinc which work as enzyme system activators; sodium, potassium and chlorine to maintain the concentration of body fluids; selenium, which works in association with vitamin E; and iodine, needed for making the hormone thyroxine.

Some of the minerals, such as sodium, potassium and chlorine, are widely distributed in the food we eat. They are freely absorbed from food and the excess is simply excreted in the urine. Other mineral substances, notably calcium and magnesium, are widely distributed, but are not easily absorbed by the body. The mineral content of foods by chemical analysis may not be a true indication of the nutritional value we can derive from them. Other minerals, including iron, are found in small amounts only. The body can also absorb only small amounts, and finds larger quantities of minerals such as copper and iron toxic.

MUESLI A breakfast dish, devised originally by the Swiss Dr Bircher-Benner at the end of the last century. In recent years, a number of commercially-prepared mueslis have been marketed. Some of these claim – untruthfully – to be based on the original Bircher-Muesli formula. The original dish contained more fruit than cereal, while most modern imitations contain predominantly a mixture of cereals. They are, nevertheless, very nourishing foods. On analysis, most mueslis contain some of the following ingredients: wheat, oatflakes, rye, barley, and millet, combined with a selection of dried fruit including apple flakes, pieces of hazelnut and almond, skimmed milk powder, honey, glucose and sugar. Served with fresh milk, a bowlful of muesli is a good dish for breakfast. It has high energy value, and is a good source of calcium, iron, thiamin, riboflavin and certain other B vitamins. The mixed cereal provides good vegetable protein, and the milk adds its own nutritional value.

Muesli may be prepared at home from similar ingredients, many of which are found in the store cupboard.

MUSHROOMS A popular vegetable with a delicate but distinctive flavour. Widely used as a garnish and as an ingredient in casseroled dishes, stuffings, flans and omelettes. Mushrooms are one of the lowest energy-value vegetables when raw, but they are frequently fried or grilled with fat, which greatly increases the energy value.

Comparison of energy value of raw and fried mushrooms

	Kilocalories	Kilojoules
1 oz mushrooms, raw	2	8
1 oz mushrooms, fried	62	256

2 oz fried mushrooms contain:

    124 kilocalories (511 kilojoules)
    1.2 g protein
    12.8 g fat
    no carbohydrate
    2 mg calcium
    0.72 mg iron
    no vitamin A
    no vitamin D
    0.07 mg thiamin
    0.40 mg riboflavin
    1 mg vitamin C

The majority of mushrooms bought today are cultivated and are available as button or open mushrooms. They are sold loose in multiples of a quarter pound. Mushrooms are also available canned.

Mushrooms should be kept in a plastic bag or in the salad drawer of the fridge. They keep fresh for several days provided they are not allowed to dry out. Mushrooms may be kept in the home freezer. They may be lightly cooked in butter, or simply wiped with a damp cloth to clean them before freezing.

Mushrooms have evolved over the last twenty years from a luxury food to one regularly included in most diets. Research into ideal growing conditions, and the application of commercial production methods to mushroom growing, have been responsible.

MUSSELS A variety of shellfish with an oval, blue-black shell. Like all shellfish, mussels are a good source of calcium and iron.

8 oz mussels, boiled (weighed with shells), contain:

    56 kilocalories (234 kilojoules)
    11.2 g protein
    1.6 g fat
    no carbohydrate
    134.4 mg calcium
    9.28 mg iron
        no figures available for vitamin content

Mussels are found in sandbanks around our coasts. Others are imported from France and Holland. They should be sold in their shells while still alive; just one dead mussel could cause food poisoning. If they are alive their 'mouths' should be tightly clamped shut. While they are still alive, mussels will keep fresh. Any open shell which does not close when lightly tapped should be discarded. Like other shellfish, mussels should be eaten on the day they are cooked.

Mussels are in season from September to March.

Mussels are also available in jars, with their shells removed, in a vinegar or brine solution. Quick frozen mussels have recently been introduced.

MUSTARD There are three types of mustard seed: white, black and brown. The black and brown seeds contain myronic oil, which gives the true piquant flavour. The white seeds have less flavour but better keeping qualities. Commercially prepared mustard powder is usually a blend of all three types of mustard seed with the addition of a cereal 'filler'. Dry mustard must be stored in an airtight container.

The name mustard comes from a corruption of 'must seeds'. The seeds were processed by the Romans by steeping them in a jar of wine known as the 'must'. Nowadays, mustard powder is blended with liquid to form a smooth creamy paste which is used as a table condiment and for flavouring various savoury dishes. It is used in such small quantities that its contribution to the diet is negligible.

Mustard is sold as mustard seed, commercially prepared mustard powder and ready-to-use blended mustard. English mustard is blended with water, French mustards with wine vinegar or grape juice. American mustard is not as hot as English, being made from the milder mustard powders.

Mustard sauce is a traditional accompaniment for baked ham and herrings. It is also a good sauce for vegetables.

Mustard seeds are also used as flavourings. The most common use is in chutneys, but the seeds may also be added to vegetable dishes, such as boiled cabbage and sauerkraut, coleslaw and potato salad.

MUTTON Meat taken from the carcase of an adult sheep. Like all red meats, mutton is an excellent source of protein, iron and B vitamins. The amount of fat varies from carcase to carcase, and between different cuts in any one carcase.

COMPARISON OF NUTRIENT CONTENT OF VARIOUS CUTS OF MUTTON (4 oz PORTIONS, WEIGHED WITH BONE)	Mutton chop grilled	Mutton, leg, roast	Mutton, scrag and neck, stewed
Kilocalories	432	332	276
(Kilojoules)	(1,806)	(1,388)	(1,154)
Protein g	17.2	28.4	20.8
Fat g	38.8	23.2	20.8
Carbohydrate g	0	0	0
Calcium mg	15.2	4.8	4.24
Iron mg	2.04	4.88	5.80
Vitamin A microg retinol equivalents	0	0	0
Vitamin D microg	0	0	0
Thiamin mg	0.10	0.10	0.10
Riboflavin mg	0.25	0.25	0.25
Vitamin C mg	0	0	0

There is little demand for mutton and it is difficult to buy in some areas. Because it is more tender and juicy, most people prefer to buy lamb, which is slaughtered before the animal is one year old. The flesh of mutton is usually darker than lamb, and the fat is harder and more yellow.

For storage, see **meat.**

 NOODLES A type of **pasta** often made with egg. This increases the overall food value of the pasta. The egg also gives the noodles a softer texture and an attractive golden colour.

Noodles are usually ribbon-shaped. They come in a variety of widths, from 'baby' noodles to 'extra broad' ones.

Noodles are a good alternative to potatoes to serve with a casseroled dish such as goulash, or to serve, like spaghetti, with a savoury sauce.

NUT The seed of certain trees or shrubs. Most nuts are highly nutritious: they are fairly rich in protein and contain a high proportion of fat. Consequently, nuts are a concentrated source of energy. They contain a number of minerals, including iron and calcium. It is not known whether these are available to the body, as nuts also contain a high proportion of indigestible fibres which can prevent mineral absorption. They are not usually eaten in great quantities except by vegetarians, who find nuts a good nutritional alternative to meat.

See also **almonds, brazil nuts, chestnuts, coconut, peanuts.**

COMPARISON OF NUTRIENT CONTENT OF VARIOUS NUTS (1 oz NUTS, WEIGHED WITHOUT SHELLS)			
	Almonds	Coconut desiccated	Peanuts roasted*
Kilocalories	164	172	166
(Kilojoules)	(688)	(722)	(697)
Protein g	5.8	1.9	8
Fat g	15.2	17.6	13.9
Carbohydrate g	1.2	1.8	2.4
Calcium mg	70	6	17
Iron mg	1.2	1	0.6
Vitamin A microg retinol equivalents	0	0	0
Vitamin D microg	0	0	0
Thiamin mg	0.09	0.2	0.007
Riboflavin mg	0.07	0.01	0.03
Vitamin C mg	0	0	0

* For values of unroasted peanuts see **peanuts.**

NUTMEG The inner seed of an apricot-like fruit borne by a tropical evergreen tree. Nutmeg is one of our most popular culinary spices. When the fruit is harvested, the dry outer husk splits, revealing the crimson covering of the nutmeg. This covering is used as another spice, mace. Nutmeg is imported from Indonesia and the West Indies.

Nutmeg is available either whole or as the ready-grated spice. Buy the ground spice in small quantities only. Like other ground spices, nutmeg loses its flavour with keeping. Both types should be in an airtight spice jar.

Nutmeg is used in both sweet and savoury dishes. It improves the flavour of egg custards and several other sweet sauces, milk and baked puddings, cakes, apple pie fillings and stewed fruits, especially prunes and similar winter compôtes. Nutmeg is also very good in creamed cheese, chicken and white fish dishes, cheese soufflés, fish cakes and with vegetables such as cabbage, spinach, carrots and green beans.

 OATS The most nutritious of all cereals. They are particularly rich in fat; the only other cereal which contains a similar amount of fat is **maize**. The husk of oats is extremely difficult to separate from the kernel, and by the ordinary methods of grinding a good deal of the husk cellulose is left in the meal in the form of small, sharp particles. These act as stimulants to the intestine and are useful in diets otherwise low in roughage, though they can prove irritating to some people.

There are various ways in which oats are prepared for human food. They may be simply cleaned and ground, the result being oatmeal of various degrees of fineness, or the branny particles may be separated to give 'oat flour'. Groats consist of oats from which the husk has been entirely removed. Groats are often used in the preparation of cereal foods for babies, and for breakfast cereals which reconstitute instantly on the addition of hot milk.

Rolling is now frequently employed as a method of preparing oats. The great pressure to which the grains are subjected between the rollers ruptures the cell walls, breaks down the cellulose, and flattens the grains out so that they are more easily softened by cooking. By the application of heat during the rolling process, the grains are at the same time partially cooked. This reduces the final cooking time, and it also alters the fat content in such a way that it is less liable to become rancid. There are several well-known brands of rolled oats available for making porridge in minutes. (Traditional porridge made with oatmeal takes as many hours.)

As with wheat flour, some of the protein and minerals are contained in the husk of the oats. When part or all of this is removed in grinding, the protein and mineral contents of the resulting oat meal or oat flour are reduced.

Oats do not contain **gluten** and oat products are suitable for use with a gluten-free diet.

THE PERCENTAGE COMPOSITION OF SOME PREPARATIONS OF OATS, UNCOOKED	Scottish oatmeal	Irish oatmeal	Rolled oats	Oat flour	Groats
Water (%)	5	5	7.8	5.8	10.4
Protein (%)	14.6	13.4	14.7	10.0	11.3
Fat (%)	10.1	8.8	6.2	5	6.5
Carbohydrates including cellulose (%)	68.2	70.1	69.8	77.9	70.4
Mineral matter (%)	2.1	2	1.5	1 3	1.7

4 oz cooked oatmeal porridge contain:

     58 kilocalories (217 kilojoules)
   1.6 g protein
   1.2 g fat
   9.2 g carbohydrate
  7.2 mg calcium
0.56 mg iron
     no vitamin A
     no vitamin D
0.06 mg thiamin
0.01 mg riboflavin
     no vitamin C

OBESITY See **Overweight**.

OEDEMA See **Water**.

OFFAL See **Heart, Kidneys, Liver, Sweetbreads, Tongue, Tripe**.

OIL A fatty substance which is liquid at room temperature. In composition, oils are like fats. They are energy-rich and composed of individual fatty acids. Most oils contain a higher proportion of unsaturated fatty acids than the true fats (see

149

fats, fatty acids). Coconut oil is the exception, containing a high proportion of saturated fatty acids. Most edible oils used are vegetable oils, derived from plants. Olive oil, corn oil, peanut (or arachis) oil, soya bean oil and sunflower oils are the most common ones.

Oil is commonly used as a substitute for animal fat in frying. As fried foods absorb some of the oil in which they are cooked. their energy value (or the number of calories they contain) increases considerably. For an example of how frying in oil can increase the calorific value of foods, see under **potatoes**.

Some oils, described as marine oils, are also derived from fish. Whale oil was widely used in the past for the manufacture of margarine. Cod and halibut liver oils are taken medicinally, as they are extremely rich sources of vitamins A and D.

See also **corn oil, olive oil**.

OLIVE These are unlike other fruits because of their high fat content.

1 oz olives in brine (weighed with stones) contains:

24	kilocalories (100 kilojoules)
0.2 g	protein
2.5 g	fat
no	carbohydrate
14 mg	calcium
0.23 mg	iron
7 microg	retinol equivalents vitamin A
no	vitamin D
no	thiamin
no	riboflavin
no	vitamin C

Olives are sold loose, bottled or canned in brine. They are either green or black. Some have the stones removed and are stuffed with pimento or almonds.

Their strong flavour makes olives excellent appetisers. They are also traditional ingredients in certain French, Italian and Spanish dishes. Black olives are also useful for garnishing a variety of dishes, ranging from flans and pizzas to open sandwiches.

OLIVE OIL A culinary oil obtained from olives. It has a high energy value but no vitamins, protein or carbohydrates.

1 oz olive oil (2 tablespoons) contains:

     264 kilocalories (1,104 kilojoules)
      no protein
    28.3 g fat (10 per cent saturated)
      no carbohydrate
     0.1 mg calcium
    0.02 mg iron
      no vitamins

Olive oil, sold in bottles and cans, is the oldest and most widely used cooking oil. Best quality oil, known as the virgin oil, is produced from selected fruit. The peeled and stoned fruit is crushed and lightly pressed at ordinary temperatures. Virgin oil is very pale in colour but has a rich, fruity flavour. Greater pressure on the crushed fruit releases the 'oil of the first pressing'. This is pale yellow in colour. The olives are then heated and subjected to greater pressure, releasing the oil of the second and third pressings. Poorer quality olive oil is produced by crushing the entire fruit, including the skins and stones. Second quality oil is greenish-yellow. It is often refined and deodorised, like other culinary oils.

The taste of good quality oil depends on where the olives were grown and the variety of the tree – over 300 different varieties are grown.

Olive oil should be kept in a cool place. It keeps its fresh flavour in the fridge, but often solidifies. Take it from the fridge for a short time before use.

Olive oil is used mainly for salad dressings, including French dressing and mayonnaise. It is also used, sometimes with butter, for frying. Its pronounced fruity flavour and comparatively low smoke-point make olive oil unsuitable for deep frying.

ONIONS A popular root vegetable, widely used for flavouring. Onions vary considerably in size, colour and flavour. Shallots, spring onions and also 'cocktail' onions also belong to the onion family. Spanish onions have a milder flavour than homegrown varieties.

**COMPARISON OF THE NUTRITIVE VALUE OF SOME ONIONS
(1 oz PORTIONS OF EACH)**

	Raw onion	Boiled onion	Fried onion	Raw spring onion
Kilocalories	7	4	101	10
(Kilojoules)	(29)	(17)	(422)	(42)
Protein g	0.3	0.2	0.5	0.3
Fat g	0	0	9.5	0
Carbohydrate	1.5	0.8	2.9	2.4
Calcium mg	8.9	6.9	17.4	38.4
Iron mg	0.09	0.07	0.17	0.35
Vitamin A microg retinol equivalents	0	0	0	trace
Vitamin D microg	0	0	0	0
Thiamin mg	0.01	trace	0	0
Riboflavin mg	0.01	0.01	0.01	0
Vitamin C mg	3	2	2	7

Home-grown onions are available from September to December, and imported onions all the year. Spring onions are available throughout the spring and summer.

With careful storage, home-grown onions may last until the new season's onions are ready. The National Vegetable Research Association is investigating improved keeping methods. The sugar in onions caramelises during frying or baking, giving their characteristic flavour. But fried or baked onions easily burn.

Certain curative properties have been attributed to onions. Eating large quantities of the raw vegetable, for example, is one old-fashioned remedy for a streaming cold.

ORANGES The most popular of all the citrus fruits. Oranges alone supply 11 per cent of the total national intake of vitamin C. The average weekly consumption of oranges is only 4 oz – one medium-sized orange. These figures emphasise the importance of oranges as a dietary source of vitamin C.

One 4 oz orange contains:

    40 kilocalories (168 kilojoules)
    0.8 g protein
    no fat
    10 g carbohydrate
    48 mg calcium
    0.4 mg iron
    8 microg retinol equivalents vitamin A
    traces B group vitamins
    56 mg vitamin C

All our citrus fruits are imported. They come mainly from Israel, Spain, Cyprus and South Africa. Oranges are harvested before they are ripe, to allow the fruit to mature slowly during transport and be ready for eating when they come into the shops. Navel and Jaffa oranges are two varieties of large, sweet, usually seedless, juicy dessert oranges.

Clementines, satsumas, tangerines and mandarin oranges are all small varieties of the orange. They are usually at their best around Christmas. Seville oranges are grown exclusively for **marmalade**. Blood oranges, known as sanguina or sanguinelli, come mainly from Spain. They are very sweet and juicy.

Although oranges are available all the year round, they are generally at their best during the winter months. In summer, they tend to be rather dry and flavourless. For storage, see **lemons.**

Oranges came originally from China, where they have been grown for many centuries. They appeared in England in the late sixteenth century, but were not widely available until the nineteenth century. Like all fresh fruit, oranges were considered potentially harmful when they were first introduced (see also **fruit**). Samuel Pepys describes his great misgivings on drinking fresh orange juice, recommended to him as a sure cure for a monstrous hangover!

OVERWEIGHT Usually defined as an excessive accumulation of body fat. (In certain medical conditions, overweight may be due to an excessive accumulation of fluid. When the condition has been corrected, the weight is usually found to be quite normal.) Degree of overweight is assessed by reference to published tables of ideal weights for both men and women of a range of heights (see page 11). In the United Kingdom, half the adult population is thought to weigh more than it should. One in every ten adults is severely overweight, or obese. Overweight is also a common problem among children, especially adolescents. Even babies are not exempt from the overweight problem.

Overweight is the almost inevitable result when energy intake from food regularly exceeds the energy output through metabolism, physical activity and heat. There are some people, usually young, very active adults, who can over-eat and yet not put on weight. It is thought that the surplus energy is burnt as heat rather than being stored as fat, which happens in the majority of people. The precise reasons why the body accumulates fat are not clearly understood. Man appears to be the only animal seriously afflicted by overweight. Basically, overweight occurs when the body's appetite control mechanism breaks down (see also **appetite**).

Severely overweight people often do not experience hunger at all. Their great desire to eat appears to spring from psychological rather than physiological urges. As hunger does not initiate the desire to eat, satiety does not stop them from eating. Many obese people are compulsive eaters. They eat when they are worried, bored, lonely, or unhappy for any other reason.

An individual's tendency towards overweight may be determined before he is born, or during the first few months after birth. At this time of life, the basic complement of body cells is established. If the child is overfed, a greater number of fat cells than normal are laid down in his body. In later life, his nutritional status affects only the actual amount of fat carried in each cell.

Bottle feeding and the very early introduction of solid foods are thought to be largely responsible for the alarming number of overweight babies. Statistics show that most children who are overweight at six months remain overweight throughout childhood. They become obese adolescents. Four out of every five obese adolescents grow into obese adults. One in three overweight adults date the onset of their weight problem to early childhood.

Overweight among girls and women is most likely to occur during periods of hormonal change. Puberty, pregnancy and menopause are the most critical times. In men, overweight commonly occurs during middle age. Increasing affluence and decreasing physical activity are the main causes.

A 10 per cent degree of overweight is recognised as a health hazard. A 20 per cent degree of overweight is considered to be a serious medical complication. Overweight people are more susceptible to diseases of the cardio-vascular system, liver and kidneys; they are more likely to develop **diabetes**: they are more prone to accidents. Overweight women are more likely to suffer from complications during pregnancy, and any surgical operation is hampered by excessive body fat.

Fortunately, the health hazards are reduced when excess weight is lost. Slimming is often a difficult and trying business, requiring encouragement and strength of mind. But an overweight person can *always* reduce to a more normal weight by sticking conscientiously to a well-balanced weight-reducing diet.

OXTAIL Contains at least 50 per cent bone, and is, therefore, only suitable for stews and soups. The meat has the same nutritive value as stewing beef (see under **beef**). It requires very long, slow cooking, but in the process develops an excellent flavour. One oxtail, stewed, will generally serve 4 people.

OYSTERS An excellent source of calcium, iron and vitamin A. Usually they are eaten raw, but can also be served cooked.

2 oz raw oysters contain:

28	kilocalories (117 kilojoules)
5.8 g	protein
0.6 g	fat
no	carbohydrate
105.8 mg	calcium
3.40 mg	iron
43 microg	retinol equivalents vitamin A
no	vitamin D
0.06 mg	thiamin
0.10 mg	riboflavin
trace	vitamin C

The flesh of some oysters is high in vitamin C: Pacific oysters have been shown to contain 22 mg per 100 g and Olympia oysters, 38 mg per 100 g.

Oysters are in season in the UK from September to April, and they are imported all year round. They have been known to man since earliest times. They were once eaten by the poor in Britain because they were cheap and plentiful, but are now regarded as a great delicacy, and their price reflects this.

Like **mussels**, they should be bought fresh and their shells should be tightly closed and intact. They are usually sold in their shells by the dozen, or out of their shells, ready prepared.

PARSLEY A well-known and widely-used herb. Parsley has a high calcium, iron and vitamin C content but contributes only very small quantities of these to the diet because it is used in such small quantities, usually as a garnish.

¼ oz raw parlsey contains:

            1 kilocalorie (4 kilojoules)
      0.4 g protein
         no fat
         no carbohydrate
      23 mg calcium
    0.57 mg iron
  95 microg retinol equivalents vitamin A
         no vitamin D
    0.01 mg thiamin
    0.02 mg riboflavin
      10 mg vitamin C

Parsley is sold fresh or dried. Fresh parsley is available from late spring until the end of the autumn. In mild winters, parsley will continue to grow throughout the winter. Parsley can be grown indoors in pots, or stored in the home freezer, to ensure a continuous supply.

Store fresh parsley in a plastic bag, tied, or in a sealed plastic container in the fridge. Some cooks like to keep a small vase with the parsley stalks standing in a little water.

PARSNIPS Root vegetables with a higher carbohydrate content than carrots, turnips and swedes.

4 oz boiled parsnips contain:

      64 kilocalories (267 kilojoules)
    1.6 g protein
         no fat

    15.2 g carbohydrate
    40.4 mg calcium
    0.52 mg iron
        no vitamin A
        no vitamin D
    0.08 mg thiamin
    11 mg vitamin C

Parsnips are available from September to April. They should be stored in a cool, dark but dry place.

PARTRIDGE One of the **game** birds which may be shot for only part of the year and which for the rest of the year are protected by law. The season for partridge is 1 September to 1 February.

Partridge contains a little more calcium and iron than chicken, but is otherwise similar in nutritional value.

8 oz roast partridge (weighed with bone) contain:

    288 kilocalories (1,204 kilojoules)
     48 g protein
    9.6 g fat
       no carbohydrate
    62.4 mg calcium
    10.48 mg iron
         no values available for the vitamin content

It is advisable to choose a young bird. The long wing feathers are V-shaped in a young bird, as distinct from the rounded ones of an older bird. Young birds have short leg spurs; their pinions and quills are pliable.

Partridges may be sold fresh or 'hung'. Before they are prepared for eating, all game birds need to be hung by their legs, complete with viscera and feathers, in a cool, airy place. Hanging tenderises the bird's flesh and gives it a better flavour. The time for hanging depends on the weather and the individual's taste, varying from a week in warm, humid weather to 2 to 3 weeks in frosty weather.

Game birds can be dry and rather tough unless they are well basted during roasting. They are best covered with strips of fat bacon. Alternatively, brush the bird with melted butter and wrap it in foil before roasting. Traditionally, a generous piece of fillet steak was placed inside the body cavity to keep the bird moist during cooking.

PASTA The staple food of the southern Italians, and consumed in large quantities everywhere in Italy. Pasta is gaining in popularity in this country, but not to the extent that it has replaced our staples of bread and potatoes. It is now both manufactured in the UK and imported from Europe.

Pasta is prepared from milled durum wheat, which is made into a dough with water before being shaped and dried. Most pasta shapes sold in the UK are formed from this basic dough. There are long, slender, round shapes, such as spaghetti and vermicelli; tubular shapes, such as macaroni; ribbon shapes, such as tagliatelle; fancy shapes, which include shells, bows, wagon wheels and alphabet letters. Green pasta is coloured a pale green by the addition of spinach to the dough.

Pasta is principally a source of carbohydrate with some vegetable protein, minerals and B vitamins.

3 oz of pasta (uncooked) per person is generally regarded as an average serving when boiled.

COMPARISON OF NUTRIENT CONTENT OF MACARONI AND 3 oz UNCOOKED SPAGHETTI		
	Macaroni	Spaghetti
Kilocalories (Kilojoules)	306 (1279)	312 (1304)
Protein g	9	8.4
Fat g	1.8	0.9
Carbohydrate g	67.8	71.7
Calcium mg	22.5	19.2
Iron mg	1.23	1.02
Vitamin A	0	0
Vitamin D	0	0
Thiamin	0.10	0.10
Vitamin C	0	0

A less popular pasta is the egg pasta which is prepared from a dough containing egg. When cooked, egg pasta has a softer, more pliable texture, and an attractive golden colour. Examples are egg noodles and lasagne.

Pasta must be stored in a dry place, where it will keep well in its own packaging. If the storage area is damp, keep pasta in storage jars or tins. Buy long spaghetti or macaroni as it is needed. (See also **noodles**.)

PÂTÉ A rich savoury dish made from well pounded or minced meat, poultry or fish. Pâté usually has a high fat content to give it a spreadable consistency.

Belly of pork, other pork cuts, ham, bacon, veal, liver, duck and goose are most popularly used to make pâtés, and the more flavoursome fish, in particular the smoked fish.

Because recipes vary so widely, it is not possible to give a precise nutritional breakdown of this food. In general terms, pâtés are high in calories (or energy value), mainly because of the high fat content. Pâtés containing liver are very rich in B group vitamins and iron. Pork pâtés also have a high vitamin B content.

The texture of pâté varies from the smooth textured pâté maison types to the coarse textured varieties usually described as pâté campagne.

Pâtés usually keep up to one week in the fridge. They should be kept covered as they are well seasoned and may pass their flavour on to other foods, and also to prevent drying out. Pâtés with brandy, and those sealed with a layer of butter will keep slightly longer.

PEACHES Large stoned fruits which may be purchased fresh and canned. They contain useful amounts of vitamin A, but not as much as apricots. A 1 oz portion of canned apricots contains 47 microg retinol equivalents of vitamin A, against the 12 found in a 1 oz portion of canned peaches.

One 4 oz fresh peach contains:	4 oz canned peaches in syrup contain:
44 kilocalories	100 kilocalories
(176 kilojoules)	(420 kilojoules)
0.8 g protein	0.4 g protein
no fat	no fat
10.4 g carbohydrate	26 g carbohydrate
4 mg calcium	4 mg calcium

0.4 mg	iron		2 mg	iron
96 microg	retinol equivalents vitamin A		48 microg	retinol equivalents vitamin A
no	vitamin D		no	vitamin D
0.04 mg	thiamin		no	thiamin
0.04 mg	riboflavin		0.04 mg	riboflavin
8 mg	vitamin C		4 mg	vitamin C

Fresh peaches are imported and are available from January to March and June to September. Canned peaches are available all year. Some fresh peaches are grown in the UK in very sheltered gardens or heated greenhouses.

PEANUT BUTTER A nutritious paste prepared from roasted **peanuts**, edible vegetable fat, sugar and salt. A very rich source of energy, peanut butter is available in the UK as a spread for bread and savoury biscuits.

Peanut butter was one of the first-ever **health foods**. It was devised at the end of the last century by Dr John Kellogg of cornflake fame. Dr Kellogg was so enthusiastic about the nutritional value of the peanut that he made peanut butter so those of his patients with poor teeth could still derive benefit from the peanut.

PEANUTS These are not true nuts, but the hard seed of a leguminous plant, also known as monkeynuts and groundnuts. They play an important part in the diet in certain African countries. They are a rich source of protein and fat, and consequently are a concentrated source of energy. They contain no vitamins A, D and C but are an unusually rich source of thiamin. They are available in their shells, shelled or roasted.

They are not eaten in large quantities in the UK except by vegetarians.

1 oz shelled peanuts* contains:

    171 kilocalories (715 kilojoules)
    8 g protein
    13.9 g fat (22 per cent saturated)
    2.4 g carbohydrate

*See also values for roasted peanuts under **nuts**.

```
17.3 mg  calcium
 0.58 mg  iron
      no  vitamin A
      no  vitamin D
 0.26 mg  thiamin*
 0.03 mg  riboflavin
      no  vitamin C
```

*75 per cent of the thiamin may be lost during roasting.

Peanuts are grown mainly for their oil, which is used to make margarine or cooking oil, often called arachis oil. In India, a successful artificial milk is being manufactured from peanuts and buffalo milk, a product which looks and tastes like ordinary cow's milk.

PEARS A very sweet and juicy fruit when ripe, but with little nutritional value. Although readily available, pears do not share the popularity of apples. In the UK the average person eats less than 1 oz of pears per week, compared with 7 oz to 8 oz of apples.

One 4 oz fresh dessert pear contains:

```
      36  kilocalories (150 kilojoules)
   0.4 g  protein
      no  fat
   8.8 g  carbohydrate
    6 mg  calcium
  0.2 mg  iron
1 microg  retinol equivalents vitamin A
      no  vitamin D
 0.04 mg  thiamin
 0.04 mg  riboflavin
    4 mg  vitamin C
```

A variety of fresh pears is available, both for dessert and for cooking. Many are grown in this country, but large quantities are also imported. They are available almost all the year, home-grown ones being supplemented by the imported ones. Pears are also available canned in syrup.

If they are for immediate use, buy fresh pears that are already soft. Generally, it is better to buy pears slightly hard and eat them as they ripen.

For long-term storage, buy under-ripe pears and keep them in a cool, though frost-free, store. Inspect at intervals and remove any pears starting to brown. Pears ripen within a few days in a warm room.

PEAS Fresh green peas, along with broad beans, contain more energy, protein and thiamin than other fresh vegetables. They also contain some vitamin C and carotene.

4 oz fresh boiled, or quick frozen boiled, peas contain:

56	kilocalories (232 kilojoules)
5.6 g	protein
no	fat
8.8 g	carbohydrate
16 mg	calcium
1.2 mg	iron
56 microg	retinol equivalents vitamin A
no	vitamin D
0.28 mg	thiamin
0.12 mg	riboflavin
16 mg	vitamin C

Quick frozen peas and canned peas, which are available all year round, are popular in the UK. The average person in the UK eats per week 0.66 oz fresh peas, 1.02 oz quick frozen peas and 3.2 oz canned peas. Fresh peas have a short season, from June to September.

4 oz canned processed peas contain:

108	kilocalories (456 kilojoules)
8 g	protein
no	fat
20.4 g	carbohydrate
32 mg	calcium
1.2 mg	iron
76 microg	retinol equivalents vitamin A
no	vitamin D
0.08 mg	thiamin
0.04 mg	riboflavin
4 mg	vitamin C

Peas are also available dried, when they become classified as a pulse vegetable. The peas are allowed to dry naturally in their pods on the plant. They may also be air-dried or freeze-dried (dehydrated); when reconstituted with water these are similar in appearance, colour and flavour to fresh peas.

Dried peas may be dried either whole or split, when they are known as split peas. They are rich in energy and protein, but other nutrients, notably thiamin and vitamin C, are lost during the slow drying process. However, before they can be used they must be soaked. When this is done the moisture content rises from 12 to 70 per cent and the energy value falls from 274 to 99 kilocalories per 100 g.

COMPARISON OF NUTRITIVE VALUE OF DRIED AND SPLIT PEAS, RAW AND BOILED; 1 oz PORTIONS OF EACH

	Dried peas raw	Dried peas boiled	Split peas raw	Split peas boiled
Kilocalories	78	28	86	33
(Kilojoules)	(326)	(120)	(359)	(138)
Protein g	6.1	2	6.3	2.3
Fat g	0	0	0	0
Carbohydrate g	14.2	5.4	16.1	6.2
Calcium mg	17.2	6.9	9.4	3.1
Iron mg	1.34	0.41	1.54	0.49
Vitamin A microg retinol equivalents	12	4	0	0
Vitamin D	0	0	0	0
Thiamin	0.2	0.03	0.20	0
Riboflavin	0.08	0.02	0.06	0
Vitamin C	0	0	0	0

PEPPERS Also known as sweet peppers, capsicums and pimentos. They may be eaten green (young) or red (ripe). They are rich in vitamin C; in fact they contain more vitamin C than any other vegetable regularly consumed in the UK.

1 oz green or red pepper contains:

11 kilocalories (46 kilojoules)
0.6 g protein

```
 0.1 g  fat
 1.7 g  carbohydrate
 5.7 mg  calcium
 0.3 mg  iron
30 microg  retinol equivalents vitamin A
   no  vitamin D
 0.02 mg  thiamin
 0.02 mg  riboflavin
 42 mg  vitamin C
```

They are cultivated in Spain, Italy, the south of France and the USA, and are available most of the year round. They are at their peak during summer and early autumn.

Choose firm, unblemished fruit. Peppers keep well in the salad drawer. They may also be quick frozen, freezing very well in cooked dishes such as ratatouille.

Peppers, especially the sweet red ones, make excellent raw salad vegetables. Peppers may also be cooked in a casseroled meat and vegetable dish, or stuffed with a savoury meat or poultry stuffing and baked.

PHEASANT One of the wild birds classified as **game**. Like partridge, pheasant contains more calcium and iron than chicken, but is otherwise similar in nutritional value.

8 oz roast pheasant (weighed with bone) contain:

```
 304  kilocalories (1,271 kilojoules)
  44 g  protein
13.6 g  fat
   no  carbohydrate
70.4 mg  calcium
  12 mg  iron
       no values available for vitamin content
```

The season for pheasant is 1 October to 1 February.

It is advisable to choose a young bird. The female bird is more tender than the male; the sexes can be differentiated by their plumage. Look for the same points as those mentioned under **partridge.**

Pheasant needs to be well 'hung', otherwise the flesh is dry and does not have such a rich flavour. When purchasing, check whether the bird is fresh or has been hung.

PICKLES Fruit or vegetables, or a mixture of both, which have been preserved in spiced vinegar. The fruit or vegetables are usually brined first to remove some of the water which might otherwise dilute the vinegar and render it too weak to act as a preservative. Very watery vegetables like marrows should be sprinkled liberally with salt and left for 12 to 48 hours.

The following fruits and vegetables may be pickled:

cucumber	beetroot
marrow	gherkins
tomatoes	green walnuts
French beans	apples, including crab apples
cauliflower	damsons
cabbage	pears
onions	peaches
mushrooms	oranges

Pickles are sold in jars and can also be prepared at home. They are usually served with cold meat and cheese.

PIGEON A small game bird which breeds in such large numbers in Britain that to some farmers it has reached pest proportions. There is no closed season for shooting pigeon, and they are not a protected species.

The nutritional value of pigeon is very similar to that of chicken (see **chicken**) except that pigeon has slightly more fat and is correspondingly higher in calories. Roast pigeon has 61 calories an ounce, while roast chicken has 54 calories an ounce.

Although available all year round, pigeon are best between March to October. They are not hung like other game birds, but eaten fresh, between 12 and 24 hours after killing. To retain their delicate flavour, pigeons should be brushed with melted butter and kept well basted during cooking. An average sized pigeon will roast in about 30 minutes.

PIMENTOS Also known as sweet peppers : see under **peppers**.

PINEAPPLES Tropical fruit which contain useful amounts of vitamin C when fresh. However, pineapple is more widely bought in the UK in the canned form.

NUTRITIVE VALUES OF FRESH AND CANNED PINEAPPLE: 4 oz PORTIONS		
	Fresh pineapple	Canned pineapple in syrup
Kilocalories (Kilojoules)	52 (217)	88 (360)
Protein g	1.6	0.4
Fat g	0	0
Carbohydrate g	13.2	22.8
Calcium mg	14	16
Iron mg	0.48	2
Vitamin A microg retinol equivalents	11	8
Vitamin D microg	0	0
Thiamin mg	0.08	0.04
Riboflavin mg	0	0.04
Vitamin C mg	28	8

Fresh pineapples are imported and are available most of the year. A pineapple is judged to be ripe for eating when one of the top leaves can be pulled out easily.

Canned pineapple may take the form of rings, chunks and pulp. Pineapple juice is also canned.

Although pineapple is best served chilled, take care not to contaminate the rest of the food in the fridge with the strong pineapple flavour. Prepare the pineapple and then place in a sealed plastic container before chilling. (Strawberries and melons should be given similar treatment.)

PLAICE One of the smaller flat fish which is gradually increasing in popularity in the UK. It is easily recognised by its spots, which range from light orange to dark brown, on the darker upper skin. Plaice has slightly more fat than haddock, but otherwise has a very similar nutritional value. (See **haddock** for nutrient analysis.)

Plaice is generally available all year round. Quick-frozen fillets are available if fresh supplies are in short supply.

Smaller fish, up to one pound in weight, may be sold and cooked whole. Larger fish, which may be up to three pounds in weight, are usually sold as fillets.

PLUMS A popular home-grown stoned fruit. Several different varieties are grown, providing plums suitable for cooking, jamming and eating as dessert. Although plums are usually sweet and juicy, their nutritional value is very low.

4 oz of plums, weighed without stones, contain:

36	kilocalories (151 kilojoules)
0.8 g	protein
no	fat
8.8 g	carbohydrate
12 mg	calcium
0.4 mg	iron
40 microg	retinol equivalents vitamin A
no	vitamin D
trace	some B group vitamins
4 mg	vitamin C

Home-grown plums are available during July, August and September, and imported plums are usually on sale from January to April.

Plums are best kept in the salad drawer at the bottom of the fridge. They also freeze well. Plums should be halved, stoned and packed in sugar syrup before freezing. A little ascorbic acid solution may also be added to prevent browning when the fruit is defrosted.

POLYUNSATURATES More correctly called poly-unsaturated fatty acids, conveniently abbreviated to PUFA, are **fatty acids** in which the carbon chain is deficient in four or more atoms of hydrogen. Main sources of PUFA in the diet are vegetable oils, in particular corn (maize) oil, soya bean oil and sunflower (safflower) oil, and certain soft margarines made exclusively with vegetable oils.

PUFA have sprung into prominence during the last 10 or 15 years since it became generally known that PUFA help to reduce the cholesterol level of the blood. Clinical studies and animal experiments suggest that when the cholesterol level of the blood is reduced, the incidence of **atherosclerosis** and **coronary thrombosis** is also reduced. Although there is no conclusive proof about this, most doctors recommend patients who have suffered from one heart attack to replace animal fats with those oils and foods containing a high proportion of PUFA.

PORK Meat derived from the pig. Pork contains more fat, but correspondingly less protein, than either beef or lamb; it contains more thiamin than most other meats.

There is a fairly large variation in the fat content found in different carcases and also in different parts of one carcase. The values given below are for meat of average fatness.

A 4 oz portion of roast pork (leg) contains:

            360 kilocalories (1,505 kilojoules)
            28 g protein
         26.4 g fat (38 per cent saturated)
            no carbohydrate
            6 mg calcium
       2.88 mg iron
            no vitamin A
            no vitamin D
         0.9 mg thiamin
         0.2 mg riboflavin
            no vitamin C

One 6 oz pork chop, grilled, contains:

            768 kilocalories (3,210 kilojoules)
         26.4 g protein
         71.4 g fat
            no carbohydrate
           12 mg calcium
       3.36 mg iron
            no vitamin A
            no vitamin D
         0.9 mg thiamin
         0.2 mg riboflavin
            no vitamin C

168

In the UK the average person eats about 3 oz pork per week. This consumption provides the following proportion of essential nutrients in the average diet: thiamin 5 per cent; protein 2 per cent; energy 2 per cent.

At one time, pork was not eaten during the summer months. This was because standards of hygiene were not as strict as they are today, and there used to be some health hazard attached to eating pork, especially if it was lightly cooked. Nowadays it is quite safe to eat pork all the year round.

When buying pork, choose meat with the lean a pale pink, moist and slightly marbled with fat. The flesh should be covered with firm white fat. The outer skin should be smooth and pliable.

For storage, see **meat**. Pork keeps fresh in the fridge for up to 3 days. Because of its high fat content, pork has a shorter freezer life than other meats. Its flavour deteriorates markedly after 6 months in the freezer.

In modern times, pigs have been specially bred to have a long, lean body shape. They are given a balanced diet to ensure optimum growth without the deposition of too much body fat. There is no question of 'fattening up' pigs in the way the old-fashioned porker was prepared for the table. Pork today also comes from very young animals, usually less than a year old.

Unlike other meats, all cuts of pork are suitable for either roasting or grilling. The fat in pork tenderises the meat during cooking, making short, dry cooking methods possible.

PORRIDGE A breakfast dish prepared from oatmeal, rolled oats or 'quick' porridge oats and water. The purchase of oatmeal and oatmeal products in the UK is declining, mostly as a result of a consumer preference for prepared breakfast cereals. Porridge supplies small quantities of protein, carbohydrate, iron and thiamin to the diet.

A 4 oz portion of oatmeal porridge, without milk, salt or sugar, contains:

    52 kilocalories (217 kilojoules)
  1.6 g protein
  1.2 g fat
  9.2 g carbohydrate
  7.2 mg calcium

0.56 mg iron
    no vitamin A
    no vitamin D
0.06 mg thiamin
0.01 mg riboflavin
    no vitamin C

The nutritional value of porridge is considerably increased if it is made with a proportion of milk instead of just water.

POTATOES The underground tubers of the potato plant. Potatoes are one of our important staple foods. In the average UK diet potatoes provide a substantial proportion of vitamin C and useful amounts of thiamin because of the large quantity regularly eaten. We eat more potatoes than all other vegetables put together.

NUTRITIVE CONTENT OF PORTIONS OF NEW AND OLD BOILED POTATOES AND CHIPPED (FRIED) POTATOES			
	New potatoes boiled	Old potatoes boiled	Old potatoes chipped (fried)
	4 oz	4 oz	4 oz
Kilocalories (Kilojoules))	84 (351)	92 (384)	368 (1,120)
Protein g	2.0	1.6	4.4
Fat g	0	0	10.4
Carbohydrate g	20.8	22.4	42.4
Calcium mg	5.6	4	16.0
Iron mg	0.52	0.40	1.60
Vitamin A microg retinol equivalents	0	0	0
Vitamin D microg	0	0	0
Thiamin mg	0.08	0.08	0.12
Riboflavin mg	0.04	0.04	0.04
Vitamin C mg*	16	4.16*	8.24*

* Vitamin C falls during storage. The concentration is highest in late summer when the crop is lifted and steadily falls during the winter and spring.

Raw potatoes	*Vitamin C mg per oz*
New (early or main crop)	9
Stored for 1–3 months	6
Stored for 4–5 months	4
Stored for 6–7 months	3
Stored for 8 months or more	2

The method of cooking potatoes also affects the final quantity of vitamin C remaining in the potato. Estimated cooking losses of vitamin C are as follows:

	percentage of vitamin C in raw potato lost in cooking
Boiled potatoes	30–50
Roast and baked potatoes	20–40
Fried potatoes	25–35

In the UK the average person eats over 46 g of potatoes each week. This consumption provides the following proportion of essential nutrients in the average diet: energy 4.5 per cent; protein 4 per cent; iron 8 per cent; thiamin 10 per cent; vitamin C 25 per cent.

As many as 40 different varieties of potatoes are grown commercially. King Edward, Redskins, Majestic and Maris Piper are good all-purpose, main crop varieties. Early potatoes include Arran Pilot, Home Guard, Grand Ulster Prince and Maris Peer.

Early new potatoes are available in July and main crop new potatoes in August and September; old potatoes are available from October to June.

Early potatoes are immature. They are lifted before the skins have set. On cooking, new potatoes are firm and waxy, not suitable for mashing or baking. They are delicious gently scrubbed and boiled in their skins.

Choose fresh potatoes free from excessive soil, without blemish, cuts and greening; they should be well-shaped, with shallow eyes. Store potatoes in a cool dark place which is also dry and airy. Sacks of potatoes should be stood on slats to allow air to circulate. Avoid bruising of potatoes, and close the sack after use. Washed potatoes do not keep as well as dry brushed ones. New potatoes do not keep for more than one week. They may be kept in the salad drawer of the fridge, though some people think they become too sweet if stored there. New potatoes also freeze fairly well.

Canned new potatoes and quick frozen chips, 'fluted fries', croquette and duchesse potatoes are all available. Some new potatoes are stored commercially each year to sell before the new season's crop is ready. These aged 'new' potatoes are characterised by the difficulty with which they are skinned.

171

For large-scale catering, ready-peeled potatoes can be supplied. An instant chip powder which is mixed with cold water and extruded as chips ready for frying is also available. Instant potato powder and flakes are also very popular with caterers.

Instant potato consists of packets of powered potato which can be simply reconstituted to mashed potatoes by the addition of hot water. Instant potatoes are very simple and convenient to prepare. Their popularity is increasing, even though they are considerably more expensive than mashed potatoes prepared in the usual way.

During dehydration, there is almost complete loss of vitamin C. As potatoes are still a very important source of this vitamin, nutritionists are concerned about the replacement of fresh by powdered potatoes on a large scale, especially as instant potatoes seem to be most popular among groups in which the vitamin C intake may be rather low: groups such as old people, large families with several young children, young people living alone with inadequate cooking facilities. Responsible manu-facturers are replacing vitamin C to ensure the nutritive value of their product. When buying instant potato, therefore, choose a brand which states on the packet that it has added vitamin C.

POULTRY Birds reared for eating, including chickens, turkey, goose, duck and guinea fowl.

Like carcase meat, poultry is an excellent source of animal pro-tein, minerals and B group vitamins. (See individual birds for their nutrient breakdown.)

The consumption of poultry in the UK has increased dramatic-ally over the last few years. The increase is due to the intro-duction of large-scale poultry rearing methods and a consequent fall in the price of chicken. The increase in price of other meats has also encouraged more people to choose chicken. In 1955, the average annual consumption of poultry (including game and rabbits) for each person in the UK was 6.4 lb. By 1972, the consumption figure had risen to 26 lb. Poultry consumption is still rising: in 1973, more poultry was purchased than any other single kind of meat. Poultry consumption overtook consumption of beef and veal for the first time.

People in London and the south-east are the main poultry eaters. Here 20 per cent to 30 per cent more poultry is eaten than the national average; in Scotland, they eat 30 per cent less than average.

See also **chicken, duck, goose, turkey.**

PRAWNS Like all shellfish they contain large amounts of calcium and useful amounts of iron and animal protein.

1 oz prawns, weighed without shells, contains:

        30 kilocalories (125 kilojoules)
         6 g protein
       0.5 g fat
         no carbohydrate
      41.2 mg calcium
      0.31 mg iron
         no vitamin A
         no vitamin D
      0.01 mg thiamin
      0.03 mg riboflavin
         no vitamin C

Prawns are available all the year round, but at their best from February to October. They are also available in cans, potted in jars, and frozen.

Fresh prawns are usually sold by volume or weight, ready-boiled either in the shell or picked. One pint of peeled prawns contains about 12 oz prawns; a pint of unpeeled prawns, about 10 oz.

Dublin Bay prawns are also known as scampi or Norway lobster. The most widely available scampi are the quick frozen variety.

PROTEINS are one of the very important major nutrients. Proteins from food are used to make the various body tissues, including skin, flesh (muscle), blood and internal organs. During growth, proteins are needed to make new tissues; during adult life, they are needed to maintain the tissues, repairing them to keep them healthy and efficient.

Plants can make their own proteins from carbon dioxide in the air, water, nitrates and other minerals from the soil. Animals cannot synthesise proteins in this way. Herbivorous animals utilise plant proteins to make their own tissue proteins. If a herbivore is eaten by a carnivore, the proteins from the flesh of the first animal will be utilised to build the tissues of the second. In this way, complex food chains can be established. Proteins made originally by plants are passed along the food chain, although they are modified by each intermediary in the chain.

Proteins are complex molecules of carbon, hydrogen and oxygen, sometimes with sulphur or phosphorus attached. The protein molecules are made up of strings of simpler units known as amino-acids. During digestion, proteins are split up into their constituent amino-acids. Then the chains are reformed according to any one of the tissue protein formulae. Only 20 different amino-acids are found in food, yet they can be combined in a great variety of different ways. These different permutations give us many different sorts of proteins. This explains why protein in flour is different from protein in beef, or why muscle protein is different from the proteins that make up the blood. Most proteins from animals (including fish, poultry and animal products such as milk and eggs) are similar to the proteins from which our own bodies are constructed. Animal proteins generally provide us with the amino-acids we need, and in the right proportions, too. Proteins from plants are not very much like our own body proteins. All of the amino-acids essential for our own good health are not to be found in any one of the plant proteins, so we could not live exclusively on one plant protein and be perfectly healthy. But we could live with only cheese, milk or eggs as the sole source of protein in the diet.

Generally speaking, animal proteins have a higher nutritional value than plant proteins (gelatine is the notable exception to this rule). The best nutritional value for money is derived from a mixed diet which supplies protein from a variety of sources, some plant and some animal. The amino-acids which may be missing from a plant protein may then be supplemented by an animal protein which is especially rich in that acid. Bread protein, for example, is short of the amino-acid lysine, which is abundant in milk and cheese. Bread and cheese, therefore, make an excellent combination. The nutritional value of the bread protein is considerably enhanced by the protein in cheese. The actual amount of protein in different foods varies quite considerably.

Recommended daily intakes of proteins are based on average figures which are thought to keep the vast majority of people healthy. Fortunately, there is little shortage of protein in the average diet in the UK.

THE AMOUNT OF PROTEIN EXPRESSED AS A PERCENTAGE BY WEIGHT IN SOME EVERYDAY FOODS	
whole, fresh milk 3.3%	eggs 11.9%
evaporated milk 8.5%	baked beans 6.0%
yoghurt 3.6%	broad beans 7.2%
Cheddar cheese 25.4%	green peas 5.8%
bacon 11.0%	roasted peanuts 28.1%
beef 14.8%	white bread 8.3%
pork 12.0%	wholemeal bread 9.6%
roast chicken 29.6%	cornflakes 7.5%
roast lamb 25.0%	white flour 10.0%
sausage 10.0%	rice—boiled 2.1%
white fish 16.0%	spaghetti—cooked 3.4%

Children, who are growing, need proportionally more protein than adults. In simple terms, children and adolescents need one seventh of their daily calorie intake to be derived from proteins. Adults are recommended to take only one tenth of their total energy intake in the form of proteins. Adults have been found to lead quite healthy lives with considerably less than this proportion of proteins. Pregnant and lactating women need considerably more protein to cover the child's requirement in addition to their own requirement. Most sedentary or moderately active men should have between 65 and 75 grams of protein each day. 55 grams of protein a day is adequate for most women; during the second half of pregnancy, women should have 60 grams of protein a day, and almost 70 grams daily if they are breast-feeding.

PRUNES Dried plums, which have a fairly high energy value and contain useful amounts of iron and vitamin A. They are usually eaten after being soaked and cooked, but may be used in the dried form in baked goods.

1 oz raw, dried prunes contains:

        38 kilocalories (159 kilojoules)
    0.6 g protein
      no fat
    9.5 g carbohydrate
    8.9 mg calcium
    0.68 mg iron

        45 microg retinol equivalents vitamin A
           no vitamin D
      0.03 mg thiamin
      0.06 mg riboflavin
           no vitamin C

4 oz stewed prunes (without sugar) contain:

        76 kilocalories (318 kilojoules)
       1.2 g protein
           no fat
      19.2 g carbohydrate
      15.6 mg calcium
      1.36 mg iron
      94 microg retinol equivalents vitamin A
           no vitamin D
      0.04 mg thiamin
      0.10 mg riboflavin
           no vitamin C

Most prunes available in this country are imported from California and are available all the year round.

Stewed prunes, like figs, are often recommended as a cure for constipation.

PULSES See under individual vegetables, e.g. **beans, lentils, peas.**

PUMPKIN A vegetable similar to, but much larger and more round than, a marrow. Not a popular vegetable in the UK, but it enjoys considerable popularity in the USA and Canada.

When served as a vegetable it is recommended that ½ lb raw pumpkin per person should be allowed.

½ lb raw pumpkin contains:

        32 kilocalories (134 kilojoules)
       1.6 g protein
           no fat
         8 g carbohydrate
      88.8 mg calcium
      0.88 mg iron

```
500 microg  retinol equivalents vitamin A
       no  vitamin D
  0.08 mg  thiamin
  0.08 mg  riboflavin
    30 mg  vitamin C
```

Pumpkin is available in the autumn. It is often used for decoration at harvest festivals and harvest suppers. In the United States, canned pumpkin is more popular than the fresh. It is mainly used for making a variety of pumpkin pies.

QUAIL One of the wild birds classified as **game**, with a nutritive value similar to that of chicken. Not as popular as pheasant and partridge, and in fact only eaten in very small quantities by a few people in the UK. They are very small birds and one is usually served to each person. Wild quail may no longer be shot and sold, but Japanese quail, reared on special farms, may be marketed in the ordinary way.

QUICK FREEZING is one of the most successful modern methods of food preservation. Its originator was Captain Clarence Birdseye. Noticing how remarkably well food kept in the extremely low temperatures of Labrador, Captain Birdseye set out to develop machinery which would simulate these cold temperatures in warmer climates. Quick freezing was first introduced into the UK in the 1930s, but quick-frozen foods were not generally available to the housewife until the early 1950s.

In any freezing process the low temperatures involved prevent the action of bacteria, yeasts, moulds and enzymes. The food remains fresh and good so long as it is maintained at temperatures low enough to prevent the action of these food spoilage organisms.

Most foods are made up of millions of small cells. The cells are filled with a watery mixture of nutrients and flavouring materials. During quick freezing the temperature of the food is very rapidly reduced to between −68°F (−23°C) and −95°F (−34°C). Tiny ice crystals form within the food, but the

177

crystals are small enough not to rupture the walls of the food cells. When the food is brought back to room temperature, it retains most of its original texture and nutritional value. The more rapid the freezing process, the smaller the ice crystals within the frozen food, and the better the food product after defrosting.

The nutritional value of most frozen foods is the same as fresh foods prepared for the table in a similar way. In order to produce a good quality product, the manufacturer has to process foods which are at the peak of perfection. This also means that the food will have the best possible food value. Ordinary foods offered for sale in the shops may not be nearly so fresh. The small but inevitable losses which occur during the freezing process are usually counterbalanced by processing food with maximum food value.

The chief nutrients affected by all methods of food preparation – domestic as well as commercial – are the water-soluble B group vitamins and vitamin C. These nutrients are dissolved out of food when it is washed, and the same vitamins are also easily destroyed by heat. Losses during quick freezing itself are very small, and they are also small during the subsequent storage of the frozen foods. Washing and blanching prior to freezing always cause some vitamin losses. Reputable manufacturers are aware of this, and can adjust their techniques to keep the losses to a minimum. For example, steam blanching causes smaller losses of vitamin C than blanching the food in hot water. Even so, nutritional losses vary considerably between batches being processed, between different brands of food, and between different food products.

Because of the convenience of buying ready-prepared, quick-frozen foods, they have been enthusiastically accepted by the consumer. Between 1960 and 1970 UK consumption of quick-frozen foods more than trebled. In the UK in 1973, a total of £345 million was spent on quick-frozen foods bought at retail outlets and in meals purchased outside the home. Freezer owners alone spent £60 million stocking their freezers with commercially quick-frozen foods in 1973.

In the home, small scale domestic freezing is becoming an increasingly popular method of food preservation. Most foods can be frozen successfully at home provided the domestic freezer can reach and maintain sufficiently low temperatures.

RABBIT Has a very similar nutrient content and appearance to chicken.

6 oz stewed rabbit, weighed with bone, contain:

    156 kilocalories (652 kilojoules)
   23.4 g protein
    6.6 g fat
        no carbohydrate
    9.6 mg calcium
   1.68 mg iron
        no vitamin A
        no vitamin D
   0.03 mg thiamin
        no vitamin C

Rabbits are available all the year round, and are sold whole or skinned and jointed. Tame rabbits, specially reared for the table, are more tender, though less flavoursome, than wild rabbits.

Store as other **meats**.

RADISH A crisp salad vegetable, rich in vitamin C and prized for its attractive colour, crisp texture and peppery flavour.

1 oz radishes contains:

    4 kilocalories (18 kilojoules)
   12 mg calcium
  0.5 mg iron
    7 mg vitamin C

Available mainly during the summer months. Buy only crisp firm radishes and store loosely wrapped in polythene or in the salad drawer of the fridge.

Radishes can be very indigestible, and are best avoided by those prone to digestive disorders.

RAISINS Like other dried fruits, raisins have a high energy value and are a good source of iron and calcium.

1 oz raisins contains:

- 70 kilocalories (293 kilojoules)
- 0.3 g protein
- no fat
- 18.3 g carbohydrate
- 17.2 mg calcium
- 0.44 mg iron
- no vitamin A
- no vitamin D
- 0.03 mg thiamin
- no vitamin C

Raisins are sold in various forms, sizes and shades. The most popular are the smaller, seedless Californian raisins and the larger, stoned (or seeded) Australian raisins. All raisins should look fresh and moist. Also available for a limited period in the year are the light brown Valencia raisins, which have the best flavour but do contain the stones (or seeds). They are usually available just before Christmas.

Unless they are sold as washed fruit (as most pre-packed raisins are today), raisins and other dried fruit should be well washed in cold water, and then dried off in a cool oven.

Like other dried fruits, raisins may be served as a dessert as well as being used in cooking.

RASPBERRIES One of the small and delicious soft fruits of summer. Raspberries are rich in vitamin C.

4 oz fresh raspberries contain:

- 28 kilocalories (118 kilojoules)
- 1.2 g protein
- no fat
- 6.4 g carbohydrate
- 46.4 mg calcium
- 1.36 mg iron
- 16 microg retinol equivalents vitamin A
- no vitamin D
- 0.04 mg thiamin
- 0.04 mg riboflavin
- 28 mg vitamin C*

* There is a 20 per cent loss of vitamin C on freezing.

Home-grown raspberries are available from June to August and frozen and canned raspberries are available all the year. When buying raspberries, choose dry and uncrushed fruit. Some raspberries tend to be maggoty, and they should be picked over carefully. Usually there is no need to wash raspberries before they are eaten.

Keep raspberries in a covered dish in the fridge, but eat as soon as possible after gathering.

Raspberries are an excellent fruit for freezing. Over-ripe fruits may be puréed and used as dessert sauce, or used to make fruit ices.

REQUIREMENTS Nutritional requirements are the daily intakes of calories (energy) and nutrients which are needed to keep an individual healthy. Quantities for different groups of people are given in the chart on page 13.

RHUBARB Usually classed as a fruit, though rhubarb is really the stem of a plant. Contains only small quantities of nutrients because of its high water content (94.2 per cent). Contains large quantities of oxalic acid which forms insoluble salts with calcium, and interferes with the absorption of calcium.

4 oz stewed rhubarb (without sugar) contain:

4	kilocalories (17 kilojoules)
0.4 g	protein
no	fat
0.8 g	carbohydrate
89.6 mg	calcium
0.32 mg	iron
12 microg	retinol equivalents vitamin A
no	vitamin D
no	thiamin
0.08 mg	riboflavin
8 mg	vitamin C

'Forced' rhubarb is available from December to March and is pink, tender and has a very fresh flavour. Home-grown outdoor rhubarb is available from March to August. This rhubarb is green, tinged with red, is firmer and has a more acid flavour. Rhubarb keeps well for up to a week in the fridge. Keep it in the salad drawer, or secured in a plastic bag. It also freezes very well.

Rhubarb is always served cooked. A proportion of raisins stewed with rhubarb offsets its acidity.

Rhubarb leaves should never be eaten, as they contain far more oxalic acid than the stalks.

RICE An important cereal which is the staple food of half the world's population, including China, India, Indonesia, Japan, Pakistan and Thailand. In poorer countries, rice is the main dietary source of protein as well as of calories, although it contains less protein than other cereals.

Rice is not eaten in large quantities in the typical western diet: the average person eats only $\frac{1}{2}$ oz each week. This amount does not contribute significantly to the overall nutritional value of the diet.

NUTRIENT CONTENT OF RAW AND BOILED POLISHED WHITE RICE		
	Rice, polished, raw, 2 oz	Rice, polished, boiled, 6 oz
Kilocalories (Kilojoules)	204 (853)	140 (585)
Protein g	3.6	2.4
Fat g	0.6	0.4
Carbohydrate g	49.2	33.6
Calcium mg	2.2	1.6
Iron mg	0.26	0.16
Vitamin A microg	0	0
Vitamin D microg	0	0
Thiamin	0.04	0.01
Riboflavin	0.02	0.01
Vitamin C	0	0

A number of different kinds of rice are available:

Round-grain rice A short, plump grain. When cooked, the grains tend to clump together. The ideal rice for milk puddings. Imported mainly from China and Australia.

Long-grain rice Grains which are 4 to 5 times longer than they are wide. Grains become light and fluffy, but stay separate when properly cooked. Most of our long-grain rice is imported from the USA. Long-grain rice is sometimes called Patna rice – Patna is an area of north-east India – but no rice has been imported into England from Patna for many years now.

Medium-grain rice is not generally available. It originally came to this country from the Carolinas, USA and is sometimes known as Carolina rice. Used at one time for puddings.

Brown rice An unmilled, or lightly milled rice, mostly sold by health food stores. Requires longer cooking, has a nutty flavour and higher food value than white rice.

Easy-cook rice Long-grain rice which has been pre-treated with steam and pressure. This aids retention of the rice's nutritive value and improves its cooking qualities. It is less likely to go sticky than plain white rice. Easy-cook rice looks a translucent yellowish-brown when raw, but changes to white during cooking.

Pre-cooked, instant or express rice Different names given to rice which has been cooked and dehydrated. The products easily reconstitute with hot water. (Follow precisely the instructions given on the pack.)

Flaked rice Another convenience form of rice which quickly cooks to make a milk pudding.

Ground rice Also known as Japanese rice. It is also used to make milk puddings, although it is not very popular today. Ground rice may also be used to replace a proportion of flour in traditional cake mixtures.

Like other dry ingredients, rice should be stored in a dry place. If there is any dampness in the store, keep rice in an airtight container such as a storage jar.

Cooked rice may be kept in the fridge for up to one week, or for three days in a cool larder. Cover the dish of rice to avoid its drying out. To reheat the rice, place in a saucepan with a little extra water. Reheat very gently. Boiled rice also freezes very well, on its own or in a mixed dish such as risotto. To use frozen rice, allow it to defrost and then reheat as above.

For one average serving of rice, allow 2 oz of raw grains. Rice trebles its weight and volume on cooking. There is no need to wash rice before cooking, or to rinse it afterwards. Washing simply removes water-soluble nutrients. Don't stir rice during cooking: this can mash the grains and make them stick together. A little oil or butter in the cooking water helps to keep grains separate.

Although we tend to think of rice being sown by bare-footed farmers in flooded paddy fields, most of the rice we eat in the UK is sown by aeroplane or tractor and is harvested by modern combine harvesters. Milling, cleaning and packing is all done by machinery. At no time is the rice touched by hand.

Rice is very easily and completely digested. This makes it a suitable food for young, old and sick people. Rice is also suitable for low residue and bland diets. Rice does not contain **gluten**, and can be used to replace other cereals in gluten-free diets. The low fat content of rice makes it particularly suitable in a low-fat diet.

RICKETS A nutritional deficiency disease caused by an inadequate intake of vitamin D. Rickets is a disease of infancy and childhood, though the deformities it causes remain throughout life. When rickets occurs, bone tissue is not correctly formed: the bones are not made strong enough to support the weight of the body. The limbs become badly deformed as the child starts to walk. The abdomen also swells and the head of a rachitic child is characteristically square.

Many paintings from the fifteenth and sixteenth centuries depict children with these characteristic features. This shows not only that rickets was known long ago, but also that the malformations which occurred as a result of rickets were considered commonplace. In a book published in 1653 the famous herbalist, Nicholas Culpeper, advocated the taking of cottonthistle as a cure for rickets.

In seventeenth-century England, rickets was perhaps more common among children from wealthy than from poor families. This may have been due to the fact that milk was considered to be a food fit only for the poor, the very young or the very old. The wealthy child would not be given milk after he was weaned. There were other misguided views on child feeding at that time, and the wealthy child was often fed a somewhat inadequate diet. The child in a poor family may have fared better, as he simply had his share of whatever food was going. If he lived in the country, he was likely to have plenty of milk.

He was also untroubled by parental views on whether a food was suitable for him: his parents' problem was to get enough of any food to eat.

Over the years, rickets continued to be an important health problem. It was widespread during the Industrial Revolution, when young children were sent to work long hours in factories and mines. A variety of treatments was tried; some of these, like the harness of iron and leather widely recommended by a Dutch specialist, attempted to straighten the limbs. At this time rickets was not associated with faulty diet. Just a hundred or so years ago, cod liver oil, a very rich source of vitamin D, was shown to cure rickets. Sir Edward Mellanby was the pioneer research worker in his field. Sunlight or ultra-violet ray therapy was found to be equally effective; these rays enable the body to make its own vitamin D.

As a result of these discoveries, rickets was eradicated from Great Britain. But in recent years, isolated cases of rickets have been reported, especially among immigrant children who have come from countries in which our staple foods are not widely used. Their own diets usually have to be adapted to British food, and vitamin D intakes are often marginal. Their customs may dictate that children are more heavily clothed, and this screens the health-giving rays of the sun. A heavily-pigmented skin also prevents the absorption of ultra-violet light from the sunshine, which in any case is less strong than some immigrants are accustomed to to. Early in 1974, the British Nutrition Foundation and the Community Relations Commission urged the Health Education Council to take more positive action in helping immigrants (especially Asians) to modify their diets and to stem the rising incidence of rickets among their children.

ROE The unlaid eggs of fish. Herring and cod roes are most common, the hard roes from the female fish and the soft roe, or milt, from the male fish. Roes are very high in nutritive value, and especially rich in proteins and B group vitamins. They are also a rich source of **cholesterol.**

The quantities of thiamin and vitamin C will be reduced in cooked roe, but it will still contain substantial amounts.

Caviar is the roe of the sturgeon. It is a great delicacy and extremely expensive to buy. 'Mock' caviars are made by colouring other fish roes.

COMPARISON OF NUTRIENT CONTENT OF COD'S ROE AND HERRING'S ROE	2 oz portions, fried	
	Cod's roe (hard)	Herring's roe (soft)
Kilocalories (Kilojoules)	118 (483)	148 (619)
Protein g	11.6	13.2
Fat g	6.8	9.0
Carbohydrate g	1.8	2.6
Calcium mg	9.6	9.0
Iron mg	0.90	0.86
Vitamin A microg retinol equivalents	0	0
Vitamin D microg	1	0
Thiamin mg	0.85	0.11
Riboflavin mg	0.57	0.28
Vitamin C mg	8	0

SACCHARIN See **Synthetic sweeteners**

SAGO is extracted from the pith of the sago palm. The starch is washed out from the pith of the felled tree. It is dried and converted into pearl sago by granulating. Commercial sago contains approximately 86 per cent starch. It has a high energy value, but very small nutrient content.

Sago is used to make milk puddings, and such dishes do, of course, contain the additional nutritive value of milk.

1 oz raw sago contains:

    101 kilocalories (424 kilojoules)
    0.1 g protein
    0.1 g fat
    26.7 g carbohydrate
    2.8 mg calcium
    0.34 mg iron
    no vitamins

4 oz sago milk pudding* contain:

    144 kilocalories (602 kilojoules)
    3.6 g protein
    4.4 g fat
   23.6 g carbohydrate
131.2 mg calcium
  0.20 mg iron

*Prepared from 1 pint milk, 2 oz sago and 1½ oz sugar.

Sago milk pudding also contains small quantities of vitamins A and D, thiamin and riboflavin.

SALMON One of the most expensive and highly prized of the fat fish. Salmon has about one third of the fat content of herring. Salmon are usually caught in rivers and coastal waters. They spend most of their lives in the sea but return to freshwater rivers and streams to spawn. Most salmon are caught on their way upstream to spawn.

4 oz fresh steamed salmon contain:

    228 kilocalories (953 kilojoules)
   21.6 g protein
   14.8 g fat
    no carbohydrate
   32.8 mg calcium
   0.92 mg iron
100 microg retinol equivalents vitamin A†
 14 microg vitamin D
  0.03 mg thiamin
  0.10 mg riboflavin
    no vitamin C

2 oz canned salmon contain:

   162 kilocalories (678 kilojoules)
  11.6 g protein
  12.8 g fat
    no carbohydrate
   38 mg calcium
  0.8 mg iron

†This is the value for Pacific fish. The value for the Atlantic variety may be considerably lower.

52 microg	retinol equivalents vitamin A
7.08 microg	vitamin D
0.02 mg	thiamin
0.06 mg	riboflavin
no	vitamin C

Fresh Scotch salmon is in season from February to August, but at its best in June and July. Imported, often frozen, salmon is available all year round. To enjoy it at its best, salmon should be eaten as fresh as possible. Buy from a reputable fishmonger and keep for no more than one day in the fridge.

Because of its excellent flavour, salmon is best poached, and served hot with an Hollandaise sauce, or cold with mayonnaise. It may be cooked whole or as cutlets. If a fish kettle is not available for poaching the fish whole, it may be cooked wrapped in a well-buttered 'parcel' of foil in the oven. Salmon cutlets may also be poached. Small salmon pieces, or trimmings, may be served in a savoury mousse or as a salmon spread.

Fresh salmon may also be smoked. This uncooked fish is considered a great delicacy, and is consequently very expensive. It is usually served in wafer-thin slices. Smoked salmon is available all year round. It should be kept in the fridge, though smoking does improve the keeping qualities of the fish.

In the UK, canned salmon is more readily available and more popular than fresh salmon. Canned salmon is usually imported from America, Canada and Japan. It is moist and flavoursome. The fish bones soften during canning; as they may be eaten with the fish, they provide a useful amount of calcium.

SALT, or sodium chloride, is one of our dietary essentials. All body fluids contain salt. Salt helps to maintain the flow of water, other minerals and metabolites around the body tissues. Sodium chloride is widely distributed in foods. The highest concentration is found in salt-cured foods, such as bacon, ham and kippers. Most packaged, bottled, canned and frozen foods have a fairly high salt content; so, too, have many cereal products and baked goods.

Although we need about 4 g of salt every day, most people take between 5 g and 20 g in their food. Not only is salt a natural constituent of food; it is often added during cooking and at the table to enhance the flavour of food. The excessive salt for which the body has no use is excreted in the urine.

Salt is also excreted as sweat. Very heavy sweating, which may be the result of hard work or strenuous physical activity, especially at high temperatures, or by normal living in a very hot climate, may deplete the body's reserves of salt. In a three-hour marathon race, an athlete may lose in sweat the 4 g of salt most sedentary people need for one full day. The lost salt must be replaced quickly or severe body cramps will occur. Salt tablets or salt drinks are usually taken to replace salt lost in heavy sweating.

Unless extra salt is needed for this purpose, a very high salt intake is not recommended. The salt may cause an increase in blood pressure, or may lead to kidney damage. The kidneys of very young babies are not sufficiently developed to deal with a high salt surplus. Early weaning foods, should not be salted, even though they may appear to be insipid to adult palates.

A salt-restricted diet or a low sodium diet may be prescribed for patients suffering from high blood pressure, heart failure, or in certain disorders of the liver and kidneys.

Salt was one of the earliest chemical preservatives used. Meat, fish and vegetables were frequently salted and served during the winter months when no fresh produce was available. The Salters Company, which supplied salt for this early food preservation, was formed as long ago as 1394.

Before vitamin C shortage was recognised as the cause of scurvy, the blame for this disease was attributed to the salt meat which formed a large proportion of the sailors' food.

SARDINES Small fatty (oily) fish which are a good source of animal protein, vitamins A and D and calcium when canned and the bones eaten.

Fresh sardines may be bought but they are not readily available. Like canned salmon, canned sardines are more popular with the majority of people in the UK than fresh sardines. Sardines are available canned in oil or in tomato sauce.

2 oz sardines, canned in oil, contain:

        162 kilocalories (678 kilojoules)
    11.6 g protein
    12.8 g fat
        no carbohydrate

             232 mg calcium
             2.2 mg iron
         18 microg retinol equivalents vitamin A
      4.24 microg vitamin D
              no thiamin
          0.12 mg riboflavin
              no vitamin C

The energy value and fat content of sardines canned in tomato are lower than that of sardines canned in oil.

SATURATED FATTY ACIDS See **Fatty acids**.

SAUSAGES Popular and traditional meat products made from minced meat, meal (or bread) and seasonings. The composition of sausages is controlled by the Food Standards Committee. Pork sausages must contain 65 per cent meat; beef sausages 50 per cent meat. Frankfurters and salami must contain 85 per cent meat, although canned versions are required to have a minimum of 70 per cent meat. These standards are minimum requirements, and many manufacturers use more meat than this. All-meat sausages are not popular in the UK. Cereal, herbs

COMPARISON OF APPROXIMATE NUTRITIVE VALUES OF PORK SAUSAGES, RAW AND FRIED, AND BEEF SAUSAGES, FRIED

	Portion—one large sausage (2 oz)		
	Pork sausage raw	Pork sausage fried	Beef sausage fried
Kilocalories	194	186	162
(Kilojoules)	(811)	(777)	(677)
Protein g	5.0	6.6	7.8
Fat g	16.4	14.2	10.2
Carbohydrate g	5.6	7.2	9.0
Calcium mg	8.6	11.2	12.0
Iron mg	1.44	1.88	2.32
Vitamin A	0	0	0
Vitamin D	0	0	0
Thiamin	0.10	0.05	0
Riboflavin	0.04	0.03	0
Vitamin C	0	0	0

and spices give the desired consistency and flavour. Sausages may also contain preservatives. The average UK consumption is between 3 oz and 3½ oz per person per week.

Grilled sausages lose more fat than fried sausages, which reduces their energy value further.

Pork and beef sausages are sold in different sizes, usually in ½ lb and 1 lb packs. The most popular are the thick or large sausages, usually 8 to the lb, or thin or chipolata sausages, usually 16 to the lb. Skinless sausages (16 to the lb) and mini or cocktail sausages (32 to the lb) are also available.

Continental-style sausages, usually ready-cooked, are often available only in a delicatessen. Popular varieties in this country include *bierwurst* and a great many other 'wursts', garlic and ham sausages, salami, frankfurters and liversausage. To be described as liversausage, the product must contain at least 30 per cent liver.

Black pudding and polony are two traditional sausage types of meat product. The colour of the black pudding is derived from the blood with which it is made. Unfortunately, the iron is not readily available from blood, so black pudding does not have a notable food value. It usually includes a large proportion of meal and fat.

SCALLOPS Shell fish, also known as *coquilles St. Jacques* because the shell was the emblem of pilgrims who visited the shrine of St. James of Compostella. Scallops are eaten in small quantities by a few people in the UK and do not, therefore, contribute significantly to the average diet. Like the other shell fish, scallops are a good source of calcium.

2 oz scallops, poached, contain:

      60 kilocalories (251 kilojoules)
  12.8 g protein
   0.8 g fat
    no carbohydrate
65.4 mg calcium
 1.70 mg iron

Scallops are in season from October to March. They are sold in their shells, but the fishmonger will open them on request. Like other shell fish, scallops should be eaten as fresh as possible. For short-term storage, keep on the top shelf of the fridge. Frozen and canned scallops are also available.

The orange part of the fish is the roe, which should be cooked with the rest of the fish. Most suitable cooking methods are poaching, grilling or baking. Often scallop dishes in restaurants are extended with coarse white fish.

See also **shellfish**.

SCAMPI See **Prawns**.

SCONES Baked flour products which enjoy a great deal of popularity in Scotland and rural parts of England. There is a large variety of recipes for scones – plain, savoury, sweet, etc.

One ($1\frac{1}{2}$ oz) plain scone* contains:

157	kilocalories (656 kilojoules)
3.3 g	protein
5.5 g	fat
24.4 g	carbohydrate
271 mg	calcium
0.28 mg	iron

*Prepared from 8 oz flour, $1\frac{1}{2}$ oz margarine, $\frac{1}{4}$ oz sugar, 5 oz milk, 4 level teaspoons baking powder to give 10 scones. Scones may be made with wholemeal flour or a mixture of wholemeal and white flours.

Small quantities of vitamins A and D and thiamin are also found in scones.

Scones differ from pastry in having a smaller proportion of fat to flour. Scones are raised with a chemical raising agent, and much of their soft texture is derived from the milk used to mix the dough. Sour milk is recommended for scones by some experts. An excellent scone may be made with a mixture of milk and natural yoghurt.

As their proportion of fat to flour is low, scones stale easily. They are best eaten either hot from the oven, or within a few hours of baking. They may be kept for a few days in an airtight tin or other container.

Newly-baked scones may also be stored in the freezer, and lightly reheated before serving.

SCURVY See **Lemons.**

SEMOLINA A granular cereal product prepared by grinding the inner part (the starchy endosperm) of hard wheat. Semolina has a fairly high protein content, about 11 per cent by weight. In the UK, semolina is used mainly as an ingredient for milk puddings. It is more widely used as a cooking ingredient in other parts of Europe. Semolina dishes are not suitable for a **gluten**-free diet.

1 oz raw semolina contains:

    100 kilocalories (418 kilojoules)
      3 g protein
    0.5 g fat
     22 g carbohydrate
  5.2 mg calcium
 0.30 mg iron
       no vitamin A
       no vitamin D
 0.03 mg thiamin
       no vitamin C

4 oz semolina milk pudding* contain:

    148 kilocalories (196 kilojoules)
    4.8 g protein
    4.4 g fat
   22.8 g carbohydrate
  136 mg calcium
 0.24 mg iron

*Prepared from 1 pint milk, 2 oz semolina, 1½ oz sugar.

Semolina milk pudding also contains small quantities of vitamins A and D and thiamin.

Semolina should be stored in an airtight container in a dry storage area. Provided it is dry, it keeps almost indefinitely.

Semolina is often used to add extra texture to cakes, puddings and biscuits. A proportion of semolina improves the texture of less rich cakes such as cherry cake.

Semolina may be used to thicken sauces and soups. It may simply be sprinkled into the hot, but not boiling, liquid, which is then reheated to boiling and stirred as the mixture thickens. Semolina is an essential ingredient in certain Continental specialities such as Italian gnocchi and the Greek halva.

SHELLFISH Very popular sea foods which are more akin to the insect world than the usual sea fish. Some shellfish, like cockles and winkles, are cheap, while others, notably oysters, are much more expensive delicacies. All shellfish are good sources of **protein**, **iron** and **calcium**. Cockles and winkles are especially rich in iron. Shellfish also contain iodine and magnesium, both of which are essential **trace elements**. (For nutritional breakdown, see individual entries for **crab**, **lobster**, **mussels**, **oysters**, **prawns**, **scallops**.)

Shellfish also contain a high proportion of **cholesterol**. Oysters contain more than 200 mg of cholesterol per 100 g, while 100 g crab, prawns, scampi or shrimps contain about 125 mg of cholesterol. See also the value given for lobster.

Shellfish are of two main types. The crustacea have legs, antennae and a jointed shell. Crabs, lobsters, crawfish, prawns and shrimps come into this group. Molluscs have a hard, unjointed shell. Bivalves such as oysters, scallops, mussels and cockles have a hinged, two-part shell. The shell of univalves, like winkles and whelks, is a solid structure.

To safeguard health, shellfish should be bought, cooked and eaten while very fresh. The flesh rapidly decomposes after death, so shellfish are often sold still alive. Because shellfish, notably cockles, breed abundantly near sewage outfalls, and because many of them act as scavengers, shellfish may be contaminated with harmful bacteria. Adequate cooking usually destroys these potentially harmful organisms. Shellfish which are eaten raw, mainly oysters, must be kept in tanks of flowing clean water to remove dirt from them. After being caught, the oysters are kept in such tanks for several days before they are sold. Cockles and similar shellfish which may be caught along our beaches should be kept in several changes of clean water for a few days before they are cooked for eating.

Some people are allergic to shellfish. Their violent reaction after eating shellfish is quite different to the food poisoning which may be traced to contaminated shellfish.

SHERRY Fortified wine. It is usually, but not always, fortified with brandy. The alcohol can be utilised as a source of energy.

THE ALCOHOL CONTENT AND ENERGY VALUE OF SWEET AND DRY SHERRY			
	Alcohol g/100 ml	Carbohydrate g/100 ml	Energy value Kilocal 100 ml (Kjoules/100 ml)
Sweet sherry	15.6	6.9	135 (564)
Dry sherry	15.7	1.4	114 (477)

There are four main types of sherry available: Fino – lightest in colour and dryest to the taste; Manzanilla – pale and slightly sharp; Amontillado – more full-bodied, rather nutty and of medium dryness; Oloroso – rich, dark-golden and sweet to the taste.

Sherries are imported mainly from Spain and South Africa. Cheaper and usually sweeter sherries are produced in Cyprus. Sherry may be blended in England from a variety of different imported sherries.

Drier sherries (best served chilled) are usually served as an aperitif. Sweet sherries may be served as dessert wines. Sherry is also popular in cooking, in both sweet and savoury dishes.

SORBITOL A carbohydrate made commercially from glucose. It is found naturally only in certain fruit berries. Sorbitol is used in place of traditional sugars in some diabetic foods. Unlike most carbohydrates, sorbitol is absorbed very slowly into the bloodstream after digestion, and unlike other sugars, it does not suddenly raise the blood sugar level which, in the case of diabetics, is then unloaded into the urine (see **diabetes**).

Sorbitol has the same energy value as glucose and other sugars, but it is not so sweet. As it is expensive to manufacture, diabetic foods containing it are also expensive. Since most diabetics have to keep to a below-average weight, sorbitol-containing foods should not be a regular part of their diet. They may be regarded as foods to have now and again.

In the past, slimmers have mistaken sorbitol-containing foods as being suitable ones for a calorie-controlled diet. This is certainly not so. It must be stressed that sorbitol has the same energy value as ordinary sugar. Sorbitol is a sugar alternative, not a sugar substitute.

SOUPS vary so much in their individual recipes, that it is very difficult to assess their nutritive value as a group. Some soups, such as minestrone, full of vegetables, pieces of pasta and thickly sprinkled with grated cheese, are almost a complete meal in themselves. Lentil or pea soup, and others made with puréed pulses, soups containing plenty of chopped meat or poultry with vegetables, fish soups like chowders or bouillabaisse also come into this category.

On the other hand, there are the thin, clear soups like broths or consommés. They contain the water-soluble extracts of meat and possibly vegetables. The nutritive value of a soup like this is negligible apart from its value as an appetite stimulant.

Because all good soups are made by long, slow cooking of the ingredients, they rarely contain more than a trace of those nutrients destroyed by heat. These include vitamin C and certain of the B group vitamins.

Stocks made with bones usually contain gelatine extracted by the long, moist cooking. This does not have the great food value many people suppose, because gelatine, although it is classed as an animal protein, is missing certain important constituents (see **proteins**).

SOYA BEANS One of the pulses, which have been cultivated and eaten by the Chinese for several thousands of years. Many traditional Chinese dishes include the soya bean as an essential ingredient. Although the soya bean is very nutritious – 40 per cent of the weight of the dry bean is protein and up to 20 per cent fat – it has not been very popular in the West until recent years. It is now being widely cultivated in the United States and processed to make artificial meat, which was devised originally for the vegetarian market, but is being readily accepted as a cheap alternative to real meat. The best soya bean products look and taste like meat and have a very realistic, meaty texture. Sometimes the artificial product is intended to replace a proportion, usually one third, of the meat in a recipe. These products are known as meat extenders.

In making synthetic meats, the protein is extracted from the soya bean. Its own characteristic flavour is removed and is replaced by meat flavours. Any flavour can be added to make products that taste like beef, chicken, bacon, ham or even crab and lobster. The protein is extruded to very fine filaments similar to strands of meat. They may be spun like synthetic fabrics to give a very realistic meat texture, or the fibres may be grouped into bundles to simulate the texture of lean meat. Additional nutrients may be added to bring the nutritive value of the synthetic products up to that of the natural meat they are to replace.

Old-fashioned soya flour has a very limited popularity owing to its strong flavour. It was promoted as a very nourishing food during the Second World War, but never became very popular. On the other hand, the synthetic meat appears to have a very good chance of being universally accepted.

SPAGHETTI See **Pasta.**

SPICE Dried and often ground parts of aromatic plants. Spices are produced from dried roots, berries, fruits, seeds, seed cases, flower buds, blossom or bark. For many centuries, spices have been sought after and highly prized. In 1000 BC, Arabs were already conducting a flourishing trade in spices, and jealously guarded the sources of their valuable wares. The merchants of Venice, much later, owed their great wealth to trading in spices with the Arabs. The purpose of many of the fifteenth-century voyages of discovery was to find the sources of the Oriental spices. Christopher Columbus himself set sail to discover a Western route to the Spice Islands, while Vasco da Gama's search for pepper lead him to round the Cape of Good Hope.

The reason for their great value was that spices were widely used as drugs and medicines, and also as preservatives, flavourings and perfumes. The spices were used as drugs before they were used in cooking. Cloves, for example, were commonly used to guard against infection, and anise was thought to prevent insomnia. Unlike any other food commodity, spices have a fascinating background of mystery and political intrigue that is belied by the innocent appearance of those small canisters sitting on the spice rack.

The imaginative use of spices in today's cooking gives pleasing individuality and extra flavour to food. Although we no longer need spices to guard against any possible food transmitted infections, their delicate flavour improves many sweet and savoury dishes. The most popular spices are pepper, cinnamon and ginger. Nutmeg, allspice, caraway, cloves, mace, saffron, paprika and cayenne pepper are also most useful for culinary use.

SPINACH A green, leafy vegetable which is gradually losing popularity. It is rich in vitamins A and C. It also contains iron and calcium, although these may not be available to the body, as they are combined with an organic substance also present in the leaves which is not digestible.

4 oz boiled spinach contain:

> 28 kilocalories (117 kilojoules)
> 5.6 g protein
> no fat
> 1.6 g carbohydrate
> 676 mg calcium
> 4.56 mg iron
> 1,100 microg retinol equivalents vitamin A
> no vitamin D
> 0.08 mg thiamin
> 0.17 mg riboflavin
> 28 mg vitamin C

Spinach is available from April to November. Buy fresh spinach which looks crisp and moist. As with other green vegetables, the vitamin C content decreases, and may be non-existent, in wilted vegetables. For short-term storage, keep in the salad drawer of the fridge. Frozen spinach is also available and spinach may be quick frozen at home.

For the best flavour and food value, lightly cook spinach in the minimum of water. Water remaining on the leaves after washing may be sufficient. Cook in a pan with a tightly fitting lid. Shake pan from time to time to avoid burning.

Overcooking or reheating leads to the development of an unpleasantly strong flavour. Overcooking also spoils the texture of spinach. These are two likely reasons for the decreasing popularity of the vegetable.

SPROUTS See **Brussels sprouts**

STRAWBERRIES A very popular soft summer fruit, rich in vitamin C.

4 oz fresh strawberries contain:

28	kilocalories (124 kilojoules)
0.8 g	protein
no	fat
7.2 g	carbohydrate
24 mg	calcium
0.8 mg	iron
4 microg	retinol equivalents vitamin A
no	vitamin D
0.04 mg	thiamin
0.04 mg	riboflavin
68 mg	vitamin C*

*There is a 20 per cent loss of vitamin C on freezing.

Home-grown strawberries are in season from late May or early June to July or early August, and there is a small late crop in September and October. Strawberries are also available frozen and canned.

Buy dry, uncrushed fruit. Avoid damaged fruit, which will soon go mouldy. Store strawberries in the fridge in a well-covered container to avoid flavour contamination of other foods.

Whole strawberries do not freeze very well as they lose their texture on defrosting. A strawberry purée, or water or cream ice, is much more successful.

Strawberry jam is also very popular. It usually needs extra pectin, especially if very ripe fruit is used (see **jam**).

STOCK An infusion of flavouring ingredients derived by long, slow cooking of selected meats, fish, vegetables, herbs and bones with water. A good quality stock is essential for all gravies, some sauces and for most soups. However delicious a stock may be, it has very little food value, being an extract of flavourings only. Even though stock made with bones contains gelatine, this is one of the poorest forms of protein and has little value. It does, however, have the indirect nutritional value of helping to stimulate the appetite, and acts as an aid to good digestion.

See also **soups.**

SUCROSE See **Carbohydrate.**

SUET A natural animal fat situated around the internal organs of sheep and cattle, sold fresh from the butcher or as packaged, ready-to-use (shredded) suet. Fresh suet should be firm, dry, sweet-smelling and free from discoloration. Suet has a high energy value and is mainly composed of saturated fatty acids.

$\frac{1}{2}$ oz suet contains:

131	kilocalories (547 kilojoules)
0.1 g	protein
14 g	fat
no	carbohydrate
0.8 mg	calcium
0.05 mg	iron
no	vitamins

Suet is better stored in a cool larder than in the fridge. If no larder is available, keep suet at the bottom of the fridge. Suet keeps well for several months provided it is kept cool.

Traditionally it was used as an ingredient of suet puddings, both sweet and savoury, for suet pastry and dumplings, and in stuffings and mincemeat, but suet is no longer very popular as a cooking fat. There is general preference for the lighter texture derived from margarine and butter. Also, we no longer need the high energy value supplied by the delicious but substantial dishes made with suet.

SUGAR White or brown, very sweet crystals derived from either sugar cane or sugar beet. About one third of all the sugar we eat is produced from home-grown sugar beet. The rest comes from imported sugar cane.

White sugar is unique in our diet, as it is one of the rare purified nutrients, being 99.9 per cent pure carbohydrate. Brown sugars contain traces of a variety of different minerals, not considered significant as such small quantities are present. There is therefore no practical difference in the food values of white and brown sugars. The main difference is in their flavours. The darker the sugar, the stronger its flavour.

White and brown sugars alike contain 112 kilocalories (468 kilojoules) per ounce.

The national average consumption of sugar each week is about 15 oz per person. Preserves, which contain a high proportion of sugar, are consumed at the average rate of 2 oz to $2\frac{1}{2}$ oz per person each week. These quantities supply roughly 10 per cent of the total energy intake of most individuals.

In recent years, the consumption of sugar has been slightly reduced. It reached its peak in 1963, when the average annual consumption of sugar, not including that eaten in biscuits, cakes and so on, was 65.5 lb for every person in the UK. The reduction in recent years may be attributed to the widespread desire to reduce body weight. A great proportion of **over-weight** can be attributed to over-consumption of sugar and sweet foods generally.

Most people are also aware of the role of sugar in causing dental caries. High sugar consumption has also more recently been cited as one of the possible causes of coronary artery disease. (There are several factors which are thought to be jointly implicated with heart disease. As yet, the evidence is far from conclusive – see also **coronary thrombosis**.)

White sugar is sold as granulated, castor, superfine, cube, coffee crystals and preserving sugar. *Demerara* sugar is a partially refined, coarse-crystalled sugar. *Soft brown* sugars are usually sold by their colour, either as light or dark brown. They are fully refined but they have a little syrup left sticking to them: *Barbados* is also a brown sugar sold either fine ground or as crystalline sugar. (Golden **syrup** is one of the by-products of sugar refining. It is the liquid which remains after crystals of white sugar have been removed.)

Sugar keeps indefinitely, but it must be kept dry, even the so-called moist sugars. Storage jars or similar airtight containers should be used if storage areas are even slightly damp.

Sugar, as it is commonly known, is the disaccharide, sucrose. Sucrose is made chemically from one molecule of **glucose** attached to another of fructose. Fructose and glucose are other, simpler, sugars. Fructose is the fruit sugar. Glucose rarely occurs in food, except in honey, where it is found with fructose. Lactose is the sugar in milk; maltose the sugar found in malt.

SULTANAS Dried fruit made from white, seedless grapes. Sultanas have a high energy value and useful amounts of calcium and iron.

1 oz sultanas contains:

> 71 kilocalories (296 kilojoules)
> 0.5 g protein
> no fat
> 18.3 g carbohydrate
> 15 mg calcium
> 0.5 mg iron
> no vitamin A
> no vitamin D
> 0.03 mg thiamin
> 0.09 mg riboflavin
> no vitamin C

Most sultanas on sale in the UK are Australian. They are also imported from Turkey, Greece and South Africa. They should be plump, golden and moist-looking.

For storage, see **currants**.

SUNFLOWER SEED OIL Sometimes known as safflower oil, it is derived from the mature heads of sunflowers, and is thus a vegetable oil. It is high in **polyunsaturated fatty acids**. Like all vegetable oils and fats, it has a very high energy value.

1 oz sunflower seed oil contains 255 kilocalories (1,070 kilojoules).

In the United States, sunflowers are widely grown as a field crop for their oil. This is used for cooking, in salad dressings and also in the production of margarine.

SWEDES Root vegetables containing some vitamin C but otherwise of little nutritive value. They contain 91 per cent to

92 per cent water, which gives them an extremely low energy value.

4 oz boiled swedes contain:

    20 kilocalories (84 kilojoules)
  1.2 g protein
    no fat
  4.4 g carbohydrate
47.2 mg calcium
0.32 mg iron
    no vitamin A
    no vitamin D
0.04 mg thiamin
0.03 mg riboflavin
  19 mg vitamin C

Swedes are available from September to April, and should be stored, with other root vegetables, in a cool, dark place.

Swedes are good flavouring vegetables for soups, stocks and stews.

SWEETBREADS The pancreas and the thymus glands of oxen, calves or lambs. They are useful and easily digestible sources of animal protein and a rich source, too, of **cholesterol.**

4 oz stewed sweetbreads contain:

  204 kilocalories (853 kilojoules)
 25.6 g protein
 10.4 g fat
    no carbohydrate
16.4 mg calcium
 1.84 mg iron
    no figures available for vitamin content

Ox sweetbreads are the cheapest but require slow careful cooking; lamb's sweetbreads are usually the most expensive and are tender and delicately flavoured.

SWEETCORN Name given to the kernels of the maize (corn) cob. See under **corn.**

SYRUP (GOLDEN) A by-product in the manufacture of sugar, taken off at a late stage in the refining process when no more white crystals can be produced. Contains 20 per cent water, and therefore has a lower energy value than sugar.

1 oz golden syrup contains:

   84 kilocalories (352 kilojoules)
  0.1 g protein
     no fat
 22.4 g carbohydrate
   7 mg calcium
 0.4 mg iron
     no vitamins

Syrup is sold in cans or jars and, like sugar, keeps indefinitely.

Syrup contains a proportion of so-called 'invert' sugar. One of its important properties is that it retains moisture easily. To make a cake which is moist and keeps well, replace a proportion of sugar with golden syrup.

SYNTHETIC SWEETENERS A number of chemical substances have a strong sweet flavour, but because they supply no energy or nutritive value of any sort, they cannot be classed as foods. At least 50 different synthetic sweeteners are known to chemists. They range from those only slightly sweeter than ordinary sugar (sucrose) to those some 4,000 times sweeter.

Saccharin is now the only synthetic sweetener which is permitted for use in foods in this country and in the USA. It is some 550 times sweeter than sucrose. There is some controversy about its safety, and it may suffer the same fate as the cyclamates in being banned. Cyclamates are rather more palatable sweeteners, and are 30 or so times as sweet as sucrose. Cyclamates were banned in late 1969 as they were suspected of producing cancer in certain experimental animals who had been fed enormous daily doses of cyclamates. More recent animal experiments have disputed this charge of carcinogenicity and steps are being taken to re-introduce cyclamates. Another synthetic sweetener known as 'aspartame' is also likely to be approved for general consumption.

 TEA The selected, dried leaves of a shrub which are infused with boiling water to make a refreshing drink. Tea has been drunk in China for thousands of years. It was first introduced into England in the middle of the seventeenth century. At first, tea, like sugar and spices, was a great luxury. When it first came on to the London market, it was sold for between £2 and £3 a pound. Understandably, it was kept under lock and key in the home, and antique locking tea caddies are now collectors' items. One hundred years later, tea still remained a fairly expensive commodity, but it was drunk by most people. Some feared that tea would finally take the place of beer in Britain. Even poor households were prepared to pay high prices for tea. A survey conducted in the late eighteenth century showed that many households with an annual food budget of only £40 were spending £2 of this on tea.

The consumption of sugar rose with the tea-drinking habit, although adding milk and sugar to tea was the custom of the poorer people only at this time. By 1871, the annual consumption of tea was nearly 4 lb per person. Many very poor people existed almost entirely on potatoes, bread and strong tea. The stimulation derived from the **caffeine** in tea was deceptively cheering. Caffeine is a mild stimulant of the nervous system, and often helps to prevent tiredness. A very high intake can cause sleeplessness and, in some people, 'palpitations'. Very strong tea can cause an over-secretion of gastric juices. It is, therefore, not recommended to anyone who is susceptible to indigestion, especially if drunk some time after food has been taken.

One advantage of high tea consumption is that tea, being one of the few foods containing fluorine, can be a useful source of this mineral. This is particularly beneficial in areas where the drinking water contains no fluorine.

Although the tea infusion itself contains very few calories, sugar is often added in large amounts, so that sweetened tea can supply a fairly large proportion of the daily energy intake of some people. Provided they keep to their daily allowance of milk – or have lemon juice with their tea – and if they use saccharin in place of sugar, tea can be drunk in unlimited quantities by slimmers. It is helpful in offsetting hunger pangs. Tea may be forbidden by the doctor for patients suffering from gastric or duodenal ulcers, and also in cases of heart failure.

TOMATOES This popular fruit is classed in the kitchen as either a vegetable or a salad. Tomatoes are useful sources of vitamins A and C. They have a high water content, and consequently a low energy value.

One 2 oz tomato contains:

8	kilocalories (34 kilojoules)
0.6 g	protein
no	fat
1.6 g	carbohydrate
8 mg	calcium
0.2 mg	iron
66 microg	retinol equivalents vitamin A
no	vitamin D
0.04 mg	thiamin
0.02 mg	riboflavin
12 mg	vitamin C

In the UK the average weekly consumption of tomatoes is about 4 oz per person.

Home-grown tomatoes are available from late April to early November. Imported tomatoes are available all the year round. Tomatoes are sold graded by size and shape; there are four grades. Like other fruits, after harvest tomatoes continue to ripen. If they are being bought in advance, it is best to buy tomatoes that are slightly under-ripe.

Tomatoes are best kept in the salad drawer of the fridge. They will keep for at least one week, or even longer, depending on their ripeness before storage. Tomatoes may be kept in the freezer, but on defrosting they are suitable only for cooking. A concentrated tomato purée may prove to be a better product for freezing. Home-grown outdoor tomatoes often do not ripen easily on the plant. They may be ripened indoors in a warm place, such as an airing cupboard or a sunny window ledge. Green tomatoes are also popular for making chutney.

Their attractive scarlet colour makes tomatoes an invaluable food for garnishing savoury dishes. They also add colour to salads.

TONGUE One of the more popular 'offal' meats. A useful source of iron and animal protein.

Bullock or ox tongue, calf's tongue or sheep's tongue are all available. Ox tongue has a good, velvety texture, and weighs between 4 lbs and 6 lbs. Calf's tongue has a very delicate flavour and texture, and weighs 1 lb to 2 lb. Sheep's tongue is much smaller, 4 oz to 12 oz.

COMPARISON OF NUTRITIVE VALUE OF PICKLED OX TONGUE AND STEWED SHEEP'S TONGUE

	4 oz portions	
	Ox tongue pickled	Sheep's tongue, stewed
Kilocalories (Kilojoules)	352 (1471)	336 (1,404)
Protein g	21.6	20.4
Fat g	27.2	27.2
Carbohydrate g	2.8	0
Calcium mg	35.2	12.8
Iron mg	3.40	3.88
Vitamin A microg retinol equivalents	0	0
Vitamin D microg	0	0
Thiamin mg	0.04	0.04
Riboflavin mg	0.35	0.35
Vitamin C mg	0	0

Ox tongues are usually pickled in brine, while sheep's tongues are often salted. Both require soaking followed by long, slow simmering. For serving as a cold dish, tongue is usually pressed or moulded in aspic. As a hot dish, Madeira sauce is a traditional accompaniment to braised tongue.

TRACE ELEMENTS Some inorganic substances are known to be essential for health, but they are needed in such minute quantities that these substances are known as trace elements. The same substances may prove to be poisonous if taken in larger than these minute amounts.

Trace elements include **fluorine, iodine,** cobalt, manganese, copper and zinc. It is quite conceivable that there are trace elements whose importance has not yet been established.

Generally speaking, the human body does not run short of the trace elements provided a varied and mixed diet is eaten. Domestic animals who are restricted to a certain area of pasture may become deficient if the ground in that area is deficient in one or more of the trace elements. Trace element deficiency diseases have been more widely studied in farm animals than in man for this good reason.

TREACLE (also known as molasses) is a by-product of the manufacture of sugar. Treacle which is very dark in colour (often referred to as black treacle) is produced at an early stage in the processing of raw sugar and retains a useful quantity of iron, calcium and other minerals.

1 oz treacle contains:

       73 kilocalories (305 kilojoules)
      0.3 g protein
       no fat
     19.1 g carbohydrate
    140.5 mg calcium
     2.60 mg iron
       no vitamins

Treacle, which is sold in cans and jars, has a much stronger flavour than golden **syrup**. Like syrup, it is a mixture of sugar and invert sugars. Because of this, treacle is used to add both flavour and moistness in baking. Ginger and chocolate cakes, for example, are greatly improved when about a quarter of the ordinary sugar in the recipe is replaced by treacle.

Treacle is also used in marinades for meat, notably for baked ham or bacon. The famous Bredenham ham derives its distinctive colour from the treacle used in curing it.

TRIPE One of the group named 'offal' meats. A useful and easily digestible source of animal protein, containing much higher levels of calcium than other meats. The calcium is derived from the lime with which it is treated during preparation.

4 oz stewed tripe contain:

      116 kilocalories (485 kilojoules)
     20.4 g protein
      3.6 g fat
       no carbohydrate
      144 mg calcium
     1.80 mg iron
    40 microg retinol equivalents vitamin A
       no vitamin D
     0.09 mg thiamin
     0.05 mg riboflavin
       no vitamin C

Tripe comes from the lining of the ox stomach. There are several different varieties including honeycomb, blanket, monk's head and book. It is nearly always sold partly cooked and blanched.

There are marked regional preferences for tripe. It is not a popular meat in the south of England. In the north, especially the north-west, tripe butchers, who sold only tripe and other 'delicacies' such as pigs' trotters and cows' heels, flourished until quite recently.

TROUT A small, round-bodied, freshwater fish, usually weighing between 6 oz and 10 oz. Caught in lakes and rivers, the brown river trout is one of our most expensive fish. Rainbow trout is a domesticated cousin of the river trout. It is raised in specially conditioned tanks, often on fish farms. Rainbow trout are quick frozen, providing an all-year-round supply.

Sea trout, also known as salmon trout, appear to be a cross between the trout and the salmon. They are larger than the river trout, but have a darker flesh. The flesh of the salmon or sea trout is paler than that of the true salmon, and is less oily.

Trout is also smoked. Being only a small fish, it is smoked whole and not as fillets, like salmon, or split, like the kipper.

All varieties of trout are a good source of protein. They have more fat in their flesh than the white fish and therefore have a higher energy value.

4 oz steamed trout contain:

    152 kilocalories (635 kilojoules)
   25.2 g protein
    5.2 g fat
     no carbohydrate
   40.8 mg calcium
   1.12 mg iron
     no vitamin A
     no vitamin D
   0.08 mg thiamin
   0.06 mg riboflavin
     no vitamin C

River trout are in season from February to early September, but at their best from April to August. Sea trout are in season from March to August. Rainbow trout are available, either fresh or quick frozen, all the year round.

Trout is best eaten as fresh as possible. It should be lightly cooked by poaching, baking or grilling to preserve its fine flavour.

TURKEY A large bird reared specially for the table. Turkeys were found in Mexico when that country was first discovered by European explorers in 1518. Modern turkeys are related to North American species brought back to this country in the sixteenth century. Nowadays, turkeys are reared and eaten all over the world. Although they are available all year round, turkey is still most popular at Christmas.

Turkey is a good source of animal protein, and contains less fat than carcase meats such as beef, lamb and pork.

4 oz roast turkey contain:

       224 kilocalories (936 kilojoules)
    34.4 g protein
      8.8 g fat
        no carbohydrate
    43.6 mg calcium
    4.32 mg iron
        no vitamin A
        no vitamin D
    0.04 mg thiamin
    0.09 mg riboflavin in breast meat
    0.20 mg riboflavin in leg meat
        no vitamin C

Turkeys are sold at various weights, but the smaller birds of 8 lb to 10 lb are becoming more popular than the larger birds of 16 lb to 20 lb or over.

Turkeys of up to 40 lb in weight are not uncommon. The larger birds are useful when catering for large numbers, but they tend to become rather dry in cooking. Smaller birds are more tender and juicy, but may have less flavour than the larger, older birds. The larger the bird, the greater the proportion of flesh to bone.

TURNIPS Root vegetables containing some vitamin C, but otherwise, because of their high water content, of little nutritive value.

4 oz boiled turnip contain:

    12 kilocalories (50 kilojoules)
  0.8 g protein
    no fat
  2.8 g carbohydrate
62.4 mg calcium
0.40 mg iron
    no vitamin A
    no vitamin D
0.03 mg thiamin
0.04 mg riboflavin
  19 mg vitamin C

Available from September to April, or until the new season's vegetables are available.

Turnips are useful as flavouring vegetables for soups, stews and so on. (See also **swede**.)

ULCER Area of damage to the lining of the digestive tract, commonly in the stomach (gastric ulcer) or the higher parts of the duodenum (duodenal ulcer). These ulcers are thought to be caused by the action of the enzyme pepsin, which is present in the acid gastric juice. Ulcers occur only in those parts of the digestive tract which come into contact with the gastric juice. Peptic ulcers – as they are collectively known – are one of the most common illnesses in the Western world; gastric ulcers are more common in lower socio-economic groups; duodenal ulcers are evenly distributed throughout the social classes. Duodenal ulcers are, however, far more common in men than in women.

Stress, strain and overwork are thought to be contributory factors. Regular hurried eating and occasional missed meals may also encourage the development of ulcers. Many ulcers disappear as suddenly as they came, without any special treatment. Patients with ulcers are usually advised to take life quietly. Physical and psychological rest are important. Four weeks' bed rest is commonly prescribed, or sedatives may be given to patients for whom bed rest is impracticable. For ulcer sufferers, a bland diet is usually helpful. Highly spiced, seasoned and flavoured foods should be avoided. So, too, should any fried food and food with a high fat content. Fibrous foods, including many raw vegetables and salads, may irritate the lining of the stomach. Coarse, wholegrain cereal foods should also be avoided.

In treating ulcers, attempts are made to reduce acid secretion, and to neutralise what acid is produced to avoid its contact with the ulcer. Small, regular meals are important. The patient should not go longer than 2 to 2½ hours without food. Milk should be taken in place of tea or coffee between meals. Only weak tea or coffee should be taken, as the caffeine they contain stimulates acid secretion. A glass of milk is also recommended for last thing at night. Alcoholic drinks, especially spirits, should be severely restricted, and cigarette smoking should be stopped.

The foods which can be eaten freely on a bland diet include milk and milk puddings; white fish, provided it is not fried; chicken, rabbit, lean ham, beef and lamb; eggs, but not fried; mild cheeses including cottage cheese; sponge cakes, plain biscuits, refined cereal products including white bread; potatoes, either mashed or boiled, but not fried or roasted; puréed vegetables and strained or puréed fruits; jellies, yoghurt and egg custards.

UNDERWEIGHT There is no hard and fast rule about how much anyone should weigh. But an individual who weighs considerably less than average for his height can be described as underweight (see table of average weights, page 11).

Provided the diet is always well balanced, with the necessary amounts of foods to satisfy the body's need for proteins, minerals and vitamins, the underweight person should be perfectly healthy. In fact, the most healthy and long-living people of all are slightly underweight. The only disease more common among underweight people is tuberculosis. Thankfully, this disease is being gradually eradicated as a result of mass screening. (Compare the list of ailments to which overweight people are more prone!) There is cause for concern if underweight is the result of poor eating habits, an inadequate diet or complete (or professed) loss of appetite. In such cases, medical help will be required. (See **anorexia nervosa**.)

Many very thin people have good appetites and eat more food than most people. They remain thin because they burn up their food very quickly. They usually lead very active and busy lives. It is very difficult for people like this to gain weight.

Other underweight people have very poor appetites. They may have no real liking for food at all. They may be best suited by taking 4 or 5 small meals a day, rather than 2 or 3 larger ones. Very heavy smoking may cause the appetite to diminish. This should be stopped, or at least cut down severely. Certainly, cigarettes should not be smoked for at least an hour before a meal. No smoking before lunch is a good rule, even if the habit cannot be broken completely.

In order to gain weight, people with small appetites should try to eat unhurried meals in a relaxed atmosphere. A short break before and after the meal is helpful. Avoid fried foods, foods high in fat, and all rich and stodgy foods. They may contain more calories, but a few mouthfuls may satisfy the small appetite. Have small helpings of light, easily digested, appetising foods. Drink plenty of milk but avoid too much tea and coffee, especially if these are made too strong. A little alcohol is helpful; too much depresses the appetite. Choose wines in preference to spirits. Avoid too many sweet foods – they fill but don't nourish very well.

VEAL Meat derived from calves less than three months old. Because it comes from a young animal, veal has a lot of bone in proportion to the meat, and very little fat. It is a useful source of animal protein.

3 oz veal cutlet, fried, contains:

> 183 kilocalories (765 kilojoules)
> 25.8 g protein
> 6.9 g fat
> 3.9 g carbohydrate
> 8.4 mg calcium
> 2.22 mg iron
> no vitamin A
> no vitamin D
> 0.05 mg thiamin
> 0.23 mg riboflavin
> no vitamin C

Veal, since it comes from a young animal, should be comparatively light in colour – fine-textured, pale pink, soft and moist. The cuts of veal available are: leg, fillet, loin, chops, cutlets, shoulder, knuckle, best end of neck, breast, and pie or stewing veal. A great deal of our stewing or pie veal comes from male calves, only a few days old, born to dairy cows.

The bones of veal make excellent jellied **stock** or gravy. This is a useful way to make use of the large quantity of bone in veal. Veal is not as popular in the UK as on the Continent. It is not always available here, as butchers do not have a great demand for this meat, which many people find insipid.

VEGETARIANS People who restrict their intake of animal foods. Ovo-lacto vegetarians do not eat meat of any kind, including carcase meat, offal, fish, poultry, or any flesh for which the animal has to be killed. They will, however, eat animal products including eggs, milk, butter and cheese. This type of vegetarianism is not very different from the normal mixed diet, from the nutritional standpoint. The animal products have a food value equal to that of animal flesh.

Vegans are more strict vegetarians who will not eat any food which has been derived from an animal. They live solely on vegetables, fruit and cereals. Many processed and pre-packed foods are forbidden to them as they contain 'hidden' amounts of products such as animal fats and milk. The vegan diet causes concern to nutritionists, especially if there have been several generations of vegans in a family. The important vitamin B_{12} is found only in animal foods. Vegan families have been found to suffer from the pernicious **anaemia** which results from a complete lack of vitamin B_{12}. Nowadays, vegans are allowed to take specially prepared extracts containing this important vitamin.

It is possible to derive adequate nourishment from plant foods alone, provided a well mixed variety of foods is eaten. The inadequacies in the protein value of one food may then be made good from the protein in another. Vegans need to eat a great deal of their chosen diet to obtain enough of the nutrients which are more highly concentrated in animal foods such as meat, milk and eggs.

VINEGAR A dilute solution of acetic acid in water with other flavourings and colouring materials. Vinegar is produced by the oxidation of alcohol in beverages such as wine or cider. In this country, malt vinegar is produced as a side product in the brewing industry.

Malt vinegar is dark brown in colour and contains a little sugary material which is derived from the malt. White or spirit vinegar is produced by distilling malt vinegar under reduced pressure. Wine vinegar is made from cheap wines. Both wine and cider vinegars retain a considerable amount of flavourings from the original wine or cider.

In the past, vinegar was widely used as a chemical preservative. Its acidity discourages the growth of micro-organisms, and for this reason it is still used today in pickles and chutneys.

Many claims are made for cider vinegar as a slimming aid or as a general tonic. There is no evidence that vinegar can help positively in slimming, although, like lemon juice, vinegar helps to suppress the appetite temporarily. Being such a dilute solution, vinegar can be considered to be virtually calorie and nutrient free.

VITAMINS Substances occuring naturally in foods which are essential for our health and well-being. Only minute quantities of more than 20 different vitamins are needed, but these amounts are essential to regulate growth of body tissues and to enable the body to use other nutrients for energy. Although vitamin deficiency diseases have been well known for centuries – accounts of vitamin A deficiency, for example, appear on Egyptian tablets and manuscripts – no one really knew what a vitamin was until the beginning of the twentieth century. Scurvy, which is caused by deficiency of vitamin C, caused the deaths and disabilities of enormous numbers of sailors for several centuries. It was the scourge of the sea until it was found to be cured by eating fresh fruit (see also **fruit**), yet vitamin C was not isolated until 1932.

Vitamin A is needed for correct functioning of the eye and also to build healthy skin and mucous membranes lining the internal tracts of the body. Vitamin A is found in butter, margarine, fat fish, cod and halibut liver oils, cheese and eggs. The orange pigment, carotene, is also converted into vitamin A in the body. Carrots, apricots, and peaches are rich in carotene; so are green vegetables, as carotene is always found associated with the green plant pigment, chlorophyll. (See also **xerophthalmia**.)

B group vitamins are needed mainly for the release of energy from food, but some are essential for blood building. All B vitamins are required for healthy growth. Thirteen different B vitamins are known (among them are thiamin, riboflavin, nicotinic acid, biotin, pantothenic acid), but many of them are found together in foods like meat, particularly offal meats like liver, kidneys and heart, eggs, some dairy produce and cereal foods, especially products made from enriched refined cereals, and wholegrain cereals.

Vitamin C is needed to make the cell binding material of all the body tissues. It also helps wounds to heal, and aids the control of the oxidative processes in individual cells. Vitamin C is found mainly in citrus and summer fruits, in green vegetables, salads and potatoes. Although most fresh fruits and vegetables contain at least traces of vitamin C, this may be lost during storage, preparation or cooking of the foods. In the average diet in the UK, potatoes are the greatest single source of vitamin C. Milk is perhaps the only animal food in the diet which contains any appreciable quantity of this vitamin. (See also entries for individual fruits, vegetables and potatoes.)

There have been many other suggestions about the role of vitamin C in the body. Most popular of all is Linus Pauling's theory that vitamin C taken in massive daily doses can cure or prevent the common cold. A great deal of work has been done on this property of vitamin C, but so far experimental evidence has been conflicting. Vitamin C is also thought to keep down the blood **cholesterol** level. A high level of cholesterol was found in animals kept on a diet very low in vitamin C, but the relevance of this to man is again uncertain.

Vitamin D is partly derived from food, and partly manufactured in the body itself when sunlight falls upon the skin. Adults may derive all the vitamin D they need from sunlight. Children, who have higher vitamin D requirements, also need regular dietary sources. So, too, do housebound adults, many old people, and anyone with a deeply pigmented skin which does not permit the penetration of the sun's rays. Vitamin D is needed, in association with calcium and phosphorus, for building bone tissue. It is important during the growing years, when new tissue is being built. Vitamin D in adult life helps to maintain the strength of the bones.

Vitamin E appears to work as an anti-oxidant in the body, but its full role is not clearly understood. We do not even know for sure that man needs vitamin E. In rats, vitamin E is needed for male animals to be fertile and for female rats to produce litters of live young. Vitamin E is used in human patients to prevent repeated abortions, but it is not certain whether it is needed for normal reproduction. Vitamin E has also been investigated in connection with muscular dystrophy, and in certain diseases of the heart and circulatory system. Again, the results are far from conclusive. Vitamin E is widely distributed in our food. The richest source is vegetable oil, especially wheatgerm oil. Vitamin E is also found in green and other vegetables, in nuts and some fruits. Most animal foods are poor sources, the best being summer butter and eggs. Severe losses of vitamin E occur during freezing, although most fresh foods keep their vitamin E very well.

Vitamin K is required to ensure that blood will clot at wounds. A deficiency of this vitamin is extremely rare, as it so widely distributed in everyday foods. The dark green vegetables are richest of all. When a deficiency is found, it is usually among premature babies or other babies who have not received the usual store from the mother before birth. Obstructive jaundice may also cause vitamin K deficiency.

VITAMIN PILLS There are today many proprietary products containing vitamins on the market. Some are single vitamin products, some are described as 'multivitamin 'pills, others combine selected minerals with the vitamins. For most people who regularly eat a well-balanced diet, there is no need at all for vitamin pills. There are certain cases where vitamin supplements can be helpful.

For growing children, vitamin D is a most essential nutrient. Children may not take enough in their food, or from their own synthesis of the vitamin in sunshine. Cod liver oil, halibut liver oil capsules and other products containing both vitamins A and D are often given to children. It is most important that the recommended dose is not exceeded. In the past, children have sometimes suffered from an illness known as hypervitaminosis, caused by an excessive intake of vitamin D. It was usually found in children with over-zealous mothers, who worked on the principle that if a little was good, an extra dose would be even better. Many baby foods, such as artificial milk powders and some cereals, have added vitamin D. This intake should be considered when doses of vitamin D supplements are being planned for babies.

From time to time, pregnant women have been found to suffer from an **anaemia** caused by a deficiency of the B vitamin known as folic acid. Most doctors now prescribe folic acid, sometimes combined with the **iron** supplements also prescribed, to all women during pregnancy. Vitamin C tablets may also be taken with iron tablets to improve the absorption of the iron they contain.

There is still debate about the efficacy of taking large daily amounts of vitamin C to prevent or cure an attack of the common cold. Fortunately, there is no risk attached to taking large doses of this vitamin. The excess is simply excreted in the urine.

Vitamin pills are often considered a general tonic or pick-me-up. Some people take them as a routine, and value them as a safeguard to health and well-being. There are certainly psychological advantages to be gained. If you think something is doing you good, it often succeeds. But for those who do not wish to spend money on proprietary vitamin products, it should be stressed that for the vast majority of people they are not necessary at all. Women who feel 'droopy' from time to time may be suffering from iron deficiency **anaemia** which is easily and cheaply cured by a course of iron, not vitamin, tablets. Consult your doctor if you are in any doubt about the need for any dietary supplement.

VODKA A spirit of 70 per cent proof produced from the distillation of fermented rye. The alcoholic strength of drinks in the UK is shown by a 'proof' measure; 70 per cent proof spirit contains 40 per cent alcohol. Alcohol is utilised in the body as a source of energy.

	alcohol g/100 ml	carbohydrate g/100 ml	energy value Kcal/100 ml (Kjoules/100 ml)
Vodka (70% proof)	31.5	Trace	222 (928)

 WALNUTS One of the most popular nuts for dessert or for cooking. Like most other nuts, they are a concentrated source of energy and contain useful amounts of vegetable protein. Walnuts contain less calcium and iron than almonds or Brazil nuts.

1 oz shelled walnuts contains:

156 kilocalories (652 kilojoules)
3.6 g protein
14.6 g fat (7 per cent saturated)
1.4 g carbohydrate
17.3 mg calcium
0.67 mg iron
no vitamin A
no vitamin D
0.08 mg thiamin
0.03 mg riboflavin
no vitamin C

Sold both in their shells or shelled, when they become walnut halves. Also available pickled. Walnuts for pickling are picked early before the shells have time to harden, and are pickled in their shells.

WATER An essential part of the diet although water cannot be classified as either a nutrient or a source of energy. The greatest part of the body is simply water. The body cells contain fluids and are also bathed in fluids. The blood, of which an adult has about 8 pints, is also largely water. Dehydration (lack of water) causes discomfort, illness and finally death much more rapidly than shortage of any other single constituent of the diet. Most adults drink about 3 pints of fluid a day, and derive a further 2 pints or so from their food.

Some fruits and vegetables, notably melon, cucumber and marrows, are almost entirely water. Juicy fruits like oranges contain 85 per cent water, while meat, eggs and milk also have a high water content. Even comparatively dry foods like bread and cheese contain about 40 per cent water.

Water shortage or dehydration may occur in cases of severe diarrhoea and vomiting, and also when the body temperature rises. Excessive sweating while working in a hot atmosphere may also cause dehydration (see also **salt**). In such cases, plenty of fluid should be consumed. Mothers who are breast feeding also need to increase their own fluid intake to maintain their milk production. Babies and young children become dehydrated more easily than adults. They should be offered water regularly, and slightly sweetened fruit juices from time to time. Recent investigations have shown that many mothers prepare powdered milk feeds incorrectly. The milk is too concentrated and can easily cause the baby to become dehydrated.

Drinking more plain water is often a simple but effective cure for constipation. A glass of water, especially if it is warm, taken before breakfast, helps to stimulate bowel movements. Increasing the water intake often helps to improve the skin, too.

The kidneys keep a very fine control of the concentration of body fluids. Except in certain medical conditions, there is no need to control the daily intake of fluid. This is true even while slimming, provided the fluids consumed do not exceed the daily calorie allowance of the reducing diet. Water taken in excess of requirements is simply excreted by the kidneys as urine. Water is also lost by sweating, from the lungs and in the faeces.

Water retention often occurs in women shortly before their periods. This may cause temporary discomfort, but usually disappears when menstruation begins. Water retention or *oedema* during pregnancy is always carefully checked. Oedema is a symptom of other complaints, including diseases of the kidneys and heart, and also occurs with some nutritional deficiencies and starvation.

WATERCRESS A green salad vegetable grown in fresh water. It contains useful amounts of vitamin C and iron and is rich in vitamin A and calcium. (The extent to which the iron may be utilised is not known.) Like most other green vegetables, watercress provides little energy, and only a small amount of protein. Owing to its high water content it is a bulky food and useful when following a low energy diet.

1 oz watercress contains:

4	kilocalories (17 kilojoules)
0.8 g	protein
no	fat
0.2 g	carbohydrate
63 mg	calcium
0.5 mg	iron
142 microg	retinol equivalents vitamin A
no	vitamin D
0.03 mg	thiamin
0.05 mg	riboflavin
17 mg	vitamin C

It is estimated that in the UK the consumption of watercress is approximately one bunch per person per year. It is available all the year round, but at its best from March to May and again in the late summer and early autumn.

Watercress should be eaten as fresh as possible. It soon turns yellow with storage. If it has to be kept, stand watercress in a glass of cold water in a cool place, or store in an airtight container in the salad drawer of the fridge.

Use watercress in salads and garnishes, and in cooking, too. Its peppery flavour lifts many dishes such as soups, sauces, flans, croquettes and pancakes. Finely chopped watercress may also be used with cream cheese or scrambled egg for sandwich fillings.

WHEATGERM is the embryo of the wheat grain. It represents about $1\frac{1}{2}$ per cent of the whole grain. Wheatgerm contains useful quantities of thiamin, riboflavin and iron, but as it is eaten in very small quantities it contributes little to the average diet. It is also a source of vitamin E.

$\frac{1}{2}$ oz wheatgerm contains:

```
   52  kilocalories (217 kilojoules)
    4 g protein
  1.1 g fat
  6.3 g carbohydrate
  7.7 mg calcium
 1.09 mg iron
   no  vitamin A
   no  vitamin D
 0.23 mg thiamin
 0.10 mg riboflavin
   no  vitamin C
```

Wheatgerm is available in a pure form and is generally sold in health food shops. It is usually served sprinkled on breakfast cereals.

Wheatgerm is removed with the bran when white flour is made. As it is comparatively high in fat, wheatgerm tends to go rancid. Wholemeal flour contains its full quota of wheatgerm and therefore does not keep as well as white flour.

Wheatgerm bread – a loaf made with white flour to which extra wheatgerm is added. Wheatgerm bread does not contain bran and is not as rough-textured as wholemeal bread. It does contain more nutrients from the extra wheatgerm.

WHISKY A spirit of at least 70 per cent proof (see **vodka**). The alcohol, derived from fermenting the carbohydrate in barley, is utilised in the body as a source of energy. Apart from this, whisky has no nutritional value.

	alcohol g/100 ml	carbohydrate g/100 ml	energy value Kcal/100 ml. (Kjoules/100 ml)
Whisky (70% proof)	31.5	Trace	222 (928)

The above values are averages for several different types of whisky; there are, however, slight variations in the energy value of different whiskys.

WHITING A round, white fish related to the **cod**, but much smaller and more delicately flavoured. Like other white fish, whiting is a good source of protein, but contains little fat and no vitamins A or D. It has small amounts of the B group vitamins and some minerals.

A 6 oz whiting, fried (weighed with bones) contains:

        294 kilocalories (1,228 kilojoules)
    26.4 g protein
    15.6 g fat
    10.8 g carbohydrate
    73.2 mg calcium
    1.08 mg iron
        no vitamin A
        no vitamin D
    0.05 mg thiamin
    0.15 mg riboflavin
        no vitamin C

Whiting are available all the year round, but are at their best from late autumn to early spring. Most fish weigh from 6 oz to 9 oz. They are usually sold (and cooked) whole.

The flesh of whiting quickly deteriorates, so whiting must be very fresh when it is eaten. For short-term storage, keep covered on the top shelf of the fridge. It is best eaten on the day of purchase.

WHOLEFOODS Usually cereal products such as breads, crispbreads, flours, meals and so on, prepared from the entire cereal grain. As nothing is removed, the product is described as a 'wholefood'. Wholemeal flour, for example, is required by law to contain all parts of the wheat. It is simply crushed and ground into flour. Nothing is removed from it, and nothing is added during manufacture. Wholefoods are usually sold by health food stores.

Products known as 'wheatmeal' or simply 'brown' have usually had the coarser outer bran layers removed during manufacture.

WINE An alcholic beverage usually produced by the natural, though controlled, fermentation of pressed fruit. Commercially, wine is produced from grapes. Large areas of prime agricultural land in Europe are devoted to growing grapes for wine making. The quality of the finished wine depends not only on the quality of the grapes, but also on the climatic conditions during the growing period. The basic difference between red and white wines is that the red wines are made from the crushed fruit complete with skin, pips and often stems of the grapes. White wines are made from either black or white grapes but the skins are separated before fermentation takes place.

According to laws passed in the major wine producing countries, wine must be made from fresh wine-grapes. Very good home wines may be made from a variety of produce, not only from fruits, but also flowers as well as grains and certain vegetables. In home wine making, yeasts must be added. In commercial wine making, natural yeasts from the grape skins produce the fermentation.

Nutritionally, wines are notable only for the energy value of the alcohol they contain. Some wines of the port wine type contain a few trace elements which may be beneficial. Alcohol taken in moderation has the advantage of stimulating the appetite (see **alcohol**). Fortified wines, including sherry, port and vermouth, to which extra alcohol is added, contain correspondingly more calories. Most table wines contain between 100 and 120 calories per glass (taken to be one sixth of a litre). The variation is due to the relative sweetness of different wines. Fortified wines contain approximately 100 calories per (much smaller) glass. Home-made wines made from vitamin C-rich fruits such as blackcurrants, raspberries, gooseberries or oranges may retain a small amount of vitamin C through fermentation and maturation.

WINKLES See **Shellfish**.

XEROPHTHALMIA A disease caused by prolonged deficiency of vitamin A. It is usually seen only in people whose diet has lacked fresh vegetables and dairy produce for long periods. With xerophthalmia the eyes become dry and infected. It is a significant cause of blindness among poorly-nourished people of the world. Xerophthalmia is classed by the World Health Organisation as one of the most widespread nutritional diseases.

It would not be encountered in this country or in other countries of the well-nourished Western world. During experiments with human volunteers (conscientious objectors in the Second World War), a dietary deficiency of vitamin A did not lead to xerophthalmia during the two-year period of the experiment, although other symptoms of vitamin A deficiency developed.

YEASTS Microscopic plants, usually unicellular, which ferment carbohydrates to alcohol. This fermentation is the yeast's natural method of deriving the energy it needs to carry out its own life processes. We utilise these reactions for our own benefit in making wines and beers. Naturally occurring yeasts, which give the 'bloom' to the grapes, are used in **wine** making. Specially selected yeasts are grown for making **beer**.

When yeasts break down the carbohydrate, they produce carbon dioxide (just as we do). We also utilise yeasts for aeration when they are used as the raising agent in **bread** and similar doughs.

224

Naturally occurring yeasts also cause a great deal of food spoilage. Their action is similar to that of mould. Yeasts usually attack sweet foods. The alcoholic taste and fizziness fruit salad develops after a few days is the work of yeasts which are normally found in the atmosphere. Food attacked by yeasts is not harmful, but they may spoil its desired flavour and texture.

Yeasts are extremely rich in B group vitamins and also in protein. Yeast tablets have been used for centuries as a general tonic. Baked products containing yeasts usually contain few of the original vitamins, which are mostly destroyed by cooking temperatures. Recently, yeasts have been grown in an attempt to find some easily produced and cheap source of protein which might be used to feed either man or farm animals. A high concentration of yeast is not very palatable, but attempts are being made to find a suitable food which might be enriched with yeast to increase the overall nutritional value of that food.

YOGHURT Most commercial yoghurt products are made from a mixture of whole milk, skimmed milk powder and liquid sucrose (sugar). Vitamins A and D may also be added. Fat free yoghurts are made with skimmed milk alone. The mixture is homogenised and then fermented with carefully selected strains of bacteria. These organisms utilise the sugar in the mixture as their own food, and produce acid as a by-product. The acidity coagulates the protein and sets the mixture. Production of bacteria is controlled to give the right degree of acidity and firmness of the curd. When this point has been reached, the yoghurt is chilled to prevent further fermentation. Yoghurt has roughly the same nutritive value as an equal amount of fresh milk. Flavoured and fruit yoghurts have added sugar as well as the flavouring fruits, juices and syrups. Many different recipes are used to prepare yoghurt and the figures given below are an average of several different types.

One 5 oz carton of natural yoghurt contains:

      80 kilocalories (334 kilojoules)
       5 g protein
     3.5 g fat
     7.5 g carbohydrate
   200 mg calcium
       no iron

              55 microg retinol equivalents vitamin A
          0.05 microg vitamin D
             0.05 mg thiamin
             0.25 mg riboflavin
                no vitamin C

The nutritional values of fruit and flavoured yoghurts vary
according to the type of fruit used. For example, more raspberries than orange are added to give a good-flavoured product.
Roughly, a 5 oz carton of fruit yoghurt contains between 140
and 150 kilocalories. Flavoured yoghurts contain about 120
kilocalories in a 5 oz carton; chocolate-topped yoghurt about
190 kilocalories.

Yoghurt is a very old food, originally devised by the Bulgarians
as a way of improving the keeping qualities of fresh milk. Over
the years, remarkable powers have been attributed to yoghurt.
The longevity of the Bulgarians was thought to be due to their
high consumption of yoghurt. But yoghurt has no mystical
powers. Its nutritional value is the same as that of the raw
materials from which it is made. It gains nothing, except perhaps an improved digestibility, during fermentation.

Health food stores often claim to sell a superior product they
describe as 'live yoghurt'. This is no different from the commercial variety; all yoghurts contain live bacteria. They can
be utilised by mixing a carton of natural yoghurt with one pint
of scalded – and cooled – sweetened milk. If this is kept in a
warm place for 3 or 4 hours, the bacteria in the bought yoghurt
multiply and ferment the extra milk. The result is a much
larger quantity of yoghurt.

Care! Do not continue for too long to make your own yoghurt
using a little of what was left over from before. Fresh bacteria
can invade the 'brew', overpowering the proper yoghurt
bacteria.

Yoghurt is an excellent food for children and old people, who
need a high consumption of milk. Yoghurt is also a good food
for babies when they start mixed feeding. In other countries,
yoghurt is more widely used in cooking than in Britain. Yoghurt
can be stirred into soups, sauces and stews for extra flavour and
richness. Plain yoghurt also makes an excellent salad dressing
– very low in calories, too. Yoghurt makes a suitable food for
convalescents. The bacteria it contains seems to be helpful in
stimulating the growth of the body's own intestinal bacteria
which may have been killed during treatment with antibiotics.

226

YOLK The yellow part of the egg is rich in fat, protein and iron. It also contains useful amounts of vitamin A and D and riboflavin. One 2 oz egg contains a yolk weighing approximately ½ oz.

One egg yolk (½ oz) contains:

50	kilocalories (209 kilojoules)
2.3 g	protein
4.3 g	fat
no	carbohydrate
18 mg	calcium
0.87 mg	iron
128 microg	retinol equivalents vitamin A
1.78 microg	vitamin D
0.04 mg	thiamin
0.06 mg	riboflavin
no	vitamin C

For consumption and availability, see **eggs**.

Egg yolk is the richest common dietary source of **cholesterol** – one egg yolk contains 215 mg. Eggs are restricted for heart patients and others wishing to keep their blood cholesterol levels normal.

Egg yolks may be kept in the fridge for several days, provided their outer membrane does not dry out. Keep the yolks in a glass covered with a little milk. Egg yolks may also be kept in the freezer. They should be lightly whisked and placed in suitably small wax cartons.

Egg yolks are often used to thicken sauces, as they have better thickening power than either whole eggs or egg whites.

ZEST The outer, aromatic layers of peel, usually of citrus fruits. Zest is rich in the essential oils which give these fruits their characteristic flavour. Finely grated peel is often described as zest in traditional cookery books. A cube of sugar rubbed over the skin of oranges or lemons also absorbs some of the zest.